'In *Transforming Criminal Justice?*, Dr Jane Donoghue packs crucial information and insights into a well-written and extremely manageable volume on problem-solving approaches to criminal justice. With a UK focus, but rich in discussion of US, Australian and other systems, Donoghue presents a sensible and balanced analysis that comes to life, with meaningful quotes from magistrates working with this material in the real world. The book should be of great interest to academics, policy-makers and practitioners alike.'

David B. Wexler, Professor of Law and Director, International Network on Therapeutic Jurisprudence, University of Puerto Rico, Puerto Rico

'*Transforming Criminal Justice?* offers a rigorous and even-handed examination of an important criminal justice reform movement. By taking a hard look at both the theory and practice of problem-solving justice, Jane Donoghue makes a significant contribution to the field. This is the place to start for anyone interested in understanding problem-solving courts, not just in the UK, but around the world.'

Greg Berman, Executive Director of the Center for Court Innovation, New York, USA

'There is much talk of "transforming" this and that within criminal justice, but rarely on transforming justice itself. This brave book, putting problem-solving at the heart of the justice process, will further enhance Jane Donoghue's reputation as one of the most original and intrepid new voices in criminology.'

Shadd Maruna, Professor and Director of The Institute of Criminology and Criminal Justice, Queen's University Belfast, UK

Transforming Criminal Justice?

Why is punishment not more effective? Why do we have such high re-offending rates? How can we deal with crime and criminals in a more cost-effective way? Over the last decade in particular, the United Kingdom, in common with other jurisdictions such as Canada, the United States (US) and Australia, has sought to develop more effective ways of responding to criminal behaviour through court reforms designed to address specific manifestations of crime. Strongly influenced by developments in US court specialisation, problem-solving and specialist courts – including domestic violence courts, drugs courts, community courts and mental health courts – have proliferated in Britain over the last few years. These courts operate at the intersection of criminal law and social policy and appear to challenge much of the traditional model of court practice. In addition, policymakers and practitioners have made significant attempts to try to embed problem-solving approaches into the criminal justice system more widely.

Through examination of original data gathered from detailed interviews with judges, magistrates and other key criminal justice professionals in England and Wales, as well as analysis of legislative and policy interventions, this book discusses the impact of the creation and development of court specialisation and problem-solving justice.

This book will be essential reading for students and academics in the fields of criminology, criminal justice, criminal law, socio-legal studies and sociology, as well as for criminal justice practitioners and policymakers.

Jane Donoghue is Reader in Law at the University of Lancaster. She has previously worked at the University of Oxford's Centre for Criminology and the School of Law at the University of Sussex. Her research interests are multidisciplinary and span criminology, criminal justice and criminal law.

Routledge frontiers of criminal justice

1 Sex Offenders, Punish, Help, Change or Control?
Theory, policy and practice explored
Edited by Jo Brayford, Francis Cowe and John Deering

2 Building Justice in Post-Transition Europe
Processes of criminalisation within Central and Eastern European societies
Edited by Kay Goodall, Margaret Malloch and Bill Munro

3 Technocrime, Policing and Surveillance
Edited by Stéphane Leman-Langlois

4 Youth Justice in Context
Community, compliance and young people
Mairead Seymour

5 Women, Punishment and Social Justice
Human rights and penal practices
Margaret Malloch and Gill McIvor

6 Handbook of Policing, Ethics and Professional Standards
Edited by Allyson MacVean, Peter Spindler and Charlotte Solf

7 Contrasts in Punishment
An explanation of Anglophone excess and Nordic exceptionalism
John Pratt and Anna Eriksson

8 Victims of Environmental Harm
Rights, recognition and redress under national and international
Matthew Hall

9 Doing Probation Work
Identity in a criminal justice occupation
Rob C. Mawby and Anne Worrall

10 **Justice Reinvestment**
Can the criminal justice system deliver more for less?
Chris Fox, Kevin Albertson and Kevin Wong

11 **Epidemiological Criminology**
Theory to practice
Edited by Eve Waltermaurer and Timothy A. Akers

12 **Policing Cities**
Urban securitization and regulation in a twenty-first century world
Edited by Randy K. Lippert and Kevin Walby

13 **Restorative Justice in Transition**
Kerry Clamp

14 **International Perspectives on Police Education and Training**
Edited by Perry Stanislas

15 **Understanding Penal Practice**
Edited by Ioan Durnescu and Fergus McNeill

16 **Perceptions of Criminal Justice**
Vicky De Mesmaecker

17 **Transforming Criminal Justice?**
Problem-solving and court specialisation
Jane Donoghue

Transforming Criminal Justice?
Problem-solving and court specialisation

Jane Donoghue

LONDON AND NEW YORK

First published 2014
by Routledge
2 Park Square, Milton Park, Abingdon, Oxon OX14 4RN

and by Routledge
711 Third Avenue, New York, NY 10017

Routledge is an imprint of the Taylor & Francis Group, an informa business

© 2014 Jane Donoghue

The right of Jane Donoghue to be identified as author of this work has
been asserted by her in accordance with sections 77 and 78 of the
Copyright, Designs and Patents Act 1988.

All rights reserved. No part of this book may be reprinted or reproduced or
utilised in any form or by any electronic, mechanical, or other means, now
known or hereafter invented, including photocopying and recording, or in
any information storage or retrieval system, without permission in writing
from the publishers.

Trademark notice: Product or corporate names may be trademarks or
registered trademarks, and are used only for identification and explanation
without intent to infringe.

British Library Cataloguing in Publication Data
A catalogue record for this book is available from the British Library

Library of Congress Cataloging-in-Publication Data
Donoghue, Jane, author.
Transforming criminal justice?: problem-solving and court specialization /
Jane Donoghue.
  pages cm. – (Routledge frontiers of criminal justice)
  1. Criminal justice, Administration of – England. 2. Criminal courts –
England. 3. Courts of special jurisdiction – England. I. Title.
  KD7876.D665 2014
  345.42'0148–dc23   2013041330

ISBN: 978-0-415-81971-8 (hbk)
ISBN: 978-0-203-67065-1 (ebk)

Typeset in Times New Roman
by Wearset Ltd, Boldon, Tyne and Wear

For my wonderful brother Jamie

Contents

Foreword: some perspective on problem-solving xiii
PROFESSOR ERIC J. MILLER
Acknowledgements xxi

1 Introduction 1
Methodology 6
Critique 7
Structure of the book 10

2 Situating problem-solving, punitivism and punishment 13
Problem-solving justice and the 'punitive turn' 18
A 'Rehabilitation Revolution'? 22
A financial imperative for change 28

3 Specialist and problem-solving courts 31
The principles and rationale of problem-solving courts 35
The 'enhanced' judicial function 37
Defence advocacy function 38
Adversarial justice 41
Problem-solving courts in England and Wales 44
The lay magistracy 47
Court centralisation and 'local justice' 50
Court review of community orders 54
Court listing practices 57

4 Drug courts and domestic violence courts 62
Sentencer continuity 64
'Voluntariness' 65
Selectivity in sentencing 67
Effectiveness 68

xii *Contents*

Court-ordered drug treatment in England and Wales 70
Intermediate sanctions for non-compliance 77
Domestic violence courts 81
Specialist domestic violence courts in England and Wales 83
Specialist sexual violence courts (SVCs) 89

5   Community courts and mental health courts   94
Community courts in England and Wales 96
Conceptualising community engagement and its outcomes 103
Mental health courts 108
Effectiveness 110
Mental health courts (MHCs) in England and Wales 111
Mental health court pilot 113
Scalability 115

6   Neighbourhood justice panels   118
Diversion and out of court disposals in England and Wales 120
Justice panels 121
Role of magistrates in NJPs 125
Pre-sentencing restorative justice 129

**7   Problem-solving and court specialisation: prospects and
      pitfalls**   133
Mainstreaming problem-solving justice 136

References   142
Index   167

Foreword

Some perspective on problem-solving

Professor Eric J. Miller

Problem-solving justice is one of the fundamental innovations in criminal justice over the past quarter of a century (Husak 2011). Originally located in certain specialised courts in the United States of America, it has outstripped these marginal spaces, and now seeks its home in more traditional locations, (Berman and Feinblatt 2002; Nolan 2003) in courts around the globe, (Nolan 2009a) often spurred by the need for new forms of criminal justice surveillance and regulation.

What is problem-solving justice? As Jane Donoghue defines it, 'a problem-solving approach prioritises efforts to change the behaviour of offenders; provide better support and aid to victims; and improve public safety in neighbourhoods' (Donoghue 2014). For the most part, however, the emphasis has most consistently been on the first of these features: problem-solving courts are primarily a means of supervising offenders in the community by monitoring compliance with conditions of release. Some policy-makers – including judges as well as legislatures – have emphasised victims and the community. But such a focus has been somewhat patchy, often operating more at the level of aspiration than implementation (Fagan and Malkin 2002).

Problem-solving justice emerges out of, but seeks to outstrip, the problem-solving court movement. The original problem-solving court is the drug court, which first appeared against the background of the massive increase in criminal caseloads experienced by the American criminal justice system starting in the 1980s. The court model developed by Judge Klein of the Florida Eleventh Judicial Circuit in 1989 was slow track, court-based and treatment oriented (Bean 1996). It set the model for future developments in problem-solving justice: mandatory treatment backed up by a vigorous programme of in-court judicial supervision of the offender (Hora *et al.* 1998). Rather than rely upon the periodic reports of probation officers, drug courts constitute the judge, treatment provider, lawyers and other treatment officials and social workers into a 'team' that reviews each case on a regular basis and provides detailed information to the judge about the offender's compliance with conditions of release (Bean 1998; Miller 2004; Hora and Stalcup 2010). These conditions, in drug court at any rate, include attending drug-counselling sessions, interviews with probation services and in-person appearances status hearings before the judge. Other types of xiv *Foreword*

problem-solving courts may vary the frequency of reporting and testing, but the court will usually require offenders to appear at least once a month. Failure to comply with the rehabilitation programme results in a series of sanctions that eventually result in short periods of jail time, or removal from the programme (Bozza 2007; Nolan 2009b; Burns and Peyrot 2008).

The politics of problem-solving justice has proven polarising; much of the contemporary literature studying the courts reflects this ideological division, falling into sometimes shrill 'camps' that toss back-and-forth overblown claims about the merits of their own position and the pitfalls of the others. In part, the debate gains much of its heat from the claim, associated with the therapeutic justice movement, that problem-solving justice is treatment-oriented (Hora 2011; Winick and Wexler 2001; Wexler 2012) (a different version of problem-solving justice avoids the putting all its eggs in the treatment basket (Berman 2004b) at 1314). In part, the debate concerns the protections available for criminal defendants through problem-solving justice (Quinn 2000; Meekins 2007). And in part, the debate concerns the methods used to achieve the court's rehabilitative and community justice ends (Hoffman 2001; Miller 2009).

The polarisation produced by the proponents and opponents of problem-solving justice replicates, even if it does not reflect, some other oppositions in the various literatures in which the study of problem-solving justice is embedded. Are the current trends in the management of criminal populations best described in globalist or localist terms? Is the state's focus on 'victims' or the consequences of crime incompatible with its attention to 'criminals' or the causes of crime? Does judicial intervention in the social welfare aspects of sentencing channel offenders out of the system or 'widen the net' to catch more within it?

A further feature complicating the study of problem-solving justice is the way in which the American criminal justice system, its practices and policies, dominate the discussion. The American model takes incarceration as the core penal practice against which problem-solving institutions are understood and evaluated. Advocates and opponents tend, by and large, to take for granted a particular historical period, (a notable exception is Mae Quinn's recent work (Quinn 2006)) and a particular political climate: the more-or-less general move to mass incarceration of American criminal policy (at the federal – and more patchy at the state – level, in particular Florida and California (Barker 2009)) against which the first drug courts emerged in 1989.

Jane Donoghue's expert study adroitly avoids the major vices of the current problem-solving literature: partisanship and parochialism. It holds out the promise and possibility of a calmer and conciliatory discussion surrounding problem-solving justice, in large part because she clearly identifies the core function of the problem-solving court, and allows for a more objective assessment of its virtues. In particular, by stepping outside the American context, she demonstrates that problem-solving justice is not a form of adjudication, operating at the trial (or in the American context, plea-bargaining) stage of the criminal justice process. Rather, problem-solving justice applies to the sentencing stage, after (or in some cases, before!) adjudication has run its course (Hora *et al.* 1998; Miller 2004). It is thus a form of justice that applies to the conditions of release of offenders who acknowledge their criminal responsibility, but identify some underlying medical or psychological factor causing their criminal conduct.

Having established that judicially monitored, de-incarcerative supervision is the central feature of problem-solving justice, we can then consider its relation to state penal policies with new clarity.

American penal policy, at least at the federal level, is usually presented as determined to increase the size and impact of the penal state at the same time as shrinking the welfare state (Garland 2001). Problem-solving justice then appears as a subversive counter-trend bucking this narrative. Problem-solving courts set out to mitigate the penal consequences of arrest and prosecution, while offering access to scarce resources, including medical and social services (Hora 2011). Whether or not the courts are as successful as some proponents claim, they are better (so the story goes) than the dominant regime (Berman and Feinblatt 2002). They provide individualised attention to criminal defendants, increasing the dignity afforded them within the system; and they provide them with access to services that are unavailable or unaffordable outside the problem-solving court. The goal, after all, is not to incarcerate, but to ameliorate the underlying social and personal factors leading the defendants down the path to crime. They are, at the least, a promising alternative to the severity state, and at worst, the only alternative, given the absence of (again, so the story goes) moderate penal policies in the United States. (For a slightly different take, see (Barker 2009; Lynch 2011).)

Another distinctively American feature of the current debate is the mostly bottom-up, fragmented, ad hoc, and low level operation of much problem-solving justice. (The exception is in New York state, which has its own problem-solving justice policymaking, court-supporting, and evaluation branch, the Center for Court Innovation (Berman 2004).) New York aside, in the American context, problem-solving courts are low-level and insurrectionary institutions, for the most part set up by local judges or court jurisdictions rather than by (and sometimes in opposition to) state legislation (Miller 2004; Burns and Peyrot 2008). These two features – fragmentation and oppositionalism – render the American experience, if not exceptional, then certainly exaggerated, even in the context of neo-liberal democracies.

Removed from the American context, however, Donoghue allows us to recognise that the use of problem-solving justice as a sentencing technique need not be dominated by the shadow of the incarcerative state, whether helping or hindering its policies. Penal policy at the state level could, after all, take a more welfarist cast (Lacey 2008; Garland 2001). In that case, the options are not between severity and some more-or-less ad hoc attempt to mitigate its impact. Instead, the options are between state-level policies that promote penal severity (responding to the consequences of crime) and policies that support social welfare interventions (responding to the causes of crime).

A less America-centric view allows us to consider what a top-down policy of problem-solving justice might look like. Problem-solving justice need not

xvi   *Foreword*

operate against the background of a state that rejects social welfare for criminals. The experience of problem-solving justice in England (Nolan 2009a) and Scotland (McIvor 2009), presents, to different degrees, an important loosening of the anti-welfare animus that goes along with American penal policy. Accordingly, changing the relationship between the state and punishment may change the nature of the justice provided.

If there is to be a clear analysis of problem-solving justice, then, it must take account of two features that Donoghue's book clarifies: the sentencing and surveillance orientation of problem-solving justice; and the relation between this type of penal policy and the more general penal goals promoted by the state. Understood in this way, there is an opportunity to find at least some common ground between proponents of problem-solving justice and those critics who believe that the problem-solving court is the handmaid of the incarcerative system. These critics point out that problem-solving justice widens the net to channel more individuals through the criminal justice system, with a longer and more intense contact with that system than their peers in other sentencing regimes, and punishing the sizable minority who flunk out of the court more harshly than they would have been had they avoided the court in the first place (Bowers 2008). Viewed from afar, however, these negative features may turn out to be more parochial than universal, a creature of the American context in which the court emerged, rather than inherent in problem-solving justice itself.

Furthermore, exploring the relationship between the style of sentencing monitoring and other features of sentencing policy may mitigate some of the overblown claims made by proponents and opponents alike. The battle over the meaning of the courts' recidivism statistics, for example, is heightened by the willingness of American problem-solving proponents to go beyond the conclusions that their mostly geographically and temporally limited studies warrant, to make universal claims about the success of the courts. We know that the courts tend to reduce recidivism during the course of the programme, and (for successful graduates) for two years after the programme ends (Belenko 2001). We do not know much more than that, in large part because there is a paucity of studies evaluating long-term client recidivism. Nonetheless, and dependent upon the goals of a penal policy, that limited period of success (approximately four years from entry into the programme to the end of most recidivism study periods) could be enough to justify this form of sentence-monitoring. But this sort of success does not demonstrate that long-term recidivism disappears, nor that participants are cured of addiction or aggression, or their inability to stay on mental health medication.

I have so far avoided the major worry raised by opponents of problem-solving justice: the attack on due process. In part, that is because I believe that, in the American context at least, structural features render this worry doctrinally marginal. It turns out that, since problem-solving justice is a form of pre- or post-adjudication monitoring of conditions of release, judicial discretion and judicial advocacy impacts many fewer constitutional rights than critics generally suppose. But doctrinal gaps may cover moral shortcomings that we ought to

Foreword xvii

address, and in a hurry. Be that as it may, there are nonetheless a variety of worries, grouped under the heading of due process or the rule of law or judicial neutrality, that we might consider inimical to the judicial role.

The two traditional concerns – partisan interventionism and lack of account-ability – present genuine problems for problem-solving justice. On the one hand, the judge is supposed to operate as advocate for the offender as they progress through the treatment programme. On the other hand, the judge is often sup-posed to operate as a surrogate for the community – as Donoghue's work shows, this can be to the extent of soliciting community sentiment on residents' experi-ences of and concerns about local crime problems (Donoghue 2012). These two interests – defendant-centred and community-centred – may on occasion conflict.

Yet another source of conflict is the judge's sense of his or her own institu-tional role and competence. Problem-solving justice often (though not always) asks the judge to step away from a posture of neutrality, one that gives Dono-ghue a certain cover and comfort when meting out criminal sentences. The indi-vidualising and interventionist posture of some forms of problem-solving justice may require the judge to undertake the role of advocate, a role that certain judges – Donoghue's example is the English magistracy – are sometimes ill-equipped to fill (in part because of inadequate governmental support for this new role).

The attempt to bring problem-solving justice into traditional courtrooms and criminal-justice settings requires a transformation in nature of authority wielded by the judge. The judge moves from having detached authority *over* others (as an umpire in adversarial contest) to a model of engaged authority *with* others (as a collaborator in team process). Furthermore, this change in the nature of author-ity is accompanied by a move from procedural justice to consequential justice; that is, from ensuring optimal procedures to producing optimal outcomes. The traditional judge is measured by success in administering fair process; the problem-solving judge is measured by success in producing long-lasting rehabil-itative change. And often the court moves from a traditional notion of disinter-ested neutrality (as umpire) to what might be called evidence-based neutrality. On the evidence-based model, the guarantee of appropriate judicial decision-making is intended to be achieved through the wealth of social scientific data, including self-studies of the court's process, to measure of effective results.

Donoghue's central question – and her focus on problem-solving *justice* rather than problem-solving *courts* – concerns whether the sort of judicial inter-vention many regard as central to the problem-solving movement is transferable out of specialised courts and into the courtroom more generally. It is generally assumed that American judges, being more experimental and informal, are more receptive to the interpersonal and rehabilitative aspects of problem-solving judi-cial engagement than foreign judges, and especially those in the more 'stuffy' courts of England, Wales and Scotland (Nolan 2009a).

Donoghue's work, both in this book and elsewhere (Donoghue 2012), reveals that this picture is overly simplistic. Donoghue has hitherto engaged in detailed ethnographic studies of English magistrates' courts. These studies both jibe and xviii *Foreword*

jar with the conversion narrative many American judges currently working in problem-solving courts tell: of being initially unreceptive to the idea of problem-solving, but once assigned to problem-solving courts, transformed by the experience. Yet – so Donoghue reveals – many judges remain unconverted and uncomfortable with the new role that problem-solving justice demands.

Donoghue's prior work on English Magistrate Courts, expertly integrated into her book, provides a fascinating account of the operation of the English and Welsh magistracy in running a community-court model of problem-solving justice. Donoghue engaged in a detailed empirical study that is unique in accessing and recording the operation of the magistrates' court to observe the government's attempt to embed a problem-solving approach to cases in these courts. In England and Wales, the British government attempted to require widespread adoption of problem-solving practices by political directive, from the top down, without any real training for the magistrates required to implement the policy. Lacking any specific direction, Donoghue found that magistrates generally resisted the informal aspects of the court – particularly interaction with communities to assess the problems presented both individually and locally by anti-social behaviour – and the formal aspects of repeat monitoring – the ability of a single magistrate within the court to track repeat offenders through the sentencing process. Instead, the magistrates reasserted their role of disinterested neutrality and detached authority and characterised the scientific and engaged aspects of the new process as requiring them to act as 'social workers' instead of 'judges'.

Donoghue's research reveals that, on the ground, impartiality and authoritarianism may be precisely the parts of the professional role that low-level court officials regard as central to their professional identity. These findings match some studies indicating that problem-solving courts are highly dependent upon the attitudes of individual judges, independent of the structure of the court (Nolan 2009b). Building upon her research into the English magistracy, Donoghue sets the stage for introducing structural solutions to the problem of judicial resistance, as well as describing the consequences of failing to properly train recalcitrant or ambivalent judges for problem-solving court practice.

The magistracy's experience in England may be symptomatic of a more general problem: the lack of training in both the theory and skills required to engage in 'social work' (Wexler 2012). The American experience is one of little or no state-sponsored training; the judiciary gets most of its induction into drug or mental-health treatment practices at annual meetings sponsored by professional associations of problem-solving judges. Often the repeated experience of engaging with drug or mental health or homelessness cases is cited as sufficient to sensitise the judge to the relevant problems (if not therapeutic techniques). Yet, with the model of problem-solving judge as engaged expert, the sheer volume of such courts – together with the 'mainstreaming' of problem-solving justice to other sites within the criminal justice – suggests that the number of judges practicing problem-solving vastly outstrips the opportunities for training (and certainly, for quality control).

Foreword xix

The worry then becomes that problem-solving judges simply mimic the dominant disciplinary practice of traditional judges, as much as (if not more than) they introduce new therapeutic techniques (Miller 2009; Burns and Peyrot 2003). And that their claims to community participation and treatment success are overblown (Fagan and Malkin 2002; Boldt 2010).

Increased sensitivity to the problems of the drug addicted or mentally ill is indeed a positive boon. Yet, while some critics of problem-solving justice call for more training, one likely result is the domination of the judiciary over the various cognate service providers and treatment specialists that is another of the important innovations of problem-solving justice. Judicial domination of social services risks the 'courtification' of service provision in ways that undermine the independence of the service provider and remove the checks that these co-equal experts can exert over the court. Call this the problem of institutional net-widening.

The checks-and-balances aspect of treatment-team authority over sentencing dispositions is one of the most promising and least comfortable aspects of problem-solving justice. Most promising because, in the ante-chamber and the courtroom, the judge is required to shed some of his or her authority and promote a more egalitarian and understanding interaction with criminal defendants, often guided by insights – or even virtual scripts – generated by treatment specialists. A positive cycle of legitimation develops, in which the offender feels 'heard' by the judge, and that the system is finally working with him; while the judge feels engaged with the offender, and gains a sense that they are indeed affecting change in the offender's life (Tyler 1992). Much of the 'legitimacy' literature addresses the positive effects of this process on the offender. Certainly, increasing access to justice has important egalitarian and democratic benefits. But a hidden subject in the cycle of legitimation is the state official (in much of the literature, the police officer; in problem-solving justice, the judge) whose sense of institutional legitimacy is also increased (Chase and Hora 2009). True believers become even more passionate about their mission and their success, increasing their willingness to push the discretion and authority inherent in such courts to the limits.

A core problem of the current system of problem-solving justice is that many judges do so without adequate institutional oversight. That worry, Donoghue suggests, is shared by judges to whom problem-solving justice is a political imperative, rather than a natural judicial style. Without institutional support, judges are cast adrift on this new wave of social monitoring and interaction, without the tools to adequately undertake their mission.

One solution – I have hinted at it, above – is to ensure that the cognate treatment professionals share decision-making power to provide checks on judicial discretion. The problem is that, as a matter of law, split decision-making power between judge and others is prohibited – to the extent that if this happens in practice, it does so under the table (Portillo *et al.* 2013). Put differently, the legal requirements of the model may have the effect of promoting 'courtification' and undermining inter-agency regulation. Because informal, such regulation must depend upon the personality of the judge.

xx   *Foreword*

A central danger of the courtification of social service provision is that, in order to increase their prestige with the court, social workers and other treatment providers will translate therapeutic concepts into legal, and in particular, criminal justice ones. The dominance of the criminal threatens to colonise these coordinate professions at the point of problem-solving provision, resulting in a novel form of net-widening, focused on institutions rather than individuals. Here, the worry is not simply that more individuals are transformed into offenders, having been caught within the criminal justice 'net' (Cohen 1985; Hoffman 2000). Rather, the worry is that access to, and the nature of, social welfare or medical treatment becomes dependent upon criminal justice concepts such as punishment, sentencing, and the amorphous and contested concept of 'risk' (O'Malley 2008; Donoghue 2008).

These may well be design issues primarily. They need not go to the heart of problem-solving justice. How things are now are not how things have to be; and the American model need not be the English (or the Scottish, or the Dutch or the Belgian and so on). What is desperately needed, and what Jane Donoghue provides, is a vision of problem-solving justice that is not beholden to the received wisdom on the American side of the Atlantic, but instead can provide more dispassionate and less parochial evaluation of the benefits and burdens of problem-solving justice.

Acknowledgements

I wish to express my sincere gratitude to all those who have participated in and assisted me with my empirical research for this book, of which there are too many people to mention individually (and some have contributed under condition of anonymity), but without whom this work would not have been possible. I am continually surprised by the willingness of so many busy individuals who generously and without condition, give up their time to assist me with my work. I know that the majority who have participated in the research have done so because they strongly believe in the value and importance of criminal justice research, especially as a tool to more effectively inform policy and practice. Many of those who have agreed to assist with my research are highly committed public servants who are dedicated to their roles and to civic duty. I very much hope that they will feel that I have produced a book that is worthy of the time that they have given up in contributing to my various projects over the years.

My great friend Eric J. Miller, who has written the foreword to this book, has been a genuine source of inspiration to me, not only in helping me to consider more deeply my perspective on problem-solving courts, but also in motivating me to interrogate the plethora of conceptual, ideological and philosophical ideas that we have discussed in our many lengthy conversations together. I owe him a significant intellectual debt, but more than that I am grateful to him for his kindness and his generosity and (although he would likely not want me to describe him as such) in acting as a mentor to me. I feel extremely fortunate to know him.

I am also most grateful to members of the Centre for Criminology at the University of Oxford, in particular Ian Loader, Carolyn Hoyle and Lucia Zedner, who provided me with invaluable feedback on a 'Brown Bag' research seminar that I gave in 2011 on my work on specialist and problem-solving courts when I was an academic at the Centre and to Julian Roberts for his comments on a working paper on problem-solving courts, which I have usefully incorporated into this book. Further thanks are due to Ian Loader for providing additional thoughtful feedback on my writing on problem-solving justice and on my empirical research funded by the Economic and Social Research Council (ESRC), which is incorporated into my arguments in this book as well as in an article published in 2012 (Donoghue 2012).

xxii *Acknowledgements*

Many thanks are due to Sean Bettinger-Lopez of the University of Miami, for his kind invitation to speak at the Law School's Bruce J. Winick Fall 2012 Colloquium on Standards in the Problem-Solving Courts. In particular, the observations of, and the conversations that I had at this symposium with Alison Redlich, Steven Belenko, Jeffrey Fagin, Mark Fondacaro and Chris Slobogin were all extremely useful. I am indebted to Gabrielle Watson for her great efficiency in helping organise my symposium on Specialist Courts and Therapeutic Jurisprudence at Balliol College at the University of Oxford in August 2012. Special thanks are due to all those who attended this symposium: Greg Berman, Judith Harwin, Gill McIvor, Eric Miller, George Mair, Matthew Millings, Toby Seddon, Cyrus Tata, Michel Vols and David Wexler. Further thanks are due to David Wexler for his support and generosity, and for inviting me to join the Therapeutic Jurisprudence Listserv which provides access to many useful resources that have assisted me in writing this book. My research has also very much benefitted from having access to the Magistrates' Open Network online forum, which I was very kindly invited to join by the forum administrator, Robert van Es. I am most grateful to Robert, not only for his invitation but also for his support in communicating information about my research to others on the Network. Magistrates' Open Network is an excellent forum for innovative and enlightened discussion and I wish him continued success with this fantastic online tool. In addition, I have had numerous extremely useful interactions with The Magistrates' Association of England and Wales. Many thanks are due to those individuals of the Association who I have been in contact with over the years. Special thanks are due to the Association for inviting me to speak at their Conference on Community Focussed Justice in London in 2011, which was an excellent event and raised many issues pertinent to my writing in this book; and to Richard Monkhouse.

I have greatly benefitted from conversations and exchanges of ideas with Phil Bowen, Director of the Centre for Justice Innovation in London, who has provided me with invaluable factual information as well as innovative explanatory and conceptual suggestions. I am grateful to Anthea Huckelsby and participants at the University of Leeds symposium on Justice in the Criminal Courts in the 21st Century for their very useful feedback and comments on a working paper that I was invited to deliver on out of court disposals and neighbourhood justice panels in July 2013. I have incorporated a number of these comments into this book.

I wish to thank Steve Broome at the Royal Society of the Arts (RSA) for our productive discussions about social sentencing and Vicki Helyar-Cardwell of Criminal Justice Alliance (CJA) for her invitation to speak about this topic at a CJA roundtable in 2012 which resulted in the generation of some new and innovative ideas around the potential and limits of our sentencing system, some of which I have referenced in this book. I am also indebted to Sarah Colover for her excellent research assistance on my Economic and Social Research Council (ESRC) funded project on Specialist Anti-Social Behaviour Response Courts. I am most grateful to Toby Seddon for his friendship and words of encouragement

Acknowledgements xxiii

during the process of writing this book and for our many stimulating conversations.

I wish to thank all those involved in the production of this book at Routledge/ Taylor and Francis. Special thanks are due to Nicola Hartley, Heidi Lee and Thomas Sutton.

Many thanks are due to Jean Spriddle for her continued interest in my work and for her positive and kind words of support over the last year and to Callum, for his love and encouragement throughout the manuscript writing process and his patience while I worked on the book throughout many consecutive weekends. I know that he will breathe a (short) sigh of relief for the respite before my next project begins...

Finally, enormous thanks are due to my mother, Moira, for being the most inspirational person I know.

1 Introduction

Why is punishment not more effective? Why do we have such high re-offending rates? How can we address the problem of courts seeing the same offenders time and time again? How can we deal with crime and criminals in a more cost-effective manner? These are some of the questions that are commonly asked about the day-to-day workings and outcomes of the criminal justice system. From the perspective of the general public, they want to know why the government is not tackling crime, and particularly repeat offenders, more effectively. Buttressed by media representations of crime which tend to report the most salacious, violent and high profile cases, and which reproduce discourses of a 'failing' criminal justice system wherein criminals are released early from prison into neighbourhoods to repeatedly re-offend, the public report concerns about fear of crime, violent crime, and about the inadequacy of effective sentences for repeat offenders. Politicians, concerned both by the social and financial costs of an ineffective approach to crime as well as its implications for their electoral appeal, increasingly place a primacy on the use of interventions that are able to statistically demonstrate reductions in rates of re-offending and which can be shown to be cost-effective, particularly in the current climate of austerity and criminal justice budget cutbacks. Crime is an issue that is high on the public and political agenda.

Yet in Britain and across much of Europe, Canada and North America, crime rates have been falling consistently since the mid-1990s. The most recent government statistics published in July 2013 show that crime in England and Wales has fallen by 9 per cent over the past year, putting the crime rate at its lowest level since the *Crime Survey for England and Wales* (formerly the *British Crime Survey*) began in 1981 (ONS 2013).[1] Police-recorded crime figures also continue to show year-on-year reductions and the latest figures for England and Wales are 38 per cent lower than 2002–2003 (Home Office 2013).[2] While the problems inherent in the interpretation and use of official crime figures are well established (Skogan 1974; Maguire 2012) and the re-categorisation of crime and changes in police practice over the last two decades, including in the use of out of court disposals, mean that such figures must be treated with some caution, nonetheless evidence from numerous empirical studies reinforce the downward trend in the overall rate of crime, both nationally and internationally (Tseloni *et al.* 2010;

2 Introduction

IEP 2013; Perreault 2013). While the factors behind falling crime rates in Britain are complex, evidence suggests that education, labour market policies, increased spending on police resources, as well as improved security technology such as car and burglar alarms, are among the reasons for the trend in falling rates of property theft and violent crime (van Dijk *et al.* 2012; Draca *et al.* 2011).[3] In particular, high income inequality and low educational opportunities have emerged as central in explaining the causes of crime (Machin *et al.* 2011; Machin and Meghir 2004). Internationally, there is also a lack of consensus on the main drivers for the drop in crime, although one of the most persuasive analyses suggests that substantive changes in the quantity and quality of security have been crucial to reductions in crime (Farrell *et al.* 2011).

However, despite evidence of falling crime rates in Britain, public perception of crime levels is often inaccurate (Duffy *et al.* 2008); fear of crime remains significant (Farrall *et al.* 2009; Brunton-Smith and Sturgis 2011); and recidivism levels, particularly for low-level offenders, are consistently high (Ministry of Justice 2013). In part (although not exclusively) a consequence of media discourses on crime, the general public are often reluctant to accept that crime is falling and tend to display inconsistency in their attitudes towards crime and justice, especially in the areas of sentencing, prison and preventative measures (Hough *et al.* 2013; Hough and Roberts 2012; Jewkes 2010). Interestingly, the public generally have more confidence in how crime is managed locally than nationally. As such a 'perception gap' exists between how safe they believe their own locales to be relative to the country as a whole (Duffy *et al.* 2008). It is also important not to overlook that street crime, violence and anti-social behaviour are more likely to be found in areas of poverty and concentrated multiple deprivation (Millie *et al.* 2005). People who live in high crime areas are more likely to be victims of crime but they also suffer the effects of criminality, including fear of crime, disproportionately and more acutely. While overall crime rates have been declining, nonetheless there remain pockets of the country characterised by social exclusion, deprivation, poverty and significant levels of criminality. There is strong evidence to suggest that high crime environments detrimentally affect families and children and lead to individuals withdrawing and isolating themselves from the neighbourhood in which they live (Ellen 2012; Shapland and Hall 2007).

One salient factor in the drop in overall crime has been major government investment in criminal justice over the last decade. Unfortunately, this level of investment has had very little impact upon recidivism levels. In England and Wales, rates of re-offending are high with around half of all crime being committed by repeat offenders. The latest government statistics show a one-year proven re-offending rate of 26.9 per cent which is a rise of 0.4 per cent compared to the previous year and only a 1 per cent fall in points since 2000 (Ministry of Justice 2013a). Thus, although the number of people entering the criminal justice system is falling, a 'hard core' group continue to re-offend at a significant rate. In the year up to 2011, more than 400 000 crimes were committed by those who had previously broken the law. For those sentenced to less than 12 months' imprisonment, 58.5 per cent had re-offended within 12 months of their release up to September 2011, which is a 1.2 percentage points increase on the previous year. High recidivism levels are problematic for politicians; not only because they suggest that the criminal justice system is failing to deter criminals and reduce victimisation but also because of the very significant cost associated with repeat offending. In England and Wales, the most recent official estimates suggest that re-offending costs the government between £9.5 and £13 billion annually. High levels of recidivist offending are also represented in criminal justice statistics internationally. For example, Canada, the US and Australia all continue to demonstrate significant rates of re-offending despite overall drops in their respective crime rates (Statistics Canada 2012; Pew Center on the States 2011; SCRGSP 2012).

As a consequence, the problem of recidivist offenders in particular has attracted much media, public, academic and political attention. This has prompted consideration and debate about a number of important overlapping issues relating to re-offending, such as levels of state investment in welfare (Young 2007; Mooney and Neal 2010); the public/private delivery of treatment and support services (Mills *et al.* 2011); criminal justice approaches to and conceptualisations of rehabilitation (Maruna 2011; Hudson 2003; Garland 2001); concern about 'meaningful' and 'productive' punishment (Broome 2012; Lacey and Pickard 2012; Husak 2011); the status of the victim in the criminal justice process (Sanders and Jones 2007; Ashworth and Redmayne 2005); the impact of high incarceration levels on local neighbourhoods (Sampson and Loeffler 2010); reform of sentencing and court practices (Ashworth 2013); and the applicability and value of non-adversarial innovations such as restorative justice (Shapland *et al.* 2006).

In recent years, the notion of problem-solving justice has emerged in response to these fundamental concerns. Problem-solving justice embodies the notion that the criminal justice system should do more than simply process cases through the courts: a problem-solving approach prioritises efforts to change the behaviour of offenders; provide better support and aid to victims; and improve public safety in neighbourhoods (Berman and Fox 2009). The concept of problem-solving justice has received increasing attention in criminal justice over the last decade. It is a term that is now routinely used by criminal justice professionals, it is deployed in political discourse, and it also features in numerous policy documents and official government publications in the United Kingdom, the United States and beyond. Problem-solving justice largely originated in America during the 1990s and its use and influence has continued to spread globally, incorporating a range of new innovations and practices including local justice centres and, most famously, problem-solving courts such as drug courts and domestic violence courts. As a theoretical concept, problem-solving justice can be located within the broader sphere of community justice. Community justice is an umbrella term used to describe innovations and policies which operate with community objectives at their core, such as improvements in safety or crime prevention, social cohesion and urban renewal. Examples of community justice

4   Introduction

initiatives include community policing, community probation, community conferencing, mentoring and community courts.

While problem-solving justice has also begun to proliferate in other jurisdictions such as Australia, Canada and the Netherlands, the problem-solving model is most developed in America. In fact, such has been the rapid growth of problem-solving justice in the US, that some scholars have even predicted that problem-solving principles will soon become the norm in every court (Hora 2011, 2009). Indeed, in the US, serious efforts have been made to assist with the embedding of problem-solving principles into mainstream traditional courts (ABACJ 2008; Casey 2006; Rottman and Casey 2005; Wolf 2009a, 2007; NLADA 2003; Clarke and Neuhard 2005). A growing body of literature suggests that US court specialisation has resulted in increased engagement between citizens and the courts, improved perceptions of neighbourhood safety, greater accountability for low level 'quality-of-life' offenders, speedier and more meaningful case resolutions, and cost savings (see for example, Wolf 2007; Henry and Kralstein 2011). In other jurisdictions too, such as Australia, Canada and the United Kingdom, the growth of court specialisation has led to the 'fusion' of court and welfare systems, and a developing welfare role for the courts (Freiberg 2003; King 2009; McIvor 2010; Holland 2011).

The primary focus of this book is to consider recent developments in problem-solving justice and court specialisation in England and Wales and to contextualise these innovations more broadly in relation to the growing international movement towards the incorporation of problem-solving practices and principles within criminal justice frameworks. Although there are a range of problem-solving models, which vary in their implementation across and within jurisdictions, there are common fundamental objectives which are characteristic of these different approaches, especially in terms of diversion from custody (at least initially) and their aims of reduced rates of recidivism. Problem-solving justice is still in its infancy in England and Wales; yet it is much more developed as a criminal justice approach in other international jurisdictions, most notably in the US.[4] Although not directly comparable, existing literature on problem-solving and court specialisation in other jurisdictions provides useful material and emerging areas of interest and critique that may inform the development and evaluation of specialist courts and problem-solving oriented approaches in England and Wales.

It is important to preface this by acknowledging that a body of scholarship has identified some of the difficulties inherent in criminal justice policy transfer (for example see Stenson and Edwards 2004). Moreover, as Tim Newburn's (2002) comparative empirical research on Britain and the US has demonstrated, in those cases where there has been significant US criminal justice policy influence, the outcomes have continued to display a number of specifically British features. National and local politics and cultures exert considerable influence on policy development and implementation. As we shall see in the pages that follow, although US-led reforms in the domain of problem-solving justice have been instrumental to the development of problem-solving and court specialisation in

England and Wales, the influence of local/national cultures (legal, political, social) has been reflected in the way that problem-solving justice has been constructed, framed and is now operating within the criminal justice system here.

The international literature also serves to highlight important critical perspectives on the problem-solving justice movement. These incorporate multiple vignettes of critique, spanning legal, criminological and practice-based analyses. Understood in their particular jurisdictional context, these different critical commentaries are both relevant and potentially helpful in informing and ameliorating the emergence and development of problem-solving practices and innovations in England and Wales. Increased awareness of documented problems (both practice and ideological) elsewhere may go some way towards encouraging efforts to ensure that these issues are not replicated, or in any event that there is at least some recognition and engagement with the dynamics of the problem-solving approach. It is also worth noting that, as Paul Holland (2011) has usefully observed in a recent article, problem-solving proponents in the US have acknowledged the limitations of previous/earlier attempts at and models of courts specialisation, and have 'internalized' and been responsive to these issues and controversies, paying particular attention to the development of court specialisation cognisant of previous failures and lack of open discourse. Greater engagement with literature identifying the difficulties in the problem-solving approach does not necessarily mean therefore that its potential utility is undermined or its value eroded – rather, it suggests that problem-solving is an innovation which can be pragmatically reformed and that it can be responsive to the demands of legal ethics and court praxis.

Finally, an important observation made by problem-solving justice advocates in England (see Bowen and Whitehead 2013) has been that there now exists a large body of empirical evidence in the form of evaluations of problem-solving innovations in the US which have contributed to an improved understanding of 'what works' in which circumstances, and for what categories of offenders, specifically in the US problem-solving domain. Although this should not be taken to mean that there is now a clear and definitive linear corollary that can be used to guarantee the effectiveness of problem-solving innovations, in the US there is nonetheless undoubtedly a more granular understanding of how problem-solving justice operates, and the circumstances in which it can be effective. In England and Wales, we are yet to develop and identify a specific evidence base with which to inform criminal justice developments in this arena. Much of the current discussion around court innovation and reform tends to coalesce around the technical aspects of court operations and the limitations that they pose for progressive reform. However, although barriers to innovation certainly do exist, we should not understand these as insurmountable constraints. By harnessing existing support within the courts and criminal justice system for new innovation and by committing to the production and analysis of appropriate and targeted empirical evidence which evaluates the factors contributing to/limiting success, we will be able to form a more rounded, complete and principled position on how we situate a

6   *Introduction*

problem-solving justice rationale within the criminal justice landscape in England and Wales.

Methodology

The research presented and discussed in this book is the culmination of a number of formal grant-funded empirical projects and informal investigative work which I first began back in 2009 when I started work on a research project, funded by the Economic and Social Research Council (ESRC), on specialist Anti-Social Behaviour Response Courts in England and Wales. This study examined recent attempts to embed a problem-solving approach in the lower courts in England and Wales and involved an observational and interview-based study with criminal justice practitioners in sites across England and Wales and an ethnographic study of cases in 22 county and magistrates' courts. The study examined the functioning and scalability of problem-solving justice in the courts in England (further details on this study are also published in Donoghue 2012). The research highlighted a number of significant opportunities and barriers to problem-solving justice, which I then explored through further fieldwork and investigation.

In the course of my fieldwork on problem-solving justice, I spoke to (by telephone and email) and met with many professionals involved in criminal justice including police, lawyers and barristers (both in-post and retired), housing practitioners, victim advocates, members of the Crown Prosecution Service (CPS) and sentencers in England and Wales.[5] Over the duration of my fieldwork, I was also very kindly invited to become a member of an online discussion network for magistrates/Justices of the Peace and judges. The network is an online forum where members of the magistracy in England and Wales, and judges from other jurisdictions including Scotland, Ireland, Serbia, Romania, Bermuda, South Africa, Canada, Italy, France, Portugal, Lebanon, Nigeria, Namibia and the US discuss matters relating to sentencing and the courts. Having access to this online forum has been enormously helpful as I was able to post discussion topics relating to my areas of research interest and engage with sentencers in detail about their responses. The network currently has more than 160 members from a wide range of international jurisdictions and so it was useful too in debating cross-jurisdictional and comparative perspectives. Given that problem-solving justice is a praxis innovation that is intended to be 'judge-led', it is perhaps then not surprising that the majority of my empirical work on problem-solving justice has been informed by my interactions with magistrates and the court system. And it is this aspect of my research which is particularly represented in the pages that follow, and I have, as appropriate included specific quotations from the magistrates that I have had verbal and email communication with over the last few years.

My arguments in this book are further informed by the exchange of empirical data and ideas that took place at an international symposium on Specialist Courts and Therapeutic Jurisprudence, funded by the University of Oxford's Faculty of Law, which I ran in August 2011. This was attended by, amongst others, Greg

Berman (Director of the Center for Court Innovation in New York), Professor Gill McIvor (University of Stirling), Professor Eric Miller (University of Loyola), Professor Cyrus Tata (University of Strathclyde), and Professor David Wexler (University of Puerto Rico), all of whose work in this area has been highly influential and of great importance in shaping my perspective on problem-solving approaches. I have also incorporated data and information disseminated by participants at a symposium on Standards in the Problem-Solving Courts at the University of Miami Law School in October 2012, where I presented data from my empirical study of specialist Anti-Social Behaviour Response Courts. The empirical data presented herein is further supplemented with information derived from a wide range of other primary and secondary sources including official government reports and publications, court reports, police records, minutes of meetings, legislation and HANSARD (the official transcript of debates in the UK Parliament).

Critique

As I have already alluded to, there are multifarious strands of critique present in the problem-solving justice literature. I wish here to provide a short summary of the main critical trajectories in order to make clear my own perspective from the outset of this book and to set out how I plan to engage with and respond to these arguments. It may be useful to think of the different types of critique of problem-solving justice as falling into two particular groups: criminological/criminal justice practice-based critiques; and critical legal commentaries. Within the former, perhaps the most fundamental genus of criticism rests on the notion that problem-solving justice has emerged in response to, and essentially to compensate for, the inadequacy of traditional state responses to crime and social problems. Numerous commentators, particularly in the US, have argued that the apparent transference of responsibility for social issues such as addiction and mental health *away from* welfare agencies *to* problem-solving courts has occurred as a result of the failure of government to invest in and support social/welfare structures. The growth of problem-solving justice is therefore seen to represent an over-reliance upon the criminal justice system to 'solve' entrenched socio-economic problems.

Although problem-solving courts are intended to operate as an alternative to incarceration, they nonetheless function as part of the criminal justice system. In the context of drug and mental health courts particularly, critics maintain that these types of courts should instead adopt a public health approach to the treatment of offenders rather than a criminal justice one, which only serves to recreate existing contours of selectivity and discrimination inherent in criminal processes. A corollary of this critique is that problem-solving courts, by their existence, create inconsistency in the treatment of offenders in the criminal justice system. For example, those who refuse to participate in the problem-solving court are then processed through the traditional court process, and so may receive different punishment to those who commit the same offence but

8   *Introduction*

instead agree to participate in the problem-solving court process. To what extent participation in treatment-oriented courts such as drug courts is genuinely 'voluntary' is also a matter of contention and much has been written about the 'coercive version of justice' that these courts arguably espouse (see for example, Miller 2009).

Although it might appear that the increased emphasis upon treatment within the court system signifies a return to the 'rehabilitative ideal' (Allen 1981), it has been argued that the existence of problem-solving courts may also provide further evidence of the *decline* of the rehabilitative ideal, whereby the most sympathetic and appealing class of criminal cases are isolated for attention, while other more complex and resource intensive cases are ignored (Casey 2004). Problem-solving courts have thus been criticised for their potential to facilitate the 'up-tariffing' of criminal justice sanctions as well as 'net-widening' through a focus on less serious offenders (McSweeney *et al.* 2008; Blagg 2008; Indemaur and Roberts 2003; Moore 2007).

An overarching concern within the critical legal scholarship has been that the growth of problem-solving justice has resulted in a concomitant movement away from the criminal justice system's adversarial tradition. As a consequence, critics maintain that the criminal justice system is being altered in fundamental ways: these changes are highly significant because the adversarial model reflects a broader ideology that inculcates important values which, if not properly protected by the system emerging to replace it, will be eroded (McEwan, 2011). Problem-solving court sceptics argue that it is not necessarily the de facto changes to the conduct of cases which threaten fair trial rights, but it is the potential for fundamental, but largely ad hoc alterations to be made to the system without proper regard for how that new system/approach will guarantee existing principles of legality and due process. They question whether developments in problem-solving justice satisfy ethical and legal practice standards and express concern that adversarial justice is being diluted, threatening the fundamental fairness of the justice system.

In the UK specifically however, there is very little academic discourse on the tensions between problem-solving and adversarial justice, and particularly how these two concepts are being reconciled within the court practices and rules of the new network of specialist and problem-solving courts. While it is certainly the case that changes can be made to trial processes and court procedures that do not undermine due process protections, there is currently a paucity of literature examining whether recent developments in England and Wales have implications not simply for court practice including traditional safeguarding procedures but also for the balance of power between defendants and the state. Developments in problem-solving justice in England and Wales also prompt questions about the role of sentencers, especially in the lower criminal courts. This relates to whether the judicial role should be conceived of as encompassing broader (social) dimensions such as leading and informing community expectations through the problem-solving justice sphere. In this context, the changing nature of the judicial role in problem-solving courts – to incorporate monitoring,

Introduction 9

reviewing and encouraging offender compliance – raises issues about judicial impartiality and independence. Critical legal commentary on problem-solving courts in other jurisdictions argues that a consideration of 'therapeutic' outcomes should not play any part at all in judicial decision-making and the 'enhanced' role that problem-solving court sentencers undertake. Legal scholars also maintain that it is problematic to transplant theories and practices from psychology and social work into the legal domain, especially when problem-solving courts lack a coherent set of theoretical organising principles. This prompts consideration of whether problem-solving justice has been rationalised in the language of pragmatism rather than the language of legal theory or doctrine.

In light of these critical criminological and legal perspectives, it is important to make clear from the outset of this book that I am an advocate of problem-solving justice and problem-solving courts. I take the view that the growth of problem-solving justice represents a progressive and viable approach to addressing crime and promoting justice. Problem-solving justice exemplifies a transformative approach to criminal justice and, although they are not a panacea, problem-solving courts are an important and innovative practice adjunct wherein the court can operate as a 'window of opportunity' in responding to recidivist offenders, including in the treatment and rehabilitation of offenders. Persuasive empirical evidence has been produced in both Australia and the US that post-sentencing oversight of offenders, particularly in drug and domestic violence court settings, leads to positive outcomes and reductions in offending. Moreover, this book argues that, through the problem-solving model, the traditional concept of adversarial justice is not undermined. While critics have suggested that problem-solving approaches have been introduced by stealth and without proper formal discussion and recognition of their potential impact/consequences for the legal tradition, I argue that problem-solving is an important and positive criminal justice innovation that, properly applied, does not undermine the adversarial tradition.

It has however been particularly important for me, in the course of writing this book, to engage with the multifarious and well-considered critiques of the problem-solving approach throughout, and I am especially grateful to my great friend and colleague Eric Miller who has provided the foreword to this text. His work, on drug courts specifically, has been enormously helpful in motivating me to evaluate my own arguments on problem-solving justice and although we disagree over both practice and theoretical aspects of the problem-solving court model, the interchange between our perspectives I think serves to highlight that there is not a strict division between those who are problem-solving court advocates, and those who are critical of their function and role within criminal justice. This is particularly important within the legal/criminological landscape where scholarship is often so polarised that there can be no positive interaction and debate between 'opposing' sides, resulting in a zero-sum approach to the exchange and development of ideas which (ultimately) has consequences for progress in the criminal justice domain.

10　*Introduction*

Structure of the book

This book sets out a 'direction of travel' on problem-solving justice, particularly with regard to its potential implementation in the English context. There are two overarching themes which inform (explicitly or implicitly) and intersect with much, if not all of the discussion presented in this text. The first theme is the significant pressure of necessary cost reductions in the administration of criminal justice; and the second is the conceptualisation of punishment and, correspondingly, justice. That an emphasis upon reductions in cost should be a central theme of this book is of course entirely to be expected given the current financial climate which has necessitated criminal justice spending cuts in jurisdictions both within and beyond those in the UK. However, it is not simply the impact of fiscal imperatives which are of interest but the way in which economic constraints have led to policy reforms which have principles of marketisation and privatisation of criminal justice services at their core. The observation that the delivery of criminal justice is now increasingly subject to processes of privatisation, links in to the second theme of this book, in respect of how we conceive of the state's role in the delivery of punishment. Problem-solving justice symbolises a new and transformative approach to punishment and the delivery of justice. Yet the implementation of problem-solving justice, and ultimately its effectiveness, will be constrained or facilitated by the criminal justice framework in which it operates. A climate of privatisation, together with the incorporation of strategies of marketisation, will undoubtedly have consequences for problem-solving praxis and outcomes.

The book begins by situating the development of problem-solving justice within the contemporary criminal justice landscape. It considers where we ought to locate problem-solving justice within the wider criminological literature which has identified a climate of 'punitiveness' in the development and articulation of criminal justice policy over the last two decades. In particular, it pays attention to recent government policy reforms which have proposed a 'rehabilitation revolution' wherein punishment is made more 'intelligent' and a payment by results (PBR) model is used to increase effectiveness in the delivery of criminal justice services such as probation, treatment and support. It then examines the concept of problem-solving justice in detail and identifies the central components and principles of a problem-solving approach to criminal justice. It reflects on how problem-solving has evolved internationally in a range of other jurisdictions and outlines areas of overlap as well as aspects of discontinuity and tension. It considers how problem-solving can be located alongside other criminal justice innovations and concepts such as community justice, restorative justice and therapeutic jurisprudence. Specialist and Problem-Solving Courts are then paid particular attention in Chapter 3. The chapter begins with a general introduction to the various features and principles of problem-solving courts before considering the development, creation and specific features of these courts in England and Wales. Fundamental to understanding the way that problem-solving justice is operating in England and Wales, is an appreciation of

Introduction 11

the distinctive role and function of the lay magistracy in the lower court system, which is discussed in detail. The existence and functioning of problem-solving courts in England and Wales is further contextualised in respect of criminal justice budget cuts which have resulted in many magistrates' court closures and significant consequences for 'local justice'; and also current policy reforms which aim to widen the skills and capabilities of magistrates in the delivery of summary justice.

In Chapter 4, Drug Courts and Domestic Violence Courts are discussed and empirical evidence on their functioning and outcomes is examined. This chapter also considers court-ordered drug treatment in England and Wales in the context of the use of Drug Rehabilitation Requirements (DRRs) as conditions of community orders; the recent introduction of combined Family Drug and Alcohol Courts in England; and it evaluates plans to create Specialist Sexual Violence Courts (SVCs) in London. It concludes by identifying the range of constraints, both practical and theoretical, that are associated with the drug court and domestic violence court model. Community Courts and Mental Health Courts are then examined in Chapter 5. The historic difficulties (in England and in other jurisdictions) of incorporating the 'community' into court processes are paid attention and current financial and organisational constraints impacting upon the work of community courts in England and Wales are discussed. The second part of the chapter examines the recent introduction of mental health courts in England and considers whether some of the practice and theoretical tensions evident in the international mental health court literature may be being replicated in the English mental health court model.

There then follows, in Chapter 6, an examination of the recent creation of neighbourhood justice panels (NJPs) in England and Wales, which is an important parallel development in the problem-solving justice domain. Problem-solving advocates in England have argued that simple summary cases should be diverted away from traditional magistrates' courts to NJPs to ensure that they are dealt with proportionately and in order to free up court resources for cases which are better dealt with in the criminal court system (Bowen and Whitehead 2013). The use and operation of NJPs in summary cases is not, however, unproblematic. This chapter draws upon my empirical research to highlight some of the tensions that exist in the functioning of NJPs, including in respect of localism agendas, the different practice frameworks and partnership arrangements that exist in these forums, and the (ir)reconcilability of NJPs as separate divisions of summary justice. The chapter also contains discussion of recent plans for the introduction of pre-sentencing restorative justice in England and Wales.

In the final chapter (Chapter 7), the prospects and pitfalls that exist to the implementation of problem-solving justice as a transformative innovation in criminal justice praxis in England and Wales are discussed. The book concludes by indicating policy implications and potential ways forward towards the reconciliation of the complex vector of legal, economic and political dynamics currently facing specialist and problem-solving courts in England and Wales and also internationally. While a number of the issues that I raise in this book have

12 *Introduction*

been acknowledged in government policy documents, as well as in publications of the Magistrates' Association, there is yet to be collective agreement (among policymakers and the professionals who work within the criminal justice system) as to a common problem-solving approach to take forward. This again highlights the difficulty in attempting to progress a problem-solving approach in England and Wales, when some of the most fundamental aspects of the model are still being debated by government, the courts and practitioners. I argue for a range of substantive changes to be made in court procedures and in the statutory provisions limiting judicial involvement in post-sentence review of offenders' progress. It recognises that the implementation of the changes to facilitate improved problem-solving justice have different timescales. However, the crucial first step is to establish the governance arrangements at a national, regional and local level to set this work in progress. Measuring progress will be vitally important in maintaining the momentum of this work to help to secure the longevity and sustainability of specialist and problem-solving courts.

Notes

1 According to findings of the CSEW, car theft has decreased by 15 per cent, vandalism has fallen by 13 per cent and burglaries have dropped by 7 per cent (ONS 2013). Official police statistics on recorded crime also support a drop in crime. The police recorded 3.7 million offences in the year ending March 2013, a decrease of 7 per cent compared with the previous year (although these statistics are contentious because of police manipulation of data to meet targets, see for example recent evidence to the Public Administration Select Committee, www.parliament.uk/business/committees/committees-a-z/commons-select/public-administration-select-committee/publications/). Notably, although there has been an overall fall in crime, there has been a 27 per cent rise in fraud. This is an important figure because although official crime statistics have their limitations, they do indicate a changing pattern in criminal behaviours. A 27 per cent rise in fraud suggests a complex mutation in criminal offending linked to the growth of an enormous shadow economy in illegal goods, which has been estimated at £3 trillion globally (Beckert and Wehinger 2013).
2 The UK is split into three main legal jurisdictions: England and Wales (54 million inhabitants: 88.5 per cent of the UK total), Scotland (5 million) and Northern Ireland (1.8 million).
3 Police numbers are at their lowest in a decade but there is no evidence of a direct causal link to the overall drop in crime. A significant proportion of crime is 'hidden' (within the home, for example) so police numbers do not have an effect on this.
4 While the US has higher levels of serious violence than other developed nations, it has similar levels of minor violence and property crime. In addition, the US can also be differentiated by its historically aggressive response to drug offences which has been a major determinant of higher prison populations (Lynch and Pridemore 2011).
5 The use of 'sentencers' refers to judges, magistrates/Justices of the Peace in England and Wales – as well as judges in other jurisdictions.

2 Situating problem-solving, punitivism and punishment

Nearly two decades ago, Carrie Menkel-Meadow (1996: 30) asked 'what would result if we re-defined our legal system to seek "problem-solving" as one of its goals rather than "truth-finding"'? She acknowledged that this suggestion would likely elicit 'huge outpourings of objections'. However, in the intervening years, there is evidence that a shift has indeed taken place, with many international jurisdictions such as the US, Canada, Australia, Scotland, England and Wales operating with some system of problem-solving justice. Problem-solving is most frequently discussed in the context of problem-solving courts. However, it is important to distinguish between problem-solving courts, and the related but separate concepts of 'problem-solving' and problem-solving justice. Problem-solving is a generic term which can be applied broadly to describe generally ad hoc attempts to find solutions to problems – its use of course extends beyond criminal justice to mathematics, economics and computer science for example. Problem-solving justice relates to problem-solving innovations in the criminal justice domain specifically, although it too is an elastic concept that has different incarnations across jurisdictions. While difficult to define, problem-solving justice has a number of overlapping principles. Problem-solving justice is in essence, about 'the community'. It is about engaging the community, involving it in efforts to reduce crime and it is about building the capacity and resilience of neighbourhoods. Problem-solving justice's focus upon the local community is important because research suggests that people who live in high crime areas are more likely to be victims of crime, they are more likely to witness a violent crime or to know someone who has been the victim of crime, and these experiences can profoundly affect peoples' outlook on life as well as their level of ambition (NHF 1999). Fear of crime is also higher in unsafe neighbourhoods and evidence suggests that individuals tend to withdraw from these communities and lead more sheltered and isolated lives (Ellen 2012). There is also strong evidence to support the conclusion that unsafe or high-crime environments detrimentally affect families and children. Exposure to crime (especially violence) can heighten stress levels in children, lower cognitive test scores and diminish performance in school (Aizer 2008; Sharkey 2010; Stafford *et al.* 2007). Elevated stress makes it difficult for children to concentrate or focus in school and learn, and it may compromise their immune systems long term, therefore increasing vulnerability to

14   *Situating problem-solving and punitivism*

disease. Crime may also profoundly affect the social structures of communities through high levels of incarceration: crime disrupts social networks, breaks up families, and weakens local institutions (Rose and Clear 2001; Donoghue 2008). Problem-solving justice is in many respects, conceived of as a response to these issues – it is about the idea that, rather than simply processing cases, the justice system should seek to change the behaviour of offenders and improve public and community safety.

The Center for Court Innovation in New York, which is a non-profit organisation that creates new programmes to test innovative approaches to public safety problems, has been a key influence and a fundamental driver in the development and growth of problem-solving justice; both in America but also in other jurisdictions such as the United Kingdom. A number of the Center's demonstration projects have received significant recognition and acclaim and they have also impacted upon the creation of problem-solving innovations in other jurisdictions. In particular, the award-winning Red Hook Community Justice Center in Brooklyn has been adopted as a model of excellence in a number of other jurisdictions. In addition, the Center has established a sister organisation in London, the Centre for Justice Innovation, which aims to improve the implementation, evaluation and dissemination of new ideas and new practices (including problem-solving justice) across the criminal justice domain in Britain. Moreover, the US has also influenced international developments in problem-solving justice because there is a very significant body of academic scholarship and empirical research on problem-solving justice and court specialisation that has examined, amongst other things, the efficacy of problem-solving courts, the benefits of problem-solving justice for victims and communities and the various implications of problem-solving courts for due process and legal ethics. Elsewhere, the body of academic literature on problem-solving and court specialisation is relatively slim in comparison to the U.S.

The Center for Court Innovation has identified six principles of problem-solving justice which have been adopted, either wholesale or in part, in other international jurisdictions (Wolf 2007: 2–8). The principles provide a useful framework for understanding the concept and praxis of problem-solving justice:

1 Enhanced information

Better staff training (about complex issues like domestic violence and drug addiction) combined with better information (about litigants, victims and the community context of crime) can help improve the decision-making of judges, attorneys, and other justice officials. High-quality information – gathered with the assistance of technology and shared in accordance with confidentiality laws – can help practitioners make more nuanced decisions about both treatment needs and the risks individual defendants pose to public safety, ensuring offenders receive an appropriate level of supervision and services.

Situating problem-solving and punitivism 15

2 Community engagement

Citizens and neighbourhood groups have an important role to play in helping the justice system identify, prioritise and solve local problems. Actively engaging citizens helps improve public trust in the justice system. Greater trust, in turn, helps people feel safer, fosters law-abiding behaviour and makes members of the public more willing to cooperate in the pursuit of justice (as witnesses, jury members, etc.).

3 Collaboration

Justice system leaders are uniquely positioned to engage a diverse range of people, government agencies and community organisations in collaborative efforts to improve public safety. By bringing together justice partners (for example judges, prosecutors, attorneys, probation officers, court managers) and reaching out to potential stakeholders beyond the courthouse (for example social service providers, victims groups, schools), justice agencies can improve inter-agency communication, encourage greater trust between citizens and government and foster new responses to problems.

4 Individualised justice

Using valid, evidence-based risk and needs assessment instruments, the justice system can link offenders to individually tailored community-based services (for example job training, drug treatment, safety planning, mental health counselling) where appropriate. In doing so (and by treating defendants with dignity and respect), the justice system can help reduce recidivism, improve community safety and enhance confidence in justice. Links to services can also aid victims, improving their safety and helping restore their lives.

5 Accountability

The justice system can send the message that all criminal behaviour, even low-level quality-of-life crime, has an impact on community safety and has consequences. By insisting on regular and rigorous compliance monitoring – and clear consequences for non-compliance – the justice system can improve the accountability of offenders. It can also improve the accountability of service providers by requiring regular reports on their work with participants.

6 Outcomes

The active and on-going collection and analysis of data – measuring outcomes and process, costs and benefits – are crucial tools for evaluating the effectiveness of operations and encouraging continuous improvement. Public dissemination of this information can be a valuable symbol of public accountability.

16 *Situating problem-solving and punitivism*

While these principles provide a framework for problem-solving justice generally, many jurisdictions which operate using aspects of the problem-solving framework also possess problem-solving courts. Problem-solving courts are frequently seen as integral to a problem-solving justice approach and often function as an ancillary component of problem-solving justice. It is important to recognise that problem-solving justice applies to the sentencing stage, post- (and sometimes pre-) adjudication (Miller 2004). Research has found that problem-solving courts may alter their focus from simply processing cases to improving outcomes for victims, communities and offenders (Kralstein 2005). Winick and Wexler (2003) note that a 'serious effort' is now being made to inculcate the principles and theories underpinning the use of problem-solving courts (namely community justice, therapeutic jurisprudence and aspects of restorative justice) into Western judicial structures.

In the United Kingdom, attempts have been made not only to develop community justice-oriented approaches, which incorporate aspects of the US approach to problem-solving justice, but also to embed a system of problem-solving courts. Interest in problem-solving courts was preceded by a range of policy innovations in Britain that repeatedly emphasised the fundamental importance of community engagement in both neighbourhood regeneration and crime control (Flint 2006; Garland 2001; Jarvis *et al.* 2011). The intrinsic value of community participation and involvement in creating sustainable, cohesive and 'safe' neighbourhoods was reiterated in numerous policy documents and guidance. These argued that failure to engage communities would make sustainable regeneration and community safety much more difficult to deliver and less likely to produce favourable outcomes (see for example DCLG 2008; ODPM 2003). The recent introduction of specialist and problem-solving courts, such as drug and domestic violence courts, as well as community courts in England such as the Community Justice Centre in North Liverpool are underpinned by a community justice model that emphasises a problem-solving approach with offenders and also with the wider community (McIvor 2010; McKenna 2007).

In 2009, the British government announced its intention to 'mainstream' aspects of problem-solving justice into the lower court system. The following core elements of problem-solving were to be introduced into magistrates' courts across England and Wales:

Identifying appropriate cases – for instance by using multi-agency meetings held prior to the court sitting to pinpoint appropriate cases and identify any services to which those individuals might be directed.

Direct judicial engagement with offenders – in court, once guilt is established, the judiciary can speak directly with the offender about why they committed the crime. The judiciary can help focus the offender on any problems that they feel have contributed to the offending, and discuss solutions in co-ordination with sentencing. Research suggests that this direct engagement by the sentencing judge or magistrates can be crucial in holding an

Situating problem-solving and punitivism   17

offender to account for their crime and sentence and getting them to take responsibility for their rehabilitation.

Problem-solving intervention – having ascertained whether there are underlying issues to be addressed, the judiciary can then direct the offender to services, often from the third sector, which will help them take action to tackle their problems.

Review hearings – Section 178 of the Criminal Justice Act 2003 provides the power for the court to review offenders' progress as they carry out Community Orders. Using the powers of Section 178, the judiciary can call an offender back to court to report on their progress both with the Community Order and with their action in addressing their problems. This has been found to work particularly well when the same member of the judiciary who passed sentence conducts the review.

(Cabinet Office 2009)

To what extent this effort to embed a problem-solving approach in England and Wales has been successful, will be considered in the chapters that follow. It is first necessary, however, to consider the background and context to this evolving interest in the concept and associated praxis of problem-solving justice. Problem-solving justice has been said to represent a direction for the law that involves using courts to

forge new responses to chronic social, human and legal problems ... that have proven resistant to conventional solutions, to broaden the focus of legal proceedings, from simply adjudicating past facts and legal issues to changing the future behaviour of litigants and ensuring the future well-being of communities.

(Berman and Feinblatt 2001: 125)

But how do we account for the growing interest in the development of this new idea over the last couple of decades and perhaps most importantly, what can we understand problem-solving justice as a response *to*?

In broad terms, explanations have tended to centre around the failure of traditional social institutions including the family, neighbourhood or community, schools and welfare bodies, to effectively support individuals and to address local social problems resulting in the appropriation of responsibility for these issues to the legal system (Freiberg 2001) – the process which Eric Miller has described as the 'courtification' of social service provision (Miller 2014). In this way, the criminal justice system becomes an important gateway for accessing services and treatment that are otherwise difficult to obtain. Indeed, numerous commentators, particularly in the US, have argued that the apparent transference of responsibility for social issues such as addiction and mental health *away from* welfare agencies *to* problem-solving courts has occurred as a result of the failure of government to invest in and support social or welfare structures (Casey 2004;

18   *Situating problem-solving and punitivism*

Daicoff 2002). However, this explanation is somewhat narrow; reasons for the growth of problem-solving courts may in fact be more nuanced than this. There are a number of other important dynamics within the context of criminal justice that might help us to explain the evolving interest in the development of problem-solving justice. Rather than viewing developments in problem-solving justice as a response to the dwindling influence of traditional institutions such as family and 'community' in the social control of behaviour, and/or as a reaction against the failure of agencies of the state to effectively address the social issues of many offenders such as addiction and mental health problems, problem-solving courts might also be seen as a 'window of opportunity' to attempt to transform the lives of those that enter the court system. In both the US and the UK, problem-solving justice is not about a wholesale departure from punishment: instead it is about transforming the substantive nature of punishment to make it more socially productive. Therefore, the development of problem-solving justice might be understood as a gradual, tacit movement *away from* 'punitiveness' (Pratt 2005) to a broader and more explicit acknowledgement that punishment must be conceived of as (socially) meaningful.

Problem-solving justice and the 'punitive turn'

Anthony Bottoms (1995) seminally introduced the term 'populist punitiveness' in an article describing the evolution of sentencing policy and the philosophy of punishment. Since then much has been written over the last two decades about the 'punitive turn' in Anglo-American criminal justice policy (Bottoms 1995; Wacquant 2004; Garland 2001; Pratt 2005; Kury 2008). Criminologists have variously observed the establishment of longer sentences and higher tariffs, mandatory minimum sentences, the creation of more crimes or law, a substantial growth in the prison population and the incarceration of increasing numbers of young people and children. Conceptually, punitivism should be understood as entailing both 'new' and increased forms of penal sanctions. New punitivism can be differentiated from increased punitivism in the respect that it is predicated upon the notion that the creation and development of penal power over the last few decades represents a radical departure from the approach(es) of the past (Pratt 2002, 2005). In particular, Jonathan Simon sees these new forms of penal power (especially in the US) as now embodying elements of cruelty wherein punishment is no longer conceptualised as being about rehabilitation but instead embodies a wish to incapacitate in an extreme way, leading to 'a willingness to degrade' (2011). On the other hand, increased punitivness is viewed as correlating with a decline in the rehabilitative ideal, the use of mass incarceration and an increased emphasis upon the rights of victims rather than offenders. David Garland in particular has identified developments in contemporary crime control as predicated upon populist punitivism, which has in turn led to:

> Harsher sentencing and increased use of imprisonment, 'three strikes' and mandatory minimum sentencing laws; 'truth in sentencing' and parole

Situating problem-solving and punitivism 19

release restrictions; 'no frills' prison laws and 'austere prisons'; retribution in juveniles court and the imprisonment of children; the revival of chain gangs and corporal punishment; boot camps and supermax prisons; the multiplication of capital offences and executions; community notification laws and paedophile registers; zero tolerance policies and Anti-Social Behavior Orders. There is now a long list of measures that appear to signify a punitive turn in contemporary penalty.

(Garland 2001: 142)

In this context, the 'revolving door' phenomenon of repeat offenders processed through the criminal justice system is viewed as a consequence of the disproportionate direction and application of penal resources and interventions against the poor and ethnic minority groups (Simon 1999, 2001; Caplow and Simon 1999). In a similar vein, Loic Wacquant (2001a, 2001b, 2006) contends that increased punitivism in neo-liberal democracies has a specifically racial dimension. He maintains that the prison has come to replace the ghetto as an institution of social control and that the presence of high numbers of African Americans in the prison population in America is an illustration of the replacement of a welfarist approach to poverty by one that is oriented around penal management. The prison and the ghetto are correlates in the sense that there is 'a functional equivalency, structural homology and cultural fusion, spawning a carceral continuum that entraps a population of younger black men rejected by the deregulated wage-labor market' (Wacquant 2001b: 95).

Thus we can observe that over the past two decades, critical criminologists have analysed punitiveness through notions of 'increased' or 'new' forms of punishment in western countries. It is argued that these developments in punitiveness have been disproportionately directed at minority social groups, the disenfranchised and the 'powerless'. On the other hand, problem-solving courts, which have been in operation in the US since 1989 and the UK since 1998, appear to have overarching therapeutic intentions, with restitution and treatment often fundamental rationales of the court process. While problem-solving courts have undoubtedly in part originated as a response to the deficiencies of existing mechanisms of social control as well as failures in state welfare provision, their introduction and evolution has also opened up space for the development of a wider discourse about the purpose of punishment, how we conceptualise it, what value it has and what purpose it serves. Thus, problem-solving courts raise important questions about how we conceptualise punishment. Since problem-solving courts have been in existence during the period of 'popular punitiveness', how then does this reconcile with the notion that both the US and the UK have been preoccupied with a law and order agenda that is intractably detached from social or welfare considerations and how do we reconcile the creation and development of problem-solving justice in a climate of 'punitivism'?

There is evidence from a number of comparative and empirical studies that punitiveness is subject to significant variation between and within countries (Tonry 2007) and that in Europe in particular, counter examples can be found

20 *Situating problem-solving and punitivism*

which do not easily fit such a bleak vision of punitiveness (Snacken 2010; Snacken and Dumortier 2011). In this regard, many developments that run counter to arguments about increasing forms of punitivism have taken place, such as the increasing prevalence of (and political legitimacy afforded to) restorative justice innovations and the introduction of diversionary non-custodial sanctions within criminal justice systems across the globe (Snacken 2010), as well as greater emphasis and recognition of the importance of treatment programmes for offenders; the abolishment of the death penalty across Europe; and the protection of prisoner rights through European legislation and case law. Moreover, although incarceration levels remain high in the US and UK, they vary greatly across the European continent, making it difficult to observe a generalised Western climate of punitiveness (Snacken 2010). Variation in the political economies of countries as well as their levels of welfare investment have been identified as of central importance to the orientation of criminal justice policies (Snacken and Dumortier 2011; Lacey 2008).

Equally important, however, is the suggestion that the commentaries around punitivism may have served to create false dichotomies and erroneous characterisations of a strict division between 'punitive' and 'non-punitive'. Roger Matthews (2005: 195–6) has persuasively articulated this point as follows:

> There is a preoccupation with limited oppositions and polarities that fail to do justice to the diversity, contradictions, reversions and tensions in current crime control policy. In this twin-track, bifurcated and zero-sum world of punitive versus non-punitive, inclusion versus exclusion, populism versus elitism, 'new' versus 'old' penologies, 'civilizing' versus 'decivilizing processes', we are in danger of becoming lost in a series of false dichotomies ... The failure to disentangle both conceptually and empirically the constituent elements of 'punitiveness' has led a number of criminologists to see the recent expansion of the crime control industry as a function of the desire to 'get tough'. Rather than seeing the growing array of agencies and institutions with their different roles, discourses and specialisms, as part of an increasingly complex, opaque and expanding network of crime control, involving a diverse range of interventionist strategies. Consequently, there is a tendency to reduce these developments to an underlying punitiveness or populism, or both ... It is not too difficult to see why penal reform groups find this type of explanation attractive, since it gives them the opportunity to present themselves as limiting the excesses of malevolent politicians on the one hand while educating a misinformed public on the other. Academic criminologists are also able to make similar claims while gaining the benefits that come from the belief that they occupy the moral high ground. However, the disproportionate focus on punitiveness may well reflect changing social sensibilities and a growing ambivalence towards the use of punitive sanctions—particularly segregative measures. Thus, rather than being in the ascendancy, punitive and emotive sanctions may in reality be becoming increasingly untenable.

Situating problem-solving and punitivism   21

Matthews' observations are important not only because they provide an important counterweight to the punitivism literature which, as Snacken (2010) has observed, has at points been unable to capture the manifestations of local dynamics and cross-jurisdictional variation evident in much crime control policy, but also because I would argue that it follows from Matthews' analysis that the *capacity* of punitivism (as a concept) to accurately represent directions in and attitudes towards crime control – and the nature of punishment – is becoming less obvious.

In the introduction to this book, I articulated that the development of problem-solving justice prompts questions about punishment, its conceptualisation and purpose. Garland (1990) maintains that criminal law is culturally embedded and that criminal justice policies inherently reflect prevailing social attitudes and traditions. With this in mind, Lacey and Pickard (2012: 8) suggest that:

> In public discourse about crime, there is an insistent worry that our capacity to hold offenders responsible and accountable for misconduct is threatened by an attitude of concern, respect and compassion. For it may seem as if these attitudes can tempt us to excuse offenders from responsibility: to hold offenders responsible, we must respond with treatment which is hard and stigmatizes – or censures, excludes, or shows no mercy.

Yet there has, over the last ten years, been evidence to suggest that Lacey and Pickard's (2012) observation that public discourse on crime continues to be dominated by these specific concerns about legitimate responses and reactions to crime, has certain caveats and limitations. We know, first of all, from influential empirical research undertaken by Julian Roberts and Mike Hough that the public are not generally as punitive as politicians believe them to be (Roberts and Hough 2011, 2005; Roberts 2008). This is also reflected in the growing popularity of informal and alternative justice innovations such as restorative justice and non-adversarial justice. Indeed this book discusses some of these recent innovations, many developed at a local level by residents themselves who not only view formal criminal justice processes as less effective than locally developed solutions, but who also emphasise the value of restorative and re-integrative solutions to local crime problems. For example, neighbourhood reparative boards and community justice panels introduced in Vermont (US) and Somerset (England), although created in different continents and at a different times, were both established in response to local residents' beliefs that a conventional, 'top-down' criminal justice approach was less effective than a local justice-oriented response. Rather than exemplifying citizens' desire for stigmatisation and retribution when holding offenders responsible for their transgressions, these innovations are instead oriented towards reparation and are perceptibly less punitive and less concerned with censure and exclusion than traditional criminal processes. I am arguing in this book that we should view the development of problem-solving justice in the context of what I see as a broader paradigm in which the concept and praxis of punishment is beginning to be transformed.

22   *Situating problem-solving and punitivism*

In this context, critics of problem-solving courts have argued that these specialist courts remain resolutely punitive because although on the face of it, they embody both legal censure *and* therapeutic elements, problem-solving court judges use coercive treatment and sanction, including the use of prison, in their decision-making. This critique perhaps somewhat misses the point however. While problem-solving justice is concerned with efforts to change the behaviour of offenders; provide better support and aid to victims; and improve public safety in neighbourhoods, it is not suggested by problem-solving justice advocates (such as myself) that problem-solving courts should not have *available* to them a punitive element to their functioning. Problem-solving justice is therefore not about a wholesale departure from punishment per se, it is about transforming the substantive nature of punishment to make it more socially productive, which includes an emphasis upon reducing the social exclusion, stigmatisation and marginalisation experienced by recidivist offenders in their neighbourhoods through treatment to address the causes of their offending; recognition of and engagement with community dynamics; and enhanced procedural justice through offender 'voice' in the court process. Problem-solving justice can therefore be differentiated from aspects of restorative justice practice because problem-solving clearly does not view the criminal justice approach (including court process) as in and of itself an exclusionary and stigmatising entity; it does not view the courts as 'ceremonies of degradation' – rather it sees courts as a 'window of opportunity'. Problem-solving court researchers in England allude to this idea, for example, when they suggest that it may be 'the physical court appearance that provides the key therapeutic moment to effect behavioural change' (Gilling and Jolley 2012). Hence, in this sense, problem-solving justice remains 'about' punishment – it is just not the type of punishment that is necessarily envisioned by those who see a continued trajectory of punitivism in which forms of punishment are reproduced which are devoid of social worth, which are almost wholly retributive and which are largely disinterested in rehabilitation. It is necessary at this juncture to provide some further context to the operation of problem-solving justice in England and Wales. Important changes have begun to occur in the criminal justice landscape, which have further altered the tone of policy and practice, and conceptualisations of 'punishment'.

A 'Rehabilitation Revolution'?

In the last few years, significant changes have begun to occur in the criminal justice system in Britain, which has seen the development of a purportedly renewed focus upon the concept of rehabilitation. Following the general election in 2010 and the formation of a Conservative-led coalition government, reforms have been introduced that fundamentally impact upon the structure and delivery of criminal justice. These reforms have largely been precipitated by economic decline and the current financial climate of austerity. Upon entering office in August 2010, the government was faced with a dysfunctional, over-centralised and expensive criminal justice system which appeared unsustainable in a country

Situating problem-solving and punitivism 23

emerging from recession. Record spending on incarceration and the doubling of the prison population over the last two decades came at enormous associated cost which was evident in a budget deficit inherited from the previous governments. In response, the Coalition prioritised a focus on reform and rehabilitation in criminal justice. However, these reforms have been extremely controversial.

In a speech to the Centre for Crime and Justice Studies at King's College London in June 2010, the Justice Secretary announced government plans for reform of sentencing and rehabilitation, which he described as a 'rehabilitation revolution'.[1] The Justice Secretary argued that significant increases in the prison population over the last two decades had been 'costly and ineffectual', and maintained that community punishment was a better alternative to prison both financially but also in respect of its potential for changing offenders' behaviour. Recognising that short prison sentences (generally of less than six months) can make it 'virtually impossible' to rehabilitate or provide training to prisoners while also negatively impacting upon their lives when they leave custody through loss of employment and/or housing, he added that the new policy also aimed at reducing the use of short prison sentences. According to official government statistics, nearly half of all offenders released from prison reoffend within a year of being released, while three quarters are reconvicted within a decade of being released (Ministry of Justice 2010c: 2). It is particularly this problem of the 'revolving door' of repeat offenders that the government's 'rehabilitation revolution' aims to address.

Further detail on the government's plans for sentencing and rehabilitation reform were then subsequently published in the Green Paper, *Breaking the Cycle*: *Effective Punishment, Rehabilitation and Sentencing of Offenders* (Ministry of Justice 2010b). The Green Paper set out six principle areas of reform: prisons and community sentences; rehabilitation; payment by results; sentencing; youth justice; and community engagement. Reductions in both inefficiency and re-offending are to be achieved through a range of processes such as reforms to community sentences by making them more onerous; enforced drug rehabilitation programmes; and the introduction of a system of payment by results for prison and rehabilitation providers. Perhaps most significantly, prisoners sentenced to less than one year in prison, who currently are not covered by rehabilitation, would in future be eligible – a potentially huge extension of the programme. The Offender Rehabilitation Bill, which is currently going through Parliament, will extend license after release to include offenders sentenced to short custodial sentences, with the aim of reducing the high re-offending rates of these offenders. The Bill will also introduce a new supervision period for the purposes of rehabilitation for this group of offenders, along with those serving sentences of 12 months or more but less than 2 years. When added to license, this supervision period will mean both groups will be subject to at least 12 months of statutory rehabilitation after release.

In 2012, the government then published a further set of reforms in the White Paper, *Swift and Sure Justice: The Government's Plans for Reform of the Criminal Justice System*. The Paper placed a particular emphasis upon more efficient

24 *Situating problem-solving and punitivism*

and reliable delivery of criminal justice to enhance public confidence, which is to be achieved through practical changes to the justice system such as increased use of technology, longer court opening times, early guilty pleas, and changes to the role of magistrates (discussed more fully in Chapter 3). The Paper also notes the government's plans, proposed in its previous consultation on reform of community sentences (Ministry of Justice 2012b), to include a punitive requirement in every community order. In this consultation, the Justice Secretary observed that:

> It's true that ... community sentences can be effective at rehabilitating offenders. But overall re-offending rates for community sentences remain too high. And ... they lack credibility as effective punishment. Sentences can involve just a weekly meeting with probation officers, or as little as six hours a week of community payback. A frustrating inability to prove offenders' means can result in fines and compensation being set at levels apparently unrelated to the swaggering lifestyles of some criminals. And, despite recent improvements, enforcement action when offenders don't turn up for community payback or bother to pay fines is still too patchy and inconsistent. I share public concern that offenders given community sentences often feel they are getting away with it, slapped on the wrist rather than properly punished.
>
> (Ministry of Justice: 2012b)

The government's position on community sentences has been somewhat disjointed however. Initially, and in the context of the publication of some positive data on the effectiveness of community sentences, the Coalition had seemed to be supportive of community sentences as having a significant and important rehabilitative role. *Breaking the Cycle* had noted that there was to be '... greater focus on rehabilitation, so that offenders who commit to reforming themselves will have a greater chance of returning to society as law abiding citizens'. Moreover, the newly enacted Legal Aid, Sentencing and Punishment of Offenders Act 2012 appeared to promote greater use of community sentencing. However, no sooner had this legislation been passed than the government introduced the Crime and Courts Act 2013, which developed proposals contained in the Ministry of Justice's consultation *Punishment and reform: effective community sentences*, and which aimed to put the emphasis back on punitive punishments within community orders. The Act *requires* a court imposing a community order either to include a requirement that fulfils the purpose of punishment in the order or to impose a fine (or do both) unless there are exceptional circumstances that would make that unjust.[2] Schedule 16 of the Crime and Courts Act 2013 (which came into force on 25 April 2013) amends the Criminal Justice Act 2003 as follows:

2   In section 177 (community orders) after subsection (2) insert—
     '(2A) Where the court makes a community order, the court must—

Situating problem-solving and punitivism 25

(a) include in the order at least one requirement imposed for the purpose of punishment, or
(b) impose a fine for the offence in respect of which the community order is made, or
(c) comply with both of paragraphs (a) and (b).
(2B) Subsection (2A) does not apply where there are exceptional circumstances which—
(a) relate to the offence or to the offender,
(b) would make it unjust in all the circumstances for the court to comply with subsection (2A)(a) in the particular case, and
(c) would make it unjust in all the circumstances for the court to impose a fine for the offence concerned.'

This could be seen as sending a mixed message about the purpose of community orders. A community sentence combines punishment with activities carried out in the community. It can include one or more of 12 requirements on an offender such as unpaid work, drug treatment and the imposition of curfews. In passing a community sentence, magistrates are able to tailor the combinations of the community order to the offender and crime committed. A number of critical commentaries have suggested that these changes to community sentences, embodied in Schedule 16 of the Crime and Courts Act 2013, will have a negative impact on judicial discretion, curtailing it in such a way to limit the effectiveness of community orders. For example, it has been argued that the new duty to impose a punitive element, will limit the discretion of judges and magistrates in setting an appropriate sentence based on the facts and circumstances of the individual case, whilst creating a false and unhelpful divide between 'punitive' and 'rehabilitative' requirements (Prison Reform Trust 2012). Interestingly, however, many sentencers interviewed for this research actually remain quite unconcerned about the new provisions and in fact see Schedule 16 as making little difference to current sentencing practices. Given the reforms have only just been implemented, it remains to be seen what impact they will have on the administration and effectiveness of community sentences, and how this will be reflected in statistics on recidivism.

Although the coalition Government has sought to distinguish its reforms as offering something 'radically different' from what has gone before, in fact much of the government's criminal justice policy rhetoric suggests clear parallels with those of the previous Labour administration(s). For example, the emphasis upon community participation through the government's 'Big Society' vision for localism in many respects mirrors the community justice approaches initiated by the Labour government as well as its 'responsibilisation' of residents in the delivery of crime 'solutions'. Prime Minister David Cameron's appeals for more 'intelligent punishment'[3] are not far removed from Tony Blair's familiar New Labour political mantra, 'tough on crime, tough on the causes of crime'. An intended significant point of difference with the policies of previous administrations however, is the Payment by Results (PbR) model, which is to be applied to

26 Situating problem-solving and punitivism

rehabilitation and probation services. As such, the Ministry of Justice (2010b: 8) noted that:

> We will signal a clean break with the controlling, centralising tendencies of the past by making a clear commitment to decentralisation. We will provide frontline professionals with greater freedoms in how they manage offenders. Local areas will focus on the criminals who cause the most problems in their communities. There will be fewer targets for providers and less prescription in the way that different agencies work together.

Yet, at the same time, the cornerstone of this new approach is the PbR model. PbR is predicated upon the notion that it is more effective for government to pay a provider of services on the basis of specified outcomes achieved rather than the inputs or outputs delivered (Fox and Albertson 2012). The government noted: 'Our decentralising approach will mean a move away from centrally controlled services dominated by the public sector, towards a more competitive system that draws on the knowledge, expertise and innovation of a much broader set of organisations from all sectors' (Ministry of Justice 2010b: 8).

However, rather than representing a substantive and genuine movement away from centralisation, towards greater autonomy for local services providers, the emphasis upon processes of marketisation represents the continuation of a trend pervasive throughout the Labour administration's terms in government (Bowen and Donoghue 2013). The probation reforms are perhaps the clearest expression of the coalition Government's continuity of a privatisation model that prefers large contract areas with long contract periods, in which central government locks money into centrally designed and centrally signed-off contracts. The probation service, traditionally a locally based servant of the court, is being divided into 21 package areas, in order to suit the needs of 'prime providers' (Bowen and Donoghue 2013). I have discussed the implications of the PbR model on criminal justice elsewhere in some detail (Bowen and Donoghue 2013) however, it is important to make clear that, in the context of criminal justice policies which both propose and require local and community justice at their core for effective delivery, PbR appears to potentially reduce opportunities for these approaches to be realised. Problem-solving justice, as we have seen, is concerned with local neighbourhoods. While the current reforms have stressed a localism agenda, and have continued to emphasise the importance of community engagement in and with criminal justice policies, the PbR model appears to undermine this local emphasis. The implications of the current privatisation model are clear: purchasing decisions are made centrally, which reduces the likelihood that budget lines will be pooled locally (Bowen and Donoghue 2013). In preventing pooling of budgets locally, this restricts the ability of decision-makers in those areas to determine best how their money is spent; and it fails to include a range of local providers in consultation and decision-making as to the purposes and services delivered by new providers locally (Bowen and Donoghue

Situating problem-solving and punitivism 27

2013). Nonetheless, the system of PbR is to be in full operation across the criminal justice system by 2015. The Justice Secretary has recently argued that evidence from PbR pilots:

> ... make a compelling case for our important reforms – re-offending rates remaining doggedly high as a hardcore of offenders continue to cause misery in communities up and down the country. Where we are seeing real improvements in tackling this problem is our through the gate Payment by Results pilots, an approach I want to see rolled out across England and Wales ... The Government is currently introducing radical reforms to rehabilitation services in England and Wales. This will see the best of the private, voluntary and public sectors working together to turn offenders away from crime for good. And we will only pay in full for services proven to cut reoffending so we only invest in what works and ensure taxpayers get better value.
>
> (Ministry of Justice 2013f)

It is too soon to say with any certainty whether the PbR model will deliver great efficiencies or greater innovation. However, as many have observed, the PbR model has to date no track record of success in the criminal justice sector. The policy of PbR has also been criticised for the methodological challenges it poses. For example, routes to desistance from offending may defy the simple pathways that a PbR model would seek to impose. Thus measuring outcomes (fiscal as well as re-offending or desistance) may be problematic. Moreover, 'gaming' of the PbR system whereby providers 'cherry-pick' those individuals who are most likely to deliver a result becomes an inevitable focus when outcomes are defined in such narrow economic terms.

There are, however, several new reforms which, although they have actually received relatively very little attention, in fact do represent important and substantive changes in criminal justice. In particular, Part 2 of the Crime and Courts Act, which received Royal Assent on 25 April 2013, creates a statutory framework for restorative justice in the courts of England and Wales. The new legislative provisions allow the courts to defer at the pre-sentence stage in order for the victim and offender to be offered restorative justice at the earliest opportunity. This is potentially a highly important development in sentencing in England and Wales. Moreover, the government has announced plans to support the creation of more restorative neighbourhood justice panels, and it is currently undertaking a review of the role of magistrates with a view to increasing their participation in community justice, as well as allowing single magistrates, rather than a bench of three, to hear cases. While Chapters 5 and 6 examine these reforms in more detail, it is fair to say that on the face of it, these reforms are, in many ways, much more significant because they represent potentially fundamental changes to the framework of the justice system which signify a more substantive break with the past, rather than, ostensibly, continuity of previous policies.

28 *Situating problem-solving and punitivism*

A financial imperative for change

While the government's reforms to criminal justice can in part be seen as an effort to ameliorate existing problems in the system and to address high recidivism levels which should, quite rightly, be a central concern of policymakers and those involved in criminal justice more broadly, there is without question a financial imperative propelling the so-called rehabilitation revolution. Previous governments in Britain spent an unprecedented amount on the criminal justice system which included higher numbers of police than ever before and neighbourhood policing as a priority, increases in average sentence lengths and the creation of a wide range of new statutory tools and legal powers to tackle neighbourhood disorder and anti-social behaviour. While it is a matter of significant debate whether this spending has contributed directly to the drop in crime rates, what is clear is that high levels of incarceration and re-offending come at enormous cost. The issue of cost has always been fundamental both to decision-making and resource allocation in the criminal justice system. However, in the current fiscal climate, economic concerns have been magnified: spending cutbacks and 'efficiency' savings loom large in the criminal justice domain. In other areas outside of criminal justice, the current economic climate has also meant that radical change to the organisation, governance and delivery of public services is taking place (Fahy 2013). This has resulted in an overhaul of the way that public services are delivered but the reforms have also challenged the nature of the relationship between the public, and the public services that they rely on (Fahy 2013).

Thus, undoubtedly, one of the key drivers for many of the government's new reforms and proposals on sentencing and rehabilitation has been the current economic climate which has created a financial imperative for more cost-effective policies. Critics have argued therefore that recent reforms appear to be based upon economic (rather than criminal justice) principles and are driven by budget cutbacks and the need to provide the same services to the public but at lower cost. For example, following the government's most recent spending review, the departmental budget of the Ministry of Justice is to be cut by 10 per cent and the Home Office resource budget is to be cut by 6 per cent (HM Treasury 2013). Cost, and reduction in expenditure particularly, has long been an issue at the heart of the criminal justice system. While the global financial downturn has brought with it a particular urgency in terms of budget reduction, cost, efficiency and resource management were also unsatisfactory prior to the recession.[4]

There are particularly important difficulties with the current approach however, which relate to resourcing, investment and implementation. These aspects will likely have considerable impact upon the extent to which genuinely rehabilitative outcomes can be delivered. By way of illustration, there have to date been wholesale cuts to initiatives that had been introduced by the previous governments and which were designed to address the root causes of crime. This includes a reduction in police numbers, large-scale cuts to Sure Start and services for young people, as well as cuts to the Education Maintenance Allowance

(EMA), which is no longer available in England. Many professionals involved in the rehabilitation sector have argued that successful rehabilitation requires resources and that without these, the reforms will not be successful in impacting upon recidivism levels. While successful rehabilitation is associated with long-term criminal justice savings (reduced spending on incarceration for example, not to mention the associated financial and social costs of crime itself), the financial imperative for immediate reductions in spending has meant that the intended outcomes of the government's reforms will likely be affected – to what degree, so far remains unclear. Moreover, no increase in budget is being made available to support these reforms and so there will be no additional money to pay for either more prisoners (at a cost to the State of an average of £40 000 a year) or for extending rehabilitation to more offenders. Therefore, genuine wholesale reform and potential successful outcomes are limited by a lack of investment.

While the government's 'rehabilitation revolution' offers very little that is new conceptually or ideologically, it does nonetheless serve to highlight a policy continuum over the last couple of decades in which, buried in the political rhetoric, is a recognition that punishment itself must become more effective and *meaningful*, as well as more cost-efficient. Over the last 40 years we can trace the discourse on rehabilitation through 'nothing works' (Martinson 1974) to an emphasis on desert-based models of punishment and 'what works' policies (McGuire 1995, Martinson 2003) informed by increased professionalisation and managerialism in criminal justice to a supposedly 'evidence-based' policy approach (Pawson 2006). According to Priestley and Vanstone (2010: 5, cited in Pycroft p. 176), with regard to mental health and substance misuse specifically, there has been a 'Babel's Tower' of different and competing approaches to rehabilitation which have at times been 'contradictory, contentious and repetitious'. Yet arguably, this observation extends more broadly than this. Although there has been evidence of a recognition from policymakers of the failure of existing forms of punishment (custody, community sentences) to make a substantive impact upon re-offending rates and to address the underlying causes of much (especially low level) criminality such as addiction and mental health problems, many of these initiatives and reforms over the years have lacked a coherent rationale. That is to say that many of the myriad different innovations and developments share an overarching concern with making sentencing more effective but there are also clearly conflicting rationale(s) underpinning these different efforts. There is often no overarching ideological agreement among those proposing change or reform. Over the last two decades there is undoubtedly evidence of efforts to try to do something 'new', and to make sentencing more socially meaningful, together with a recognition that the revolving door of repeat offenders is not improving. As we shall see in the next chapter, problem-solving justice has come to feature prominently in these debates. There is not one simple solution to the UK's high rates of re-offending and so, as I have stated in this book's introduction, problem-solving justice should not be viewed as a panacea. It does, however, provide a conceptual and praxis framework around which to base reform. With this in mind, the following four chapters give

30 *Situating problem-solving and punitivism*

examples of how specialist and problem-solving courts are operating in different jurisdictions, an examination of salient practice and ideological implications, with a particular insight into how these courts are currently functioning in England and Wales.

Notes

1 Ken Clarke served as the Justice Secretary from 2010 to 2012. He was succeeded by Chris Grayling.
2 The Crime and Courts Act 2013 also builds on the provisions of the Legal Aid, Sentencing and Punishment of Offenders Act 2012 to extend the length and duration of curfews and introduce a new foreign travel prohibition, alcohol abstinence and monitoring requirements as well as giving discretion for sentencers to impose treatment requirements for offenders with mental health needs or problems with alcohol or substance misuse.
3 A recent example of an attempt to make punishment more 'meaningful' has been illustrated by changes made under the Justice Secretary, Chris Grayling, to prisoner privileges such as automatic access to TV and prison gyms. The changes will add a new 'entry' level for all male prisoners for the first two weeks of their sentence in which their privileges, including access to private cash and wearing their own clothes, will be restricted. All convicted male prisoners are to be required to wear prison uniform for the first two weeks of their sentence while offenders in privately run prisons will also lose access to satellite subscription channels. Offenders returned to prison for breaching license conditions will also be placed on the new entry level for two weeks. According to the Ministry of Justice, those prisoners who do not cooperate or who fail to engage in rehabilitation by the end of the entry-level period, will drop to a basic level with associated lack of privileges. The rationale for these changes is on the face it, a populist one, with the Justice Secretary stating that: 'It is not right that some prisoners appear to be spending hours languishing in their cells and watching daytime television while the rest of the country goes out to work … This cannot continue. Prisoners need to earn privileges, not simply through the avoidance of bad behaviour but also by working, taking part in education or accepting the opportunities to rehabilitate themselves.' Penal reformers have argued that these changes, while undoubtedly appealing to the broader public, represent a narrow interpretation and understanding of how punishment can be made more meaningful. Broader issues relating to overcrowding, together with significantly reduced prison budgets and staffing numbers impact fundamentally upon the rehabilitative capacities of prisons.
4 For example, substantial pressures were placed upon sentencers in the magistrates' courts in 2006 to stop using custody when sentencing as the prisons were at capacity. In order to ease overcrowding in prisons in England and Wales, the Home Office engaged an emergency measure under The Imprisonment (Temporary Provisions) Act of 1980, which enables prisoners to be held by police if there is no room for them to enter the prison system. Rapid increases in the prison population had meant that some jails across the country were badly affected and unable to house any more offenders. Magistrates were concerned about the impact that pressure not to use custody placed upon their independence, particularly in those cases where custody was the most appropriate sentence. Interestingly, changes have since been made in the structure for assault cases which appear to make custody a less likely outcome. Similarly bail has also changed quite significantly, again potentially reducing the likelihood of remand in custody.

3 Specialist and problem-solving courts

Over the last decade in particular, the United Kingdom, in common with other jurisdictions such as Canada, the US and Australia, has sought to develop more effective ways of responding to criminal behaviour and social disorder through court reforms designed to address specific manifestations of crime (for selected examples of the broad cross-jurisdictional appeal of criminal court specialisation for example, National Crime Council 2007; Goldberg 2005; Hora and Stalcup 2008; King *et al.* 2009). Specialist and problem-solving courts operate at the intersection of criminal law and social policy and appear to challenge much of the traditional model of court practice (Berman and Fox 2009). The established roles of lawyers and judges in the judicial process are modified and problem-solving courts often expressly reject a style of practice that could be fitted within a mainstream, rule of law approach to adjudication (Miller 2012). Judges assume an arguably more subjective role in the justice process which encompasses monitoring, evaluating and rewarding offender compliance (Mair and Millings 2011). Judicial power in problem-solving courts has expanded into areas in which sentencers have traditionally provided relatively little oversight: namely, diversion and probation (Miller 2012), while the function of the criminal defence lawyer encompasses 'team' co-operation (Kerr *et al.* 2011). Frequently underpinned by principles of restorative justice or therapeutic jurisprudence, the courts shift their focus from sentencing to a broader problem-solving methodology that is designed to enable sentencers to address the social and personal issues of offenders through an intersection with service frameworks outside the justice system in order to develop more effective solutions to criminal behaviour (Wexler 2010; Chase and Hora 2000). Moreover, problem-solving courts emphasise the importance of 'community engagement' with judicial processes (Berman and Fox 2009).

For the purposes of clarity, it is important from the outset to define what is meant by court specialisation and to identify the distinction between specialist and problem-solving courts. Problem-solving and specialist courts both address specific types of offences/offenders and are designed to provide a tailored and specific response to particular types of criminality (drug related offences, domestic violence, and so forth). However, while specialist courts appear to operate using a problem-oriented rationale, as we shall see in the pages that

32 Specialist and problem-solving courts

follow, not all specialist courts operate using what would generally be regarded as 'problem-solving' principles. Sir Robin Auld, in his *Review of Criminal Courts in England and Wales*, considered calls for specialist courts in England and Wales, and observed that there is a wide variation in what is understood by the term specialist court (Lord Justice Auld 2001). The *Auld Report* identified at least three senses in which the term specialist court is used: to refer to courts where specialist knowledge is required because the decision-making requires particular expertise, or where the sentencing regime requires access to specialist support workers; to refer to courts that depart from the traditional adversarial model and focus on a problem-solving approach; and in concentrated listing of particular types of cases (as a matter of convenience). Since the publication of the *Auld Report* in 2001, and the subsequent creation and development of court specialisation in England and Wales, a significant body of literature now exists that reinforces and extends the *Report's* earlier definition of specialist courts (Tata 2013).

Hence, specialist courts are not necessarily 'problem-solving' in nature, as they may have a narrower remit, with objectives centred upon efficient and consistent dispute resolution ('fast track' courts), rather than addressing structural inequalities and neighbourhood concerns.[1] They might also not consider rehabilitation as part of their remit. The purpose of specialist courts is generally to enhance the speed and efficiency of court processes and to bring about improved judicial decision-making by virtue of the judiciary's specialist experience, together with greater consistency in sentencing outcomes. The objectives of problem-solving courts are however, much broader. It is now generally accepted that specialist courts possess either limited or exclusive jurisdiction in a specific field of law where the presiding officer has direct expertise in that field (Clinks 2011; Nolan 2002). In the UK and beyond, specialist courts which operate using a problem-solving rationale have aimed, variously, to use the authority of the court to address the underlying problems of individual litigants, the structural problems of the justice system and also the social problems of communities (Miller 2007, 2012). Therefore, specialist or 'fast-track' courts should not be confused with courts which are specifically 'problem-solving' in nature, although there can be some overlap between the two. This is especially true in England and Wales, where courts such as Specialist Domestic Violence Courts (SDVCs) aim to incorporate aspects of the problem-solving model but currently fail to include certain fundamental elements critical to the problem-solving approach and so cannot be described as genuinely problem-solving in nature (this is discussed more fully in Chapter 4). It is also important to recognise that the notion of 'problem-solving' that these courts adopt is not an uncontested term within legal and criminological scholarship. Mae Quinn (2009), amongst others, has argued that 'problem-solving' is fundamentally problematic because many courts do not solve the social problems that they originally set out to address.

While the vast majority of court specialisation is within the criminal law domain, there are also a limited number of examples to be found within the civil law tradition. For example, the growth of specialised business and commercial

Specialist and problem-solving courts 33

courts has occurred in many jurisdictions in recent years, including England and Wales, Canada, Hong Kong and the US. Specialist business/commercial courts use specialised judges and expedited case management procedures to provide an expert and faster dispute resolution process. The courts are typically ancillary to a larger court and are characterised by a 'a jurisdiction limited to some, but not all, kinds of business disputes, presided over by only a few specialist judges, with an emphasis on aggressive case management and use of alternative dispute resolution (ADR)' (Peeples and Nyhein 2008: 35).

As described previously, the US has been at the forefront of the development of problem-solving courts. It is important to note that it was judges themselves who were pivotal to the emergence and development of the US problem-solving court movement, and elsewhere the commitment of individual judges to a problem-solving rationale has been identified as critical to the success of problem-solving courts (Nolan 2009). For example, in his analysis of the introduction during the 1980s and 1990s, and subsequent proliferation of US drug courts, Goldkamp notes that the courts:

> Were established because of the emergence of a small network of committed officials, judges, administrators, treatment providers, prosecutors, and defenders who shared their experiences and newfound expertise, who travelled to one another's courts at their own expense to observe or provide assistance.
>
> (Goldkamp 2000: 947; see also Hora 2011)

In America, judges themselves had acknowledged that an alternative to traditional case processing methods was necessary to deal effectively with drug cases (Bean 1996). Moreover, interest in the development of a problem-solving approach was further supported by key criminal justice representatives at the Conference of Chief Justices and Conference of State Court Administrators in August 2000, which passed a resolution to:

> Encourage, where appropriate, the broad integration over the next decade of the principles and methods employed in the problem-solving courts into the administration of justice to improve court processes and outcomes while preserving the rule of law, enhancing judicial effectiveness, and meeting the needs and expectations of litigants, victims, and the community.
>
> (2000: 22–3)

Subsequently, problem-solving justice became formally accepted as an important element of the US justice system when, in February 2007, the American Bar Association (ABA) adopted the new ABA Model Code of Judicial Conduct which states that:

> Judges in problem-solving courts may be authorized by court rules to act in non-traditional ways. For example, judges presiding in drug courts and

34   *Specialist and problem-solving courts*

monitoring the progress of participants in those courts' programs may be authorized and even encouraged to communicate directly with social workers, probation officers, and others outside the context of their usual judicial role as independent decision makers on issues of fact and law.

(CPS 2007: 10)

The new Model Code also states that a judge may 'initiate, permit or consider ex parte communications expressly authorized by law, such as when serving on problem-solving courts' (CPS 2007: 24). Consequently, the problem-solving approach has become part of mainstream US justice (Berman and Fox 2009). Elsewhere, aspects of the problem-solving court model have been transplanted to other jurisdictions internationally, including Australia, New Zealand, Canada, Scotland and Ireland (National Crime Council 2007; Goldberg 2005; Hora and Stalcup 2008; King *et al.* 2009).

In his comparative work, James Nolan has observed that the growth of problem-solving courts both nationally and internationally has meant that indicators of 'success' and determinations of efficacy are very much culturally defined as a consequence of the different contexts in which problem-solving courts exist (Nolan 2009). Some courts embed a therapeutic rationale which may result in measurements of success that are at odds with traditional criminal justice indicators such as reduced rates of recidivism and lower crime figures. Given that most problem-solving courts are concerned with the 'treatment' of offenders, the different philosophies underpinning the disparate range of treatment programmes necessarily inform notions of success and efficacy in the operation of these courts (Nolan 2009). Notions of success and efficacy are therefore contingent upon the underpinning philosophies of individual courts and the court practitioners operating in these domains which influence and shape treatment rationale and standards required in programme outcomes. With these constraints in mind, the relative effectiveness of different categories of problem-solving court are considered in more detail in Chapters 4 and 5, which pay close attention to the methodological difficulties that have been exemplified in some of the existing literature.

Although there is some clear variation in the different aspects and manifestations of problem-solving that these courts embody (Nolan 2009), there are nonetheless overarching guiding principles that inform the development and the rationale behind their creation. The following sections will endeavour to outline these general principles and to identify the main criticisms that have been made of their application in practice. Given that the vast majority of the available literature on problem-solving courts is within the American domain, much of the concerns that are examined relate to the functioning of US problem-solving courts, although there are a number of important studies which have been undertaken in other jurisdictions such as Scotland, Australia and New Zealand which are also included in the discussion. Understanding how these articulated concerns may serve to inform the development of problem-solving courts in England and Wales is, of course, a primary focus of this book. Chapters 4 and 5 explore

Specialist and problem-solving courts   35

in greater detail how these areas of tension may be replicated or guarded against in the English and Welsh context and the comparative differences in the functioning of problem-solving courts in England and Wales.

The principles and rationale of problem-solving courts

The principles underpinning the work of problem-solving courts include a team-focussed approach where social agencies and other support/treatment services such as drug agencies, employment and training organisations, housing providers and debt advice agencies work collaboratively with the courts and other key criminal justice agencies such as police and probation to increase efficiency and effectiveness in the delivery of justice. This collaborative approach includes enhanced information sharing about defendants, victims and neighbourhoods. A number of courts, most notably community courts, also seek to enhance neighbourhood engagement and to align their work with community contexts and local dimensions of crime. One of the fundamental principles of problem-solving justice is the explicit incorporation of the community into the judicial process as a means of increasing the efficacy of the criminal justice system in responding to local crime problems. Many problem-solving courts adopt, either explicitly or implicitly, principles and practices consistent with restorative justice or therapeutic jurisprudence (Took 2005; McNeill 2011; McIvor 2009; Nolan 2003).

Therapeutic jurisprudence first originated in the US in 1987 and is defined as the study of the role of law as a therapeutic agent (Wexler 1990, 1992; Winick 1997). It can be located as part of a broader movement in law alongside the other principal revisionary trajectories such as restorative justice (O'Hear 2009; Wenzel *et al.* 2007), and problem-solving justice (Holland 2011; Burns 2011). Both interdisciplinary and empirically focussed, therapeutic jurisprudence should be understood as a heuristic set of organising principles – rather than as a distinctive theory – for understanding the content of law and legal processes. In this way, it is 'not so much a body of substance as it is an approach (through careful analysis and empirical research) to creating a body of substance' (Stolle *et al.* 2000: 34). Those responsible for the creation and development of therapeutic jurisprudence undoubtedly view its utility in and function for, at least to some degree, law reform (Wexler and Winick 1996: xvii). Slobogin (1995: 219), for example, asserts that '[t]herapeutic jurisprudence, carefully pursued, will help produce a critical psychology that will force policymakers to pay more attention to the actual, rather than the assumed, impact of the law and those who implement it.' In this respect, therapeutic jurisprudence is oriented towards the promotion of greater cognisance of the de facto operation of the law *in practice* and its multifarious outcomes.

Clearly therapeutic jurisprudence is not an end in itself – it is not an algorithm for generating improved administration of justice, nor does it provide solutions to achieving fairer outcomes. In essence, therapeutic jurisprudence is a lens through which to view the interplay of legal rules, legal processes and legal actors within the justice system, and the resulting determinate substantive effects

36 *Specialist and problem-solving courts*

upon the social, psychological/emotional and physical well-being of those affected by its outcomes – namely litigants, their families and associates and more broadly, the neighbourhoods in which they reside. Therapeutic jurisprudence emphasises the 'human element' in lawyering and seeks to highlight the frequent disjuncture between the aspirational rhetoric surrounding the provision of legal services and their substantive consequences – which can have negative outcomes for the community of law's stakeholders. While these elements have long been recognised by practitioners and scholars alike, and multifarious efforts have been made to incorporate a 'human element' into the application of the law, Wexler argues that therapeutic jurisprudence represents an explicit attempt to order and conceptualise these disparate practices and insights as a unique field of inquiry (Wexler 1995: 236).

Similarly, it has been observed that specialist and problem-solving courts may also draw upon elements of restorative justice (Feinblatt 2000). The theory and practice of restorative justice have emerged largely as a result of concerns about the status of the victim within the criminal justice system (Wright 1996). Although there is not a specific consensual definition of restorative justice (Gavrielides 2008), one can summarise that restorative justice practices generally adhere to three main principles. First, restorative justice practices aim to repair the harm to those affected by crime or conflict. Second, they bring together all those who are considered stakeholders in the consequences of the crime (including victims and offenders), who should be included in the restorative process as soon and as often as possible. Third, restorative justice practices emphasise partnerships between government and community in order to enhance the role of community involvement in restorative processes. John Braithwaite observes that therapeutic jurisprudence and restorative justice are both concerned with highlighting 'the enormous impact the justice system can have on people's psychological and physical well-being' and that both traditions share an interest in 'how to overcome the problem of criminal offenders denying the pain of their victims, both for the sake of healing the offender and preventing further victimisation' (Braithwaite 2002: 244).

Yet while it is clear that restorative justice and therapeutic jurisprudence are related phenomena, for conceptual purposes it is important to distinguish problem-solving justice from therapeutic jurisprudence and restorative justice. Problem-solving justice should be understood as a legal praxis innovation whereas therapeutic jurisprudence and restorative justice are both theoretically grounded academic conceptualisations of justice (Nolan 2009). Some tensions also exist in the use of the term 'therapeutic jurisprudence' among those in the court community. Although Wexler and Winick have long maintained that therapeutic jurisprudence considerations should be prudently and selectively invoked, and in those cases where they are compatible with evidence-based judicial decision-making, they should be incorporated (where appropriate) into legislative interpretation, scholars have noted the potential irreconcilability of therapeutic jurisprudence principles and values both internally and, in their application to legal decision-making (Slobogin 1995; Davis 2003).

The 'enhanced' judicial function

The growth of problem-solving courts has brought about a changed orientation in the way that some polycentric disputes (involving legal and non-legal systemic issues) are being managed and resolved by judicial forums. Structural developments in the criminal courts which embed a problem-solving approach in justice processes have altered the function of judicial officers. The role of the judiciary in problem-solving courts differs significantly from traditional courts in that sentencers must consider a range of broad issues such as, for example, the defendant's physical and mental health, diversion and community related issues such as local neighbourhood demographics and crime trends. Although problem-solving courts in Britain were established around different objectives in relation to the relevant offender groups, they all share the common theme of *greater involvement* of sentencers in addressing the problems and factors that contribute to offending, and the specific strategies that might divert offenders away from future crime. This approach is based on evidence which indicates that greater interest by sentencers in the personal circumstances of offenders appearing before them was a motivating factor in offenders' determination to desist from crime (see for example, King and Batagol 2010; Gottfredson *et al.* 2007). Research findings suggest that the behaviour of a judge at sentencing can have a substantive effect upon an offender's compliance with the terms of their probation (Wexler 1993). For example, by communicating the conditions of the probation in simpler and more comprehensible terms directly to the offender, or by invoking judicial praise as a means to motivate an offender to abide by the terms of their probation, judicial behaviour can play a central role in buttressing criminal justice objectives (Wexler 2010). Shadd Maruna observes that judicial involvement can promote rehabilitation by contributing to 'desistance narratives' that can help to bring about and sustain desistance from crime (Maruna 2001; see also Maruna and LeBel 2002). There is also evidence to suggest that judicial-defendant exchanges may assist with the process of denial minimisation, encouraging offenders to take responsibility for their actions (Gebelein 2000). While sentencing in the courts in England and Wales engages with these issues to some degree already, the role of the problem-solving court judge is intended to be much broader, facilitated by judicial continuity in order to ensure that there is the opportunity for a more substantive relationship to be developed between sentencer and offender.

One leading advocate of problem-solving justice in Australia, Michael King, has proposed a judicial monitoring approach in specialist family violence courts that emphasises the role of the offender in resolving their criminal behaviour and its underlying issues (King 2009). Drawing upon transformational leadership as well as feminist theory, the approach suggested, broadly speaking, is for judges to engage with defendants and to actively involve them in decision-making about their rehabilitation; to take an active interest in and support their progress; engage 'techniques' that might assist offenders in responding to similar future events/problems; include the victim(s) directly in the court process and expressly

38 *Specialist and problem-solving courts*

take into account their views at sentencing (King and Batagol 2010). Aspects of these different components may however be viewed as irreconcilable with the doctrine of the criminal law (Ashworth 2004a, 2004b).

It has also been suggested that judicial techniques of this type may in some circumstances be potentially counter-productive, hindering offender motivation and reducing the effectiveness of mandated court programmes. Research in the US indicates that problem-solving court judges may probe into defendants' personal lives in ways that are 'inappropriate' under the problem-solving approach (McCoy 2003). Critics maintain that the 'therapeutic' rhetoric of problem-solving court practices could in fact serve to buttress pre-existing power dimensions, reinforce professional sensibilities and bias(es) and place in jeopardy individual liberties and their status within legal processes. For example, in specialist mental health review tribunals in New Zealand, Diesfeld and McKenna (2007) suggest that lawyers have vitiated their advocacy role for defendants and instead have adopted the use of therapeutic language in mental health review tribunals in New Zealand, while the tribunal itself has begun to use therapeutic language in its decisions. While the use of such language may be facilitative of a more 'human' approach to resolving defendants' issues related to their mental health, which are intended to support and encourage individuals in their journey towards recovery/improved health, legal scholars argue there are clear difficulties inherent in legal representatives' adoption of therapeutic language in place of their advocacy function. Therefore, critics maintain that the application of therapeutic language in legal forums has the potential not only to unduly influence decision-makers through professionals'/clinicians' perspectives but also risks the judiciary becoming engaged in covert paternalism concealed by therapeutic language (Freckelton 2007).[2]

Defence advocacy function

Another distinctive characteristic of the operation of problem-solving courts that requires attention is the role of defence counsel. As the problem-solving approach emphasises team working as paramount, there are then potentially opportunities for defence solicitors to find themselves with concurrent conflicts of interest in problem-solving courts. Critical legal commentary on US problem-solving courts has suggested that the function and responsibilities of the defence when they are acting on behalf of an individual defendant are fundamentally different from those that they assume when operating as part of a team. When functioning as part of a team, the defence's allegiance is no longer to their individual client in the protection of confidential information, the pursuit of their client's wishes, and the duty to avoid interests that may conflict with those wishes: the defence's role is transformed when they operate within a problem-solving paradigm. They contend that team working requires that defence lawyers act in accordance with the collaborative interests of non-clients (such as probation and treatment agencies for example) and that ultimately they demonstrate fidelity to the collective goal of the team for success in a reduction of offending/treatment.

Specialist and problem-solving courts 39

This necessitates open and full sharing of information and the pursuit of interests other than those solely of their client.

The criminal process in the lower courts is, instrumentally and symbolically, heavily dependent on defendants pleading guilty (Tata 2008). It is central both to the practical operation and to the legitimacy of the criminal process that the decision as to how to plead is seen to be freely made by the defendant. In practice however, the choice to plead guilty is limited by a significant number of key determinants. Evidence suggests that guilty pleas are influenced by a broad range of factors including a pervasive legal/court culture of the presumption of guilt (McConville *et al.* 1994; Baldwin and McConville 1977; Sanders and Young 2007); an 'ideology of triviality' (McBarnet 1981); the standard and quality of lawyer's advice (Goriely *et al.* 2001); and defendant displays of emotion/ remorse and judicial responses to these (Anleu and Mack 2005).

Summary courts rely on the expeditious production of guilty pleas. For example, almost all cases in the magistrates' courts in England and Wales end in a guilty plea and evidence suggests that defendants can have a poor understanding about the facts of their case and what they have pled guilty to (Tata *et al.* 2004). Moreover, in the US, coercion (and undue influence) appears to be a characteristic of some problem-solving courts where defendants can be pressurised to take the option of pleading guilty and accepting treatment instead of proceeding to trial and hearing the evidence against them, albeit with the overarching threat of imprisonment (Freckelton 2007). Furthermore, some reports suggest that proceedings in specialist homeless courts in the US tend to be largely informal and that as a result, there is little opportunity for client and attorney to develop any meaningful relationship and as a consequence, the defendant's wishes are not necessarily represented fully or accurately (Meekins 2006). Since many jurisdictions, including problem-solving courts in England and Wales, require that a defendant is only permitted to have their case heard by a problem-solving court or to enter treatment once guilt has been admitted, it follows that due process rights must be assured.

In the US, it has been observed that the reduced advocacy role of the defence in problem-solving courts may impact upon counsel's role in providing advice to clients about the legal consequences of the court's treatment regime, and in being able to supply an independent check upon the court's decision-making (Meekins 2007; Pinard 2004). Indeed, by invoking a 'teamwork' approach to case processing, defence solicitors may necessarily impinge upon their most fundamental duty to zealously pursue and protect the best interests of their clients (Quinn 2000). In problem-solving courts, the defence moves from being a dynamic advocate engaged with and persevering in contest and argument with the legal system, to a 'team player' who will undertake collaborative discussions with both prosecutors and judges, as well as other members of the court 'team' (Spinak 2003). The traditional function of the criminal defence solicitor moves from advocacy to cooperation. This undoubtedly raises important questions in respect of defendants' reduced confidence in case outcomes.

40   *Specialist and problem-solving courts*

However, perhaps the most significant potential repercussions of the changes made to the role of the defence may impact upon those who are already over-represented within the criminal justice system (Kennedy 1997). Empirical research continues to sustain the conclusion that certain ethnicities and social groups are disproportionately represented within the criminal justice system (Shute *et al.* 2005). A recent evaluation found that 71 per cent of drug court participants in England did not possess any educational qualifications (Kerr *et al.* 2011: 10). In the US, evidence suggests that defendants from racial and ethnic minorities are frequently over-represented in problem-solving courts (see for example, McKeana and Warren-Gordona 2011; Wolf 2009b; Beckerman and Fontana 2002). Correspondingly, minority social/ethnic groups are more likely to encounter, and are more vulnerable to, the threats posed by unequal repres-entation such as harsher treatment during the criminal process and potentially racially motivated sentencing decisions (Shute *et al.* 2005; Hough and Roberts 1999; Johnson 1987; Kane 1993). Where defence solicitors do not zealously advocate for their client's interests, critical legal commentators have argued that due process protections and other legal rights may be jeopardised. For example, defence solicitors should be proactive in exposing police abuse of powers, they should be instrumental in voicing the defendant's position and their rights within the legal process and they should challenge any case which is wrongfully brought. In this regard, issues of competence, ethics and zealousness of advo-cacy are all salient (Meekins 2006).

The enhanced judicial role requires that judges engage in interactions with the defendant which will involve judicial praise and encouragement, but equally, judicial disapproval and reproach. That defence lawyers cannot, or ought not, intervene to protect the interests of their clients during these interactions has been criticised for limiting the defence attorney's activist role in the criminal process (Meekins 2006). However, this critical legal commentary on the role of defence counsel has developed largely in response to the operation of problem-solving courts in the US. Although defence lawyers in England and Wales possess particular responsibilities under the Criminal Procedure Rules (2013), which highlight their duties in respect of their clients, the operation of problem-solving courts in England and Wales nonetheless raises important questions about overlapping responsibilities under the problem-solving court model. Treat-ment providers participating in drug courts in England have reported, for example, that the traditional advocacy role of the defence has been significantly altered in these courts. Such observations are not unexpected however, as the problem-solving approach appears to represent a shift away from the traditional adversary model of justice, towards a more 'collaborative' case processing. To what extent this places adversarialism in jeopardy has been a central concern of critical legal scholars engaged in debate about the problem-solving court movement.

Adversarial justice

The growth of court specialisation has been characterised as embodying a 'paradigm shift' in the criminal justice system (Nolan 2001), with problem-solving courts having variously been described as 'mutations' (Casey 2004), juridicial 'experiments', and a legal 'revolution' (Hora 2011). In the US, critics have suggested that the problem-solving court movement is but another process of 'criminal court experimentation' situated within a long and checkered history of such endeavours.[3] Some scholars have gone as far as to argue that specialist and problem-solving courts in the US have 'abandoned' the notion of adversarial justice in favour of a therapeutic jurisprudence approach (Meekins 2006). This is in part because traditional courts operate in a primarily adjudicatory fashion and possess an adversarial environment, a reliance upon positive law, appellate review and a static operational model. In contra-distinction, problem-solving courts rely upon sociological theory, function in a collaborative environment, exist within an adaptive operational model and possess no appellate review (Casey 2004). Moreover, justice is a subjective term and can be applied subjectively within problem-solving courts as much as in other types of courts (Smith 2003). However, it has been observed that justice in US problem-solving courts is more oriented towards *results than process*, with successful outcomes variously identified as reductions in recidivism, and the completion of treatment programmes (Hardcastle 2003). Critical legal scholars suggest that this conceptualisation of justice may impede procedural fairness.

Hora *et al.* (1998: 453) usefully identify the main characteristics of problem-solving courts as: 'immediate intervention; non-adversarial adjudication; hands-on judicial involvement; treatment programs with clear rules and structured goals; and a team approach that brings together the judge, prosecutor, defence counsel, treatment provider and correctional staff'. They contrast this with the key characteristics of the adversary process as: self-initiation by the parties, 'whether civil litigant or public prosecutor'. The court does not seek business and it is up to the parties to come forward with the evidence. The judge is passive; it is objective in the sense that the decision is based upon the evaluation of materials presented by the parties; it is an all or nothing outcome; and it is authoritative in that judgment carries the force of law. However, the concept of adversarialism is hermeneutically contested and it does not necessarily follow that problem-solving approaches operate in opposition to the adversary system. It may be that they operate as an adjunct to it. Some commentators contend that adversarialism is a term devoid of value because the traditionally posed opposition of adversarial and inquisitorial procedures is a false dichotomy: no one jurisdiction displays all the characteristics of one or other model (Cappelletti and Garth 1976). Accordingly, in the absence of a 'pure' example of either model, each existing system can be viewed as a composite of a range of different procedural elements: attempting to distinguish between the two is therefore tautological.[4] On the other hand, an 'ideal' adversarial/inquisitorial model may provide instrumental value as a conceptual tool or theoretical paradigm (Chase 2002).

42   *Specialist and problem-solving courts*

Yet, adversarialism is more than a framework for description and analysis. Ideologically, it attests to a fundamental and irrebuttable commitment to the protection of parties from the power of the state by allowing them to direct proceedings. The adversarial system is viewed by many lawyers, judges and legal scholars as a vital tool in curtailing governmental and corporate arbitrariness, in challenging bias, abuses of power and errors by law enforcement agencies (Luban 1983). It has been described as the 'best system for protecting individual dignity and autonomy' (Sward 1988). Thus, in ideological terms, debates about the intrinsic value of the adversarial model appear to hinge on notions of the appropriate function of criminal proceedings and the importance attached to truth-finding versus the operation of the criminal trial as a limiter of state power (McEwan 2011, see also Goodpaster 1987). Conferring power upon the parties to an action functions as a level of protection against the over-extending reach of state power, and it is for this reason that the primary justification of the adversary system is the protection of individual rights and freedoms (Burns 2009). As Jenny McEwan (2011) observes on recent developments in England and Wales:

> The adversarial tradition takes account of the difficulty of ensuring fairness between the participants when one is the state itself. Criminal cases are unlike civil ones in that in the former it is always the defendant who has most to lose.

Those that are critical of adversarialism, seek judicial restraint and not judicial activism, which is why legal reformers are likely to view recent developments in problem-solving justice with trepidation and scepticism. The adversarial system, as a form of 'responsive law', has been characterised as a 'high risk strategy of governance' which can be readily exploited for pragmatic, financial gain (through private claims) and which is unpredictable and often inefficient in delivering justice (Nonet and Selznick 1978). Moreover, there are matters (both civil and criminal) which are not suited to a binary (right/wrong, win/lose) resolution. The complex and multifaceted nature of disputes can often require complex and multifaceted solutions which critics argue, the adversarial system is inadequate at providing (Menkel-Meadow 1984, 1996). The development and widespread acceptance of Alternative Dispute Resolution (ADR) within the legal profession demonstrates recognition of the non-binary nature of many disputes, although there is evidence that some of these processes retain adversarial values (Stempel 2010; Rabinovich-Einy and Tsur 2010).

The criminal law is both cumbersome and susceptible to inconsistent and unequal treatment. Legal scholars have long questioned the complex, lethargic and resource-intensive nature of the adversarial system (Miller 1984); its legitimacy as a determiner of truth (Kagan 2003; Fisher 1993; Freedman 1975; Gerber 1987; Frankel 1974); and its efficacy (Menkel-Meadow 1996). Robert Kagan (2003: 4) maintains that adversarialism 'inspires legal defensiveness and contentiousness, which often impede socially constructive co-operation, governmental action, and economic development, alienating many citizens from the law itself.'

Specialist and problem-solving courts 43

These have collectively been recurrent and overlapping themes evident in legal scholarship on adversarialism in both the US and in Britain (Devlin 1979; McConville *et al.* 1994; Langbein 2003). It has also long been observed that the adversary function of prosecuting and defence lawyers may serve to obfuscate fact determination because 'frequently the partisanship of the opposing lawyers blocks the uncovering of vital evidence or ... distorts it' (Frank 1973). That client interest may not be best served by adversary discourse and structure has been a point well made within the dissenting literature (Zacharias 2009a, 2009b; Sahl 2011; Aspen 1993).

The adversary system is not the only system capable of guaranteeing principles of legality and due process of course. However, any alterations to the adversarial system of justice must also guarantee the protection of rights to ensure that fundamental due process values are not threatened (McEwan 2011). This had led some to question, in view of the concerns highlighted in the pages thus far, whether the development of problem-solving justice been accompanied by profound consideration of the values that underpin traditional legal structures.

While attempts have been made to demarcate the 'adversarial system' from what is not, such attempts have encountered heuristic and philosophical difficulties. King *et al.* (2009), for example, posit a dichotomous relationship between adversarialiam and non-adversarialism but concede that most legal processes do in fact combine aspects of both adversarial and non-adversarial practice to varying degrees. The primary difficulty in attempting to ascertain or differentiate the adversarial system from what is not, lies with the lack of specificity evident in any such categorisation. The 'adversarial system', as King *et al.* (2009) recognise, is capable of evolving, of expanding and of synthesising to incorporate or reject particular processes or vectors within it. That there is no authentic and distinct exposition of what constitutes 'the adversarial system', therefore means that it is problematic to argue that new vectors such as problem-solving justice, explicitly do not form part of the adversarial process, particularly in view of the fact that the adversarial system is capable of embodying and approbating elements which at least prima facie appear to be non-adversarial (Dewhurst 2010). While problem-solving justice undoubtedly represents a significant change to the operation of the legal system wherein the traditional roles of lawyers and judges in the judicial process are modified, it does not necessarily follow that adversarial justice is being undermined. Eric Miller argues in the introduction to this text that because problem-solving takes place either pre- or post-adjudication, due process criticisms perhaps do not hold as much weight as some critics might suggest. Moreover, the expansion of court specialisation and problem-solving justice should not necessarily be seen as a direct result of dissatisfaction with the adversarial system.

Another salient feature of lower level criminal courts is the informal authority exerted by magistrates and other 'repeat players' within the criminal court process such as lawyers and criminal justice professionals. However, rather than creating opportunities for increased/improved forms of negotiation consistent

44 *Specialist and problem-solving courts*

with rule of law governed, adversarial criminal justice, the dominance of repeat players in the criminal court instead engenders 'an intimate exchange between familiars competing over plural conceptions of justice', while reproducing and further entrenching existing deficiencies in lower level criminal court praxis (Miller, 2012). In this regard it might be argued that the introduction of problem-solving courts, although expanding judicial supervision to diversion and probation, has not brought about a substantive change in the adjudication of the lower level criminal courts – rather, problem-solving courts share, and may in some instances serve to further entrench the legitimacy problems already in existence in magistrates' courts particularly. According to Eric Miller, it follows that the central innovation of problem-solving courts 'is to reclaim power' for the court judge 'as a therapeutic or problem-solving expert who dominates [the] court' (Miller 2012). Consequently, Miller observes that problem-solving courts represent a change in emphasis more than a change in structure. The crucial point is however, that problem-solving justice operates pre- or post-judicially. Therefore due process issues associated with substantive adjudication are less significant than may be the case if problem-solving formed part of adjudication.

Problem-solving courts in England and Wales

Strongly influenced by developments in US court specialisation, problem-solving and specialist courts including domestic violence courts, drugs courts, community courts, anti-social behaviour response courts, family drug and alcohol courts, mental health courts and youth courts have proliferated in Britain over the last few years. This evolution of the criminal court system has occurred in response to public and professional dissatisfaction with the legal process. This is particularly with regard to the perceived failure of traditional magistrates' courts: to deal effectively with offenders by responding to the underlying causes of criminal behaviour; impact upon recidivism levels and the 'revolving door' phenomenon of repeat offenders; and improve sentence completion and compliance. Court reformers have identified long-standing complaints that the court system is overburdened, lethargic, expensive and that it places substantial limits upon public access to justice (Tomasic and Feeley 1982), while court formality has been viewed as a barrier to the identification of the root causes of interpersonal disputes and problem behaviour (Cabinet Office 2009). Consequently, the belief that the legal system had become too complex and unresponsive to meet community needs for justice resulted in calls for court procedures and structures to be streamlined and simplified, and for the creation and development of specialist and non-juridical/informal dispute resolution forums.

The introduction of the Crime and Disorder Act 1998 signalled an attempt by Tony Blair's New Labour government to test alternative approaches to problems such as drug addiction, youth crime, domestic violence, anti-social behaviour and a lack of public trust in the criminal justice system (Ashworth 2010; Berman and Fox 2010). The development of court specialisation and problem-solving justice was intended to narrow the gap between top-down bureaucratic control and participatory local democracy as well as addressing low levels of approval in local courts. Court specialisation began to evolve in 1998 with the creation of the first two drug courts in England, located in Wakefield and Pontefract, West Yorkshire, which were based in large part upon the US drug court model.

Following the creation of the Yorkshire drug courts, the *Auld Report* examined the arguments for the wider introduction of both drugs and domestic violence courts in England and Wales. The *Report* acknowledged that there are some features of domestic violence offences that may make them unsuitable for conventional courts and referred to a pilot domestic violence court in Calgary that aimed to bring as many agencies as possible together to discuss appropriate treatment. While it was acknowledged that full evaluation of the pilot was not available, the *Report* concluded that: 'like other "restorative" approaches [...] in North America, its success appears to be, not so much in devising alternative procedures, but in gathering together the resources of a number of concerned agencies and focusing minds on the issue' (p. 5). With regard to the lower courts' response to domestic violence in England and Wales, it was noted that efforts were already being made to improve inter-agency working but there remained 'the need for all agencies to match their stated policies with action' (ibid.). While urging that immediate efforts be focussed elsewhere, the *Auld Report* left open the question of specialisation and made no recommendations for the introduction of domestic violence courts.

The issue of court specialisation resurfaced again however in 2002, in the criminal justice reform White Paper *Justice For All* which stated that the Government would 'consider the scope for introducing a greater degree of specialisation within the criminal court system' (Home Office 2002). Its proposed strategy was to see if there were advantages to handling domestic violence cases together in a dedicated specialist court. The White Paper stated that:

> Specialisation could increase the throughput of cases, secure more effective outcomes, allow more convenient and less burdensome arrangements to be made for victims, witnesses and lawyers, and use court time more effectively. But it does depend on having sufficient cases to justify the special arrangements, and on the availability of suitably trained judges, magistrates, and staff.
>
> (Home Office 2002: 26–30)

Following the publication of *Justice For All* and under the direction of the newly created Courts Innovation Branch, which was responsible for developing problem-solving approaches to the way in which courts dealt with issues such as domestic violence, drugs and anti-social behaviour, specialist courts then began to proliferate under the Labour Government, with the structure and composition of the courts continuing to be strongly influenced by US problem-solving court models – the most obvious example of this being the Liverpool Community Justice Centre which is based upon the Red Hook Community Centre in New York. Community justice centres operating with ancillary problem-solving

46 *Specialist and problem-solving courts*

community courts were created in Liverpool and Salford in 2004 with expansion to a further 11 additional jurisdictions in 2006. In addition to the introduction of these courts, government intended that a problem-solving approach would be further facilitated by the introduction of section 178 of the Criminal Justice Act 2003. This contained provisions for magistrates' courts to bring back before them offenders sentenced to community orders to review progress made in complying with the requirements of the order. Dedicated drug courts were launched in magistrates' courts in Leeds and West London in 2005, with the Ministry of Justice outlining plans for further expansion of problem-solving drug courts in 2008. In October 2009, Her Majesty's Courts Service launched a six-month pilot project to implement a problem-solving approach in magistrates' courts in six Local Criminal Justice Board areas. Although these courts adopted a problem-solving approach, they did not include some key features of community justice courts. Section 178 of the Criminal Justice Act 2003 was not implemented, hence there was no provision for regular review of offenders subject to community supervision, and services were not co-located at the court. Across England and Wales there are now currently 141 specialist domestic violence courts: 13 community justice courts (located in Birmingham, Bradford, Plymouth, Hull, Leicester, Merthyr Tydfil, Middlesborough (Teesside Magistrates' Court), Nottingham, North Liverpool, Salford, and three locations in London: Haringey, Newham (Stratford Magistrates' Court) and Wandsworth (South Western Magistrates' Court), six drug courts (located in Leeds, London, Barnsley, Bristol, Cardiff and Salford), two mental health courts (located in Stratford and Brighton), and two family drug and alcohol courts (based in Gloucester and at the Inner London Family Proceedings Court).

The distinction between therapeutic jurisprudence and problem-solving discussed earlier is important in the context of the existence of broader policy intentions to (re)orientate the lower courts around problem-solving practices: criminal court reform in England and Wales has not only focussed on the creation of specialist courts but has also been concerned with establishing the existence of a wider problem-solving framework for the operation of all magistrates' courts. In recent years, numerous government policy documents and guidance have argued that the operation of the lower courts and the decision-making of magistrates must be (re)aligned around a problem-solving approach to cases (Home Office 2005; Cabinet Office 2009). Further plans to expand and entrench 'problem-solving justice' into the criminal justice framework in England and Wales were set out as a strategic priority in Her Majesty's Courts Service (HMCS) Business Plan 2010–2011 which identified the importance of the establishment of a framework to facilitate mainstreaming the approach across *all magistrates courts* in England and Wales. In May 2012, the Magistrates' Association stated its support for the establishment of problem-solving in all magistrates' courts as a strategic priority (Magistrates' Association 2012). However, the reconfigured or 'enhanced' relationship that exists between judge and offender in problem-solving courts clearly represents a significant departure from the traditional functions of lay magistrates and district judges and which necessarily has

Specialist and problem-solving courts 47

implications for judicial training, local court practices and judicial independence. These aspects, which will shortly be examined in detail, have for a number of reasons only been considered and addressed in a perfunctory manner by government, and by policymakers. Moreover, the implementation of plans for further reform in this area is further circumscribed by a number of practical issues relating to the operation and administration of the magistrates courts, as well as by changes to the duties of lay magistrates, which require detailed consideration.

The lay magistracy

Fundamental to understanding the way that problem-solving justice is operating in England and Wales, is an appreciation of the distinctive role and function of the lay magistracy in the lower court system. The English and Welsh legal system is highly distinctive in comparison with many other jurisdictions in its use of 'lay' (non-professional) justices in the lower criminal courts. Lay magistrates are essentially volunteer judges, who are made up of members of the general public, and who operate in the magistrates' court in England and Wales. (Scotland has its own separate legal system with legally qualified Sheriffs adjudicating in the lower courts.) There are presently 23 500 lay magistrates who sit across adult, youth and family courts, which hear around 98 per cent of criminal cases (Ministry of Justice 2013b). Lay magistrates decide on matters of fact and law (guilt and innocence), and they also impose sentences. So, in this respect, they perform both the functions of judge and jury that are undertaken in the Crown Court. Thus magistrates have very significant power within the criminal justice system and correspondingly, 'over the lives of others' (Berlins and Dyer 1989: 75).

Magistrates have been commissioned to keep the peace in England since 1195 (Derbyshire 2011). Their role became formalised in the Justices of the Peace Act 1361 which devolved power to members of the community to administer justice. Hence, this system of administration by lay justices is one of the oldest legal institutions in the country (Derbyshire 2011). The lay magistracy is intended to be representative and inclusive of all sections of society, therefore no formal qualifications are required to apply to join the magistracy. The only specified requirement is that applicants be of good character.[5] However, although the lay magistracy is gender balanced and ethnically representative at the national level, data on the current composition of the lay magistracy indicates that they are largely made up of individuals from professional occupations and managerial positions (Morgan and Russell 2000), and increasingly, retired professionals (Ministry of Justice 2013b). The age of eligibility for appointment is between 18 and 65 years old and presently over half of serving magistrates are over the age of 60.[6] Lay magistrates are required to stop hearing cases at the maximum age of 70, at which point they are moved to the supplemental list. Magistrates are required to sit for a minimum of 26 half-day sittings (13 days) per year. This can be more if they also sit in other courts such as family or youth courts. The average number of sittings per year is approximately 35 and magistrates should not sit more than 70 times a year. Under the Employment Rights Act 1996,

48 Specialist and problem-solving courts

magistrates' employers have a legal duty to provide their employees with the requisite time to sit as lay magistrates.

Magistrates sit as a bench of three in court. All three magistrates on a bench have equal decision-making powers but only the chairman will speak in court and preside over the proceedings. In a magistrates' court, District Judges (DJs) also hear cases. These are full-time members of the judiciary who usually deal with longer and more complex cases coming before the court. Magistrates are generally cheaper than the use of a single, salaried DJ (Ames *et al.* 2011). Magistrates hear a broad spectrum of cases including less serious criminal cases such as motoring offences, and failure to pay council tax or TV licenses, but they also deal with cases at the more serious end of the range of criminality such as causing death by aggravated vehicle taking, assaults, sex offences, drug offences, frauds, theft and burglaries. In addition, magistrates consider bail applications, deal with fine enforcement and grant search warrant and right of entry applications. Magistrates' courts will also hear cases brought by bodies such as the DVLA and RSPCA, and also some civil and family matters.[7] For a single criminal offence committed by an adult, magistrates have the power to impose a period of not more than six months in custody (or a total of 12 months for multiple offences). Their sentencing powers also include the imposition of fines up to £5000 and community penalties. Over 80 per cent of cases in the magistrates' court involve guilty pleas, therefore magistrates' work is predominantly concerned with sentencing rather than determining innocence or guilt (Davies 2005).[8]

Over the years, the training of lay magistrates has greatly improved following criticism that there were insufficient monitoring and assessment procedures in place to determine whether training had been properly understood and implemented by individual magistrates (Huxley-Binns and Martin 2013). In 1998, a formal framework for magistrates' training was introduced, the Magistrates New Training Initiative (MNTI), which was subsequently refined in 2004 by the Magistrates National Training Initiative (MNTI). The framework introduced four basic 'competences', which form the basis of magistrates' current training. Competences are essentially a description of the required knowledge and understanding that magistrates must be able to demonstrate, and a checklist of observable behaviour necessary to fulfil the role (Magistrates' Association 2013). As part of the required competencies, new magistrates must be able to demonstrate competence in being able to manage themselves; being able to work as a member of a team; and competency in making judicial decisions. It is currently the responsibility of the Magisterial Committee of the Judicial College (formerly the Judicial Studies Board) to ensure that magistrates (and District Judges in magistrates' courts) are adequately trained to fulfil their judicial roles and functions, and to ensure consistency in magistrates' training at local, regional and national level (Judiciary of England and Wales 2013).

Before sitting in a court, magistrates will receive induction and core training lasting the equivalent of 3 days (18 hours), which is delivered by the Justices' Clerk (a legally trained adviser) at the local magistrates' court. Over the first

Specialist and problem-solving courts 49

year, magistrates undertake further training, including for example, visits to prisons or young offender institutions, and each new magistrate is assigned to a mentor who oversees their personal development and guides their progress in the first few months following their appointment. Although this formal training is provided to new magistrates, magistrates will build their competence 'on the job' as they begin to hear more cases, for different offences. It is because the 'on the job' aspect of building competency is viewed as central to the development of magistrates' abilities that there has been resistance to calls from some commentators for a reduction in the number of days that magistrates are required to sit. Further consolidation training takes place after a year which is normally the equivalent of 2 days (12 hours) and an appraisal is also undertaken where the magistrate will be observed to determine whether the new magistrate is demonstrating competence in the role. Following successful completion of the appraisal, the magistrate is deemed fully competent. Further on-going training is intended to take place throughout the magisterial career, including update training on new law and procedures (Ministry of Justice 2013c).

In the course of my research, I have found that most magistrates are generally very open to the idea of more training, and they believe that it is particularly necessary when new provisions have been enacted (see for example, their generally positive responses to suggestions of training in restorative justice, Chapter 6) although there was evidence that some of these types of training initiatives are better received than others, particularly when magistrates feel that the challenges that they face in the operation of the court system are not being properly recognised. For example, a number of magistrates criticised the *Stop Delaying Justice* case management training initiative which was undertaken in 2012, on the basis that they felt that magistrates were being unfairly 'singled out' as responsible for delays in the court process and insufficient recognition was paid to issues surrounding the practices of solicitors and the CPS, as well as problems in court listing systems. In the present economic climate however, there is a significant shortage of available funding for magistrates' training beyond the basic provision for new magistrates. This has meant that peripheral training is now virtually non-existent and that budgets do not extend to incorporate additional training in other areas that may usefully be developed such as problem-solving techniques and community engagement. Although the magistrates' association runs a number of successful projects such as the *Magistrates in the Community* initiative, which aims to increase public awareness of the role of magistrates, funding for broader training initiatives is heavily circumscribed. Many magistrates are employed in the professional training industry and it has recently been suggested by the Chairman of the Magistrates' Association that some of these skills could usefully be harnessed in developing further training initiatives for the lay magistracy, which would in turn take some of the onus off the magistrates' court service in the provision of training, although it is unlikely that HMCTS would approve such a move.[9] It has also been suggested that, given the budgetary constraints upon greater formal training, magistrates attendance at conferences and symposiums could potentially form part of magistrates' competences, as another

50 *Specialist and problem-solving courts*

avenue for developing magistrates' knowledge and skills through alternative (non-HMCTS organised) forums and events.[10] At present, the centralised arrangements governing the operation of individual courts limits their autonomy in being able to introduce new practices (Bowen and Whitehead 2013). Her Majesty's Courts and Tribunals Service (HMCTS) currently oversees the administration of Courts in England and Wales and evidence suggests that this body frequently denies local courts the flexibility and the authority to adapt and introduce new local innovations (Gibbs 2013). Moreover, the increasing centralisation of the administration of the courts (and criminal justice more broadly) has a number of important ramifications for the work of lay magistrates and their ability to deliver 'local justice'.

Court centralisation and 'local justice'

The value of a lay magistracy as an embodiment of citizen participation in justice is a cornerstone of the philosophical underpinnings of the magistracy in England and Wales. Many have observed the important symbolic role that the lay magistracy embodies within the English legal system. Magisterial justice has been described as:

> Not simply a quicker, cheaper, form of 'proper' justice. It has the potential to be a qualitatively different form of justice. It is based on the assumption that there exists an entity called 'the community' ... which is reflected in the administration of justice rather than being constructed by it.
>
> (Worrall 1987: 108)

Historically, there has been recognition by politicians of the central role that lay participants play in the delivery of justice to local communities. More than a decade ago, a report commissioned by the Home Office, *The Judiciary in the Magistrates' Courts*, found that 'Successive governments ... have favoured the encouragement of active citizens or of an active community. The lay magistracy, whatever its imperfections, is a manifestation of those concepts' (Morgan and Russell 2000: 117). The recognition of the central role played by magistrates as a manifestation of the democratic involvement of citizens in their local communities appears to receive continued support from government (Ministry of Justice 2013b). However, a number of important changes in recent years have significantly reduced opportunities for the delivery of genuinely 'local justice' in the communities that magistrates serve. Furthermore, the continued existence of lay participation in summary justice itself is under threat, and it is not clear whether the lay magistracy will continue to be a feature of the English legal system in years to come.

Local justice embraces the idea that the power and authority for the administration and decision-making made in the justice system should be invested in bodies close to local communities. In England and Wales, it is primarily a movement associated with the transference of power from central government to local

Specialist and problem-solving courts   51

authorities (Bowen and Donoghue 2013). The delivery of local justice is intended to be a fundamental objective of the role of magistrates, wherein magistrates 'bring common sense and knowledge of the locality and the local community to the criminal justice process' (Davies 2005: 113). This might include, for example, knowledge of local economies, social demographics and cultures, as well as the availability and infrastructure of local treatment and support services, unemployment levels and the prevalence of various types of offences. Although the concept of local justice is not uncontested and it has been accompanied by both philosophical and practice-based critiques, evidence suggests that local justice is important because it embodies decentralisation, openness, and accountability, which are welcome hallmarks of a modern democratic state. However, a number of changes have taken place over the last fifteen years, which have progressively undermined its potential effective implementation in the lower courts.

Much academic attention has been devoted to the trend of centralisation and managerialism that came to be associated with the Labour administration under Prime Ministers Tony Blair and Gordon Brown respectively As a consequence of New Labour's reform of the public sector, a 'new managerialsm' evolved which incorporated the imposition of professional standards of management on public services and which involved the enormous expansion of centrally imposed targets. This was accompanied by the incentivisation of senior and middle managers in public services to achieve what were at times viewed as erroneous outcomes/goals. There was correspondingly some evidence of perverse effects, notably 'gaming' of the system, particularly by the police, to achieve performance targets (Raine and Keasey 2010). As part of the drive towards greater professionalisation and managerialism, local, and at times fragmented, organisational structures were subsumed within nationally administered, 'coherent' frameworks. In 2001, local probation areas were rationalised and put within a national framework for the first time. Magistrates' courts committees were abolished and a new centralised agency to manage all the courts and a number of new local boards and committees were created. The introduction of the National Offender Management Agency in 2004 layered even more command and control over prisons and probation. New regimes of performance targets strengthened Whitehall's ability to exert control through accountability. The police were set targets in the National Policing Plan and the new Police Performance Assessment Framework. Probation performance was measured over about 30 key performance indicators. The relationship between the centre and the local was being dramatically shifted, with central government departments pouring over data to better understand and intervene in local performance (Bowen and Donoghue 2013). While the current Coalition government has sought a movement away from the managerialist approach of successive Labour administrations through for example, the creation of police and crime commissioners (PCCs) and the removal of centralised targets, and it has emphasised its commitment to reintroducing localism as a central part of its current policy agenda, there remain strong and fundamental facets of centralised control evident in the criminal justice system. This is exemplified by the current privatisation model (and its impact

52   *Specialist and problem-solving courts*

upon Probation), as well as in the continued centralised administration of the courts system (Padfield, 2011).

Prior to 2003, magistrates were required to live within 15 miles of the area in which they worked. Following the introduction of the Courts Act 2003, no such provision now exists (Huxley-Binns and Martin 2013). Significant numbers of court closures have taken place over the last ten years which means that many magistrates no longer live near the court in which they sit, resulting in a reduction in magistrates' knowledge of local areas and local problems. The most recent programme of court mergers and closures in 2012 resulted in a significant reduction in the number of Local Justice Areas (LJAs). The court system is organised around LJAs which are used to determine which magistrates' courts may hear a particular case. At the same time, the Senior Presiding Judge, Lord Justice Goldring, stated that every Justice must be prepared to sit anywhere in the LJA if required. The distances between courthouses can be daunting and, outside of London, can reach distances of nearly 80 miles between courts in the same LJAs. It is then perhaps not unexpected that a recent report found that centralisation has resulted in 'unnecessary court closures, the disempowerment of magistrates, the disappearance of the justices' clerk as a powerful local figure, courts become distanced from local government, reduced local accountability and low morale among court staff' (Gibbs 2013). Thus, the importance and value attached to local justice appears to have been reduced as national consistency has increased.

Moreover, amongst the magistracy themselves, there is debate – and some tension – about the concept of local justice and how it applies, and how it ought to apply, to the work that magistrates undertake. While the effect of court closures and mergers has obvious implications for local justice, which magistrates emphasise, there are also concerns that a focus on 'local' decision-making leads to inconsistency in sentencing, potentially undermining public confidence in the court system (Magistrates' Association 2012). Inconsistency in sentencing has been an area of concern among legal commentators for some time (Ashworth 2004a). Significant efforts have been made to address this issue, through in particular the introduction of sentencing guidelines. Yet, these too have potential implications for local justice and a number of magistrates involved in my research have criticised the introduction of sentencing guidelines for impacting on their ability to deliver local justice. One magistrate in the South West remarked that:

> Where there may have been a local outbreak of a particular crime, particularly those that encouraged copycat behaviour, early versions of the guidelines did give local benches some scope to give heavier sentences to strengthen that deterrence, latter ones did not and the guidelines became tramlines that turned sentencing into a tick box affair. When coupled with a flurry of benches being combined for the sake of economy, the public once again saw the court as being an enforcement arm of the state that had more to do with maintaining state power than it did to solving the social problems

Specialist and problem-solving courts   53

that faced some local residents on a daily basis. 'Us' and 'Them' had returned in a big way. Justice was no longer seen to be done because, where once the local townsfolk could pop into the local court to see how those that had committed crimes that may have affected their daily lives were dealt with, they now had to travel at least ten miles – in our area – to one of the few court houses left open, at great cost and inconvenience, very often in areas where no public transport existed.

Many magistrates feel increasingly disempowered and report that their professional autonomy is being undermined, especially through court centralisation and efforts such as sentencing guidelines aimed at increasing their 'professionalisation' (Gibbs 2013). But given that the lay magistracy is largely made up of participants from the professional classes and those over the age of retirement, critics have argued that the status quo of a partially professionalised lay body provides neither genuine lay participation nor the most effective form of professional participation (Davies 2005; Gibbs 2013). The logical corollary of this argument is that the magistracy should become a fully professionalised body. Yet this has significant associated problems of principle (Davies 2005). Lay magistrates provide an important check on the dominance of professional/expert power. Attempts to 'professionalise' the lay magistracy through increased training risks removing the 'community' dimension from the majority of criminal cases (Davies 2005). Moreover, because magistrates sit as panels of three, judgment of law and fact does not rest with a single individual, thus providing an important oversight and accountability function.

Nonetheless, further changes to the role of the lay magistracy are now being considered as a consequence of the current Coalition government's drive to increase efficiency in the magistrates' courts, as a result of current fiscal imperatives and the need to reduce expenditure in the criminal justice system more broadly. The Government's White Paper *Swift and Sure Justice*, set out proposals for single magistrates to deal with low-level, uncontested cases such as shoplifting and criminal damage offences, where the defendant has been charged with the offence by the police and a guilty plea is anticipated (para 119). Other regulatory offences such as cases relating to TV licenses, vehicle excise duty and fare evasion were identified in the White Paper as those which:

> Need not take up valuable space in magistrates' courtrooms and … could also be dealt with by a single magistrate, in a way that is both swifter and involves less bureaucracy, whilst still maintaining the defendant's right to a fair and open hearing.

Similarly, in 2013, the Ministry of Justice, in its *Reforming the Role of Magistrates* consultation, outlined plans to ensure 'maximum use is made of the skills and capabilities of magistrates so they are routinely dealing with serious and complex cases, within their powers, rather than committing them to the Crown Court for sentencing' (Ministry of Justice 2013b). This is to involve unclogging

54 *Specialist and problem-solving courts*

magistrates' courts through, for example, dealing with 'the 500 000 or so simple road traffic offences out of the traditional process, freeing-up time for magistrates in courtrooms to deal with more serious offences' (Ministry of Justice 2013b). These proposals have been met with some alarm from magistrates who question the impact that these changes will have on the fairness of hearings. While it has been observed that in the vast majority of TV license cases, for example, a single magistrate could reasonably be used, there are also concerns about fairness when magistrates are involved in these type of 'bulk cases' where they report that it can occasionally be 'easy to make a mistake'. The bench of three magistrates is an important check on fairness and moderation to ensure consistency, which may be affected in these sorts of cases.

Most significantly, however, are plans to place 'the magistrate at the heart of the criminal justice system in their communities' and to involve magistrates in 'cutting crime locally' through, for example magistrates scrutinising the police's use of out of court disposals, and engaging with local community initiatives. In addition, the Offender Rehabilitation Bill, currently before Parliament, introduces new powers to enable magistrates to impose short periods of custody for any offender who breaches their new supervision period, following a sentence of less than 12 months in prison. Although driven by 'efficiency' savings,[11] these reforms have highly significant ramifications for the role of magistrates which will impact upon their ability to deliver problem-solving justice, since the concept of problem-solving justice proposes the explicit incorporation of the community into judicial process as a means of ameliorating the criminal justice system and 'empowering' communities (Cabinet Office 2009; Ministry of Justice 2011, 2012a).

Court review of community orders

As briefly mentioned above, an important development in problem-solving justice was the introduction of powers to provide for court review of community orders under section 178 which was contained in the Criminal Justice Act 2003. On the face of it, section 178 powers appeared to signal an opportunity for courts to systematically adopt processes of review of offender compliance that are integral to the problem-solving court model. The legislation provides that:

(1) The Secretary of State may by order—
   (a) enable or require a court making a community order to provide for the community order to be reviewed periodically by that or another court,
   (b) enable a court to amend a community order so as to include or remove a provision for review by a court, and
   (c) make provision as to the timing and conduct of reviews and as to the powers of the court on a review.

Therefore, under section 178, powers are given to certain courts by the Secretary of State to enable the judiciary to make an order allowing or requiring a court to

Specialist and problem-solving courts   55

review the progress of an offender under a community order. This involves the offender returning to the court at each review to discuss his/her progress with the judiciary. Under Section 178, the court also has the power to attach or remove a review provision from a Community Order, and regulate the timing of reviews. Her Majesty's Court Service had initially appeared to be enthusiastic about the development of a problem-solving approach, which was to be buttressed by the use of section 178 powers. In 2009, for example, HMCS Annual Report observed that:

> This year we began developing the core principles of this approach to determine how it might be rolled out to all magistrates' courts across England and Wales. The potential for this work is significant. In the community justice courts, HMCS facilitates the use of the judicial power to review offenders' progress on community orders, under Section 178 of the Criminal Justice Act 2003. These powers could potentially benefit the problem-solving approach. However, legislation currently only permits the use of this power in the 13 community justice courts. The benefits of using Section 178 can be transformative. For example, a 28 year-old male with a long history of offending was called back before magistrates under Section 178 to review his Community Order. The court identified social and health problems including severe alcohol dependency and homelessness. He was assessed, in court, by a specialist alcohol worker and referred to Alcohol Dependency services. During subsequent Section 178 reviews to monitor his progress, the defendant appeared to have turned his life around and had re-established his relationship with his parents. His accommodation needs had been met and he was alcohol-free. In another case a 19 year-old male given a Community Order had three reviews scheduled during the period of his order. The first review was positive. He had been attending the learning support he had been referred to and was even enjoying the unpaid work imposed by his order. However, by the second review he was in breach of the order. His explanation to the court for not attending probation appointments was that he was being bullied by other offenders in his group, something he had failed to report to his probation officer. The court was able to order another review in two weeks time to allow discussions to take place with his probation officer. By the final review he had successfully completed his hours of unpaid work and was voluntarily accessing education and employment services. We are exploring how these ways of working might be a feature of a broader problem-solving approach.
>
> (Her Majesty's Courts Service (2009: 14–15))

However, since that time, although section 178 powers have been invoked in a number of courts in England and Wales, including drug courts, their use has in fact been extremely limited overall. There are a number of explanations for this. The most significant reason is that many magistrates are not familiar with the power to review community orders under section 178 of the 2003 Act. Despite

56 *Specialist and problem-solving courts*

these powers being introduced a decade ago, over the course of my research it became clear that most magistrates were not aware that the powers existed at all and that the use and applicability of these powers was not a subject that was ever discussed with colleagues. Other important factors contributing to the limited use of section 178 powers were cost; and the attitudes of and implications for Probation. Magistrates who are aware of the power to apply for review of community orders under section 178 have identified that the use of such powers comes with associated costs, as well as requirements for the availability of magistrates to hear the reviews. Scheduling review hearings requires additional court time and resources, which have been under significant pressure for a number of years. A number of magistrates have identified the primacy of cost based concerns in the review of community orders. One magistrate observed that:

> Previously, the question of cost was uppermost in magistrates' minds when they were involved in courts designated to the review of community orders because they were invariably being requested to end a community sentence early as the offender was "doing fine now". I always had concerns about this as I felt it was a decision being taken purely on cost – although we were being told the rehabilitation was successful. I suppose it's no different to prisoners being released early on license.

The issue of cost has always been fundamental both to decision-making and resource allocation in the criminal justice system. However, in the current fiscal climate, these issues have been further magnified. There is also the issue of ensuring the availability of magistrates for reviews, which can be problematic given the part-time nature of magistrates' work. Nonetheless, there is significant support from magistrates for judicial involvement in review of community orders. One magistrate reported positively on a visit that magistrates from their court had undertaken to the US the previous year where they had visited a District Court and had seen the way that community orders were discharged by the Judge ordering them and the way that the offender was required to provide proof it had been completed. It is clear that some magistrates do not wish to see judges having greater involvement in the implementation or monitoring of sentences. They take that view that magistrates are deployed most effectively in the court process and the sentence is most effectively monitored and supported by the appropriate agency that is employed to do this. However, there are many magistrates who do see constructive value in sentencers playing a greater role in reviewing community orders.

There is a tension evident in the potential for section 178 powers to be viewed as a challenge to or criticism of Probation's professional judgment and so for there to be an element of resistance towards greater use of the powers, since it is Probation who would traditionally put these cases into the court list for review in the first place. For example, one magistrate, who had sat in a court which had been operating a 'Community Justice' scheme and had used section 178 powers reported that they had worked successfully, but that 'it does use up court time and CPS and Probation Officer time [and] Probation might think we were checking up on them or usurping their role'. As part of this court's community justice initiative, magistrates visited Attendance Centres to talk with clients during their term on a community order. The magistrate reported that they found the interactions with clients very useful but also 'uncomfortable' in the way that it may have appeared to undermine Probation's authority.

It also appears that there has been a degree of cultural resistance or ambivalence towards greater use of section 178 powers from within HMCTS and/or the Ministry of Justice. Magistrates report that 'non-one [within HMCTS] made any effort to try to implement this' while another sentencer suggested that 'the provision was widely ignored by HMCTS/Ministry of Justice because they didn't agree with it! So much for the will of the people expressed in Parliament.' The very limited use of section 178 powers is significant because it provides a substantive route into a problem-solving approach. Without court review of sentences and judicial engagement with offender progress, the problem-solving model does not operate. Undoubtedly, it is not appropriate for all community orders to be subject to review under section 178 powers, however a significant number of cases would certainly benefit from the judicial oversight that the powers permit. Problem-solving court advocates argue that there is no appropriate response from the Ministry of Justice as to why this approach is not feasible.

Court listing practices

Inadequate and ineffective court listing practices are a significant barrier to magistrates' courts being able to realise problem-solving objectives in England and Wales. In some courts there is resistance to the creation of listing practices ensuring continuity of sentencer on the basis that this might impact upon judicial neutrality since magistrates are obliged to treat each case impartially. For example, one magistrate recalled a case which they believed served to illustrate the problems associated with sentencer continuity:

> It is impossible to be completely unaffected by cases ... Some magistrates may state that they "put personal angst to one side" and make appropriate decisions. But I would argue that this is impossible. And I shall give a personal example, a defendant admitted animal cruelty and we referred the case to probation for a report. The case in question was horrendous. I personally did not wish to come back and sentence and would have requested not to ... Some people may argue – that is the very reason why I should have returned on the case.

Other courts continue to operate using archaic and outdated listing practices; some courts report they have little money to update their systems with new technology; that the costs of continuity in cases is not matched by the benefits; and that it is 'so difficult in the current cut back climate, it is virtually impossible for magistrates to come back on a case'. Magistrates in other courts report a frustration at their

58   *Specialist and problem-solving courts*

obsolete rota systems and what they observe as a reluctance or unwillingness by others to attempt a new approach. Replacing the scheduled bench can also be unpopular because of the shortage of available sittings. Court centralisation has also had a significant impact, limiting as it has done, individual courts' autonomy and budgets. This frustration was expressed by one magistrate who noted:

> The amalgamation of courts' administration is not helping the listing situation. Magistrates would welcome the opportunity to 'seize' themselves to sentence complex cases which they have decided upon. It would only be desirable to automatically be given cases where complex issues had to be decided which would not be apparent to a purely Sentencing Bench.

Another significant barrier however is the volume and type(s) of cases heard in the lower courts, together with the part-time nature of lay magistrates' participation, which some argue precludes the creation of a case listing system which enables judicial continuity. In particular, magistrates recognised that this may be a specific difficulty for those sentencers who were in full-time employment and would not be able to be as flexible in their availability:

> We do sometimes return as a bench to deliver a sentence by taking over another court for a short while to deal with a single case before handing the court back to the bench listed for the day. It is possible for all sentencing that requires a full report beforehand be handled by a special sentencing court where benches just turn up to deal with their outstanding sentencing issues. For example, the first hour every Friday is a sentencing court where sentencing magistrates could sit for as little as ten minutes just to deal with the outstanding case. Now that is all very well for those of us that have retired but for the others who have to arrange time off work, they may find it a little difficult.

There are a number of courts, however, which have proactively tried to improve listing practices to enable greater continuity. One magistrate in the Midlands told me that it was:

> ideal for the Bench which has ordered a pre-sentence report following a plea of guilty or having sat on a trial or Newton hearing to return to sentence the defendant. It is more likely that a different Bench will read the report and impose a sentence although in [area deleted] we are fortunate in having a group of Justices with sufficient flexibility and commitment to sit on a particular case when consistency is required – even if it means turning up at court to sit on just one case.

Elsewhere, in London, another magistrate noted that:

> The roster is always a major headache for court staff. Judicial continuity is always a problem because magistrates are not always available. But this

could be improved by better use of technology and on the day arranging for the current bench to adjourn with the case. We did this in the family court to a useful degree.

One magistrate usefully described to me a possible way of setting out criteria for a bench to return for sentencing. They observed that benches may decide that they want to return to sentence for a variety of reasons, including, to avoid the following bench having to repeat the evidence where the case involves complex issues; where the evidence of live witnesses gives a greater depth to the decision-making process than a mere report of the facts at a later hearing could; and in those circumstances where the hearing bench feels that a later sentencing bench would not be able to understand the subtleties of why the hearing bench had asked for a serious disposal. It was suggested that it may be possible to organise a criteria for a bench to return for sentencing, based on these different circumstances. They observed that 'the existing system whereby benches that want to return to sentence sort out a convenient date in court on the day that the report is asked for works reasonably well but it would it would be nice to have it formalised a little.'

Thus, in order for problem-solving to be mainstreamed and undertaken effectively in magistrates' courts generally, the listing of court cases requires very significant improvement. The co-ordination and administration of court lists to effectively group cases that would benefit from problem-solving would be necessary. To create consistency in the relationship between sentencer and offender so as to ensure that magistrates are able to establish effective communication with offenders over successive reviews (and develop the sort of relationship envisaged by problem-solving practices), court systems would need to be introduced to allow sentencers to be automatically given cases which they have previously heard. The selected quotations from magistrates discussed above, give a flavour of some of the relatively complex barriers that exist to creating such a system. Yet they are not insurmountable barriers. Magistrates who are keen to see listing practices revised to enable greater continuity, suggest a range of possible techniques to improve current systems. It is clear however, that the most important factor is the 'buy in' of sentencers themselves and a concomitant commitment from them to try new practices, to generate and share information about their innovations, and to prioritise a system which can produce more continuity, even when resources are scarce.

Notes

1 For example, in England, a network of specialist traffic courts is currently being introduced as part of the Government's *Criminal Justice Strategy and Action Plan*. This will result in a specialist traffic court in every police area by 2014, which will operate using specialist prosecutors.

2 Although it is worth contrasting these concerns with observations made by legal commentators in other jurisdictions. For example, Stuart Field (2006: 522) has argued that in the French inquisitorial criminal process, evidence of the defendant's 'character' is

60 *Specialist and problem-solving courts*

pervasive and visible, particularly in the most serious cases, and its relevance is more broadly defined. Moreover, in court

> its presentation is shaped by a developed and positive conception of the French citizen ... As a result, the legitimacy of trial is seen in terms of the rehabilitation of the accused as a citizen of the state rather than simply the punishment of a particular infraction.

3 See Mae C. Quinn, *The Modern Problem-Solving Court Movement: Domination of Discourse and Untold Stories of Criminal Justice Reform*, 31 Wash. Univ. J. Law and Pol, 58 (2009) (noting that progressive efforts to reform the court process through the introduction of specialised criminal courts had first been made by Judge Anna Moscowitz Cross during the first half of the twentieth century. The courts were however largely criticised and ultimately abandoned.). Further discussion of the problems encountered by such attempts at reform can be found in Mae C. Quinn, *Revisiting Anna Moscowitz Kross's Critique of New York City's Women's Court: The Continued Problem of Solving the 'Problem' of Prostitution with Specialized Criminal Courts*, 33 Fordham Urban L. J. 665 (2006). *See also*, Timothy Casey, *When Good Intentions Are Not Enough: Problem-Solving Courts and the Impending Crisis of Legitimacy*, 57 S.M.U. L. Rev. 1459, 1464 (2004) (suggesting that the juvenile courts were 'the original problem-solving courts'), and for an indication of the problems encountered in juveniles courts, see *re Gault*, 387 U.S. 1, 17–18 (1967). The landmark Supreme Court decision held that juveniles in criminal proceedings must be afforded the same due process rights as adults. Mr Justice Fortas observed that

> the highest motives and most enlightened impulses led to a peculiar system for juveniles, unknown to our law in any comparable context. The constitutional and theoretical basis for this peculiar system is – to say the least – debatable. And in practice ... the results have not been entirely satisfactory.

4 For example, in the US, an extremely high number of federal criminal cases are resolved by pleas rather than by trial and which could be said to utilise procedures that are not manifestly different from those applied in problem-solving courts (Kempinen 2011). Kempinen notes that according to the U.S. Sentencing Comm'n, Sourcebook of Federal Sentencing Statistics (2009), the number of federal criminal cases resolved by plea rather than trial was 96.3 per cent. By 2010, this had risen to 96.8 per cent, Sentencing Comm'n, Sourcebook of Federal Sentencing Statistics (2010).

5 As part of this criteria, there are a number of restrictions on eligibility, however, and those who have been declared bankrupt, police officers, traffic wardens, those currently serving in the army, and individuals with criminal convictions are currently unable to serve as magistrates.

6 One potential explanation for the unequal representation of particular social demographics within the lay magistracy results from the selection process for potential applicants (Davies 2005). Appointment of lay magistrates is made by the Lord Chancellor, who selects candidates from shortlists composed by local Advisory Committees. The assessment and selection of applicants is based on an evaluation of a number of key skills. It may be that candidates working in professional domains are more familiar with and experienced in communicating their abilities to satisfy such criteria and it might also be the case that many of the skills required of lay magistrates 'fit more comfortably into the self-evaluation of someone with a professional or managerial background' (Davies 2005: 96). We should also not forget the historical continuity of evidence documenting the more limited engagement of individuals in formal criminal justice from socio-economically deprived backgrounds.

7 The Crown Court deals with more serious criminal cases such as murder and rape which are referred from magistrates' courts.

8 Davies (2005: 109) notes that it is important to make clear this aspect of the work of

magistrates because magistrates 'are often compared unfavourably with lay juries in the Crown Court. However, in reality, magistrates are far more often called upon to do the equivalent work of the salaried judge in his or her sentencing role, rather than the work of the jury'.

9 Comment made by Richard Monkhouse at the launch of the *Better Courts: Cutting Crime through Court Innovation* symposium, London September 2013.

10 Comment made by Richard Monkhouse at the launch of the *Better Courts: Cutting Crime through Court Innovation* symposium, London September 2013.

11 Last year around 9800 defendants were convicted by magistrates and then were committed to the Crown Court for custodial sentences. Out of this number, 40 per cent received up to six months' imprisonment, meaning that these are offenders who could have been sentenced in the magistrates courts, where the cost of a typical sitting day is significantly cheaper – on average this is £1400 per day in the magistrates' court compared to £2150 per day in the Crown Court.

4 Drug courts and domestic violence courts

The creation and development of drug courts can be understood as a largely practical response to rising levels of incarceration and prison overcrowding, but they are also the result of a growing international consensus that punitive criminal justice sanctions, as a first response to addressing problems associated with drug addiction, are inappropriate and ineffective. Sending drug-addicted offenders to prison often does little to address their drug dependency and is also likely to increase their exposure to and interaction with criminal networks. Evidence suggests that much drug dependency is associated with acquisitive crime and so a failure to address the underlying causes of such criminality will likely be ineffective in reducing levels of recidivism. The economic cost of acquisitive crime linked to drug abuse is high, impacting significantly upon local and national economies, as well as policing and other criminal justice resources. Policy documents often highlight that drug abuse is associated with violence in communities, unemployment and chaotic lifestyles. Therefore drug-related crime, and drug-addicted offenders, raise questions about the administration of the criminal justice system that are of fundamental significance. The issues that they raise reflect and remake the public and political concerns about criminal justice that were outlined at the start of this book.

Drug courts are intended to offer an alternative (at least in the first instance) to incarceration. While these courts originated in the US, specialised drug courts are now in operation in a number of countries across the world including Canada, Australia, New Zealand, Ireland, Scotland, the Caribbean, South Africa and Europe. Although there are a range of different drug court models, with varying types of implementation across, and within, jurisdictions, there are common fundamental objectives that are characteristic of all drug courts. A central concern of drug courts is to keep drug dependent offenders out of prison by mandating treatment instead of imprisonment, as well as reducing criminal justice system overload and prison overcrowding (Cooper *et al.* 2010). Effective drug treatment as a pathway to reduced recidivism is also a shared objective of drug courts. The notion that drug dependence is intrinsically linked to crime is thus a central theme. Although researchers within the field of addiction have sought to highlight the complex nature of the link between drugs, treatment and crime (see for example Sparrow and McIvor 2013; Stevens *et al.* 2005), there is

Drug courts and domestic violence courts   63

nonetheless a significant body of empirical work suggesting the potential for appropriate treatment to lead to reductions in both drug use and crime (Lösel *et al.* 2011; Holloway *et al.* 2008).

While drug courts are treatment oriented, their mode of operation tends to be judicial in nature. Drug courts are not responsible for determining an offender's guilt as they must usually already have pleaded guilty in order to meet the eligibility criteria for the drug court. Thus, drug courts are not concerned with determining guilt or innocence, but with the sentencing aspect of proceedings. As outlined in previous chapters, the judge is the central figure in the drug court model but functions as part of a 'team' of other criminal justice professionals including lawyers, treatment service providers, social workers and probation. The courts operate using systems of rewards and sanctions to promote compliance. Mandatory urine testing is a feature of drug courts, as well as review hearings to establish the offender's levels of compliance with their treatment. Offenders who are referred to a drug court do not receive a custodial sentence (or the sentence is suspended) but are instead entered into a court-ordered drug treatment programme. Provided that they comply with the conditions of their sentence, the offender is able to avoid imprisonment. If the offender fails to abide by the terms of their treatment, they will be returned to court where they will face re-sentencing and possible imprisonment (provided that the original offence committed was eligible for a custodial sentence).

In the majority of jurisdictions, drug courts deal with offenders who are engaged in committing minor crimes which are a consequence of their drug dependency (Belenko 1998). In England, for example, drug courts are used for drug-misusing offenders who commit low-level acquisitive crime (such as shoplifting) to fund their addiction. Similarly, US drug courts tend to exclude any offenders who have committed violent crimes and/or who have serious mental health issues, and focus on offenders who have committed non-violent crimes such as property crime and who have relatively few prior convictions for serious offences (Kalich and Evans 2006). However, there is some variation in terms of the types of offenders that drug courts in other jurisdictions will target. Most notably, courts vary in terms of whether they will only accept low-level non-repeat offenders, or whether offenders are permitted to enter into a drug court programme if they have committed violent crimes. In both Canada and Australia, drug courts will accept repeat offenders who have committed relatively serious crimes, although they do not accept offenders who have been accused of violence against the person.

Drug courts operate pre or post judicially, and so procedures for referring offenders to drug court vary across jurisdictions. Offenders are either diverted to the drug court before being sentenced, in which case they only return to court for sentencing if they fail to successfully complete the drug court programme; or they enter drug court after sentencing (where guilt has been admitted) and their sentence is suspended pending successful completion of the programme. To what extent abstinence is a requirement of drug courts, also varies again according to jurisdiction. While the majority of drug courts emphasise abstinence-based

64　*Drug courts and domestic violence courts*

treatment, especially in the US, there are also examples of other courts which use methadone maintenance programmes and where a reduction in the drug court participant's substance misuse will be accepted by the court (McIvor 2006). James Nolan (2009: 58) has identified the distinctive British approach to 'harm reduction' in the drug court setting, whereby reduced use as opposed to complete abstinence can be accepted by a court, and which tends to be at odds with the US approach where total abstinence is a common goal and requirement of drug courts and where 20 per cent of American drug courts specifically prohibit any type of pharmacological intervention. However, recently there appears to be increasing distance between the emphasis upon 'treatment' and 'punishment' in US drug court praxis (Murphy 2012; Hunter *et al.* 2012; Belenko *et al.* 2011).

Sentencer continuity

A growing body of empirical work has begun to evidence the importance of the role of the sentencer in drug court review hearings, and particularly the effect on compliance of the levels and types of interactions that take place between judge and offender (McIvor *et al.* 2003, 2006). Recent empirical research on the operation of drug courts in Britain reinforces the salience of the relationship between judge and offender. In Scotland, drug courts were first piloted in 2001 and shared many characteristics in common with drug courts in other jurisdictions such as England, the US and Australia, including integration of substance misuse treatment with criminal justice processing; frequent testing for illicit drugs; on-going judicial review of participants' progress; and partnerships with other relevant agencies to provide continuous support for participants (McIvor 2010).[1] Research findings on Scottish drug courts indicate that the interactions that took place in court between offenders and judges encouraged increased compliance and supported offenders in their efforts to address their drug use and associated offending (McIvor 2010). It was reported that 'the success of the drug courts was dependent to a large extent on the attitudes and approaches of the [judges]' (McIvor 2010: 31). Furthermore, in an evaluation of drug courts in England (which will be discussed further in the following pages), it was found that continuity of a judge across court appearances was associated with enhanced compliance with court hearings, lower levels of positive drug tests for heroin, an increased rate of completion of orders and a reduced frequency of conviction (Matrix Knowledge Group 2008).

Indeed, in other jurisdictions too, there is evidence that judges play a central role in assisting drug-misusing offenders to lead law-abiding lives. In 2007, one of the most important evaluations of US drug courts was published by the National Institute for Justice (Finigan *et al.* 2007). While the general study findings suggest that drug courts can potentially be effective in reducing recidivism and lowering cost, the researchers found that a drug court's 'success' was largely affected by the role assumed by the judge and the nature of offender interactions with the judge. Similarly, in a US randomised control trial on the long-term effects of participation in the Baltimore City drug treatment court, Gottfredson *et al.* (2007) observed that judicial review was directly correlated with reduced drug use and, moreover, that it indirectly reduced criminal behaviour by increasing participants' perceptions of procedural fairness. Gonzales *et al.*'s (2006) literature review of drug court evaluations also found evidence to suggest that drug courts can potentially reduce recidivism and promote other positive outcomes. Again, it was reported that offenders' interactions with the judge are one of the most important influences on the experience they have while in a programme.

'Voluntariness'

The 'voluntary' nature of offenders' participation in drug courts has been subject to significant scrutiny and critique, particularly from legal scholars reflecting on the operation of the US drug court model (see for example Miller 2004; Quinn 2000). Michael King has observed the way in which the rationale of US drug courts differs substantially from the approach taken in other jurisdictions such as Australia and Scotland. In America, drug court practices evidence the responsibilisation of the defendant and the use of (judicial) power and coercion to ensure compliance with perceived 'therapeutic' goals or outcomes. Petrila (1993: 882) maintains that:

> While often cloaked in the language of autonomy and choice, [a 'therapeutic' approach] simply reinforces the existing distribution of power in the relationship between treater and treated. In some critical areas, it will result in even more power accruing to professional interests.

Other scholars too have observed the potential for a 'therapeutic' approach to buttress pre-existing power dimensions and to reinforce professional sensibilities and bias(es) (Arrigo 2004). Accordingly, these critical commentaries have sought to draw upon Foucauldian notions of power and agency and have compared drug court methodology with 'the imposition of the will a powerful individual on that of a powerless one' (Allen 2002: 132).

These observations tie in with existing praxis-based critiques which contend that drug courts are not 'treatment' based as their rationale suggests but are in fact wholly punitive criminal justice innovations which are able to exploit the marginal position of those that are subject to their remit. For example, although not currently possible in English and Welsh drug courts, drug courts in other jurisdictions are able to impose intermediate sanctions for failure to comply with the terms of treatment. As a consequence, a central critique of the drug court model has been the potential for such courts to result in drug court participants spending more time in prison than they would have if they had been processed through the ordinary court system. There is also evidence that those who are expelled from drug courts for failure to successfully complete their treatment requirements, are in turn subject to harsher sentencing than they would have

66   *Drug courts and domestic violence courts*

received if they had not entered the drug court originally (DPA 2011). A recent meta-analysis of US drug courts found that while the use of the courts:

> Significantly reduced the incidence of incarceration on the precipitating offense, corresponding to a reduction in confinement from 50 per cent to 42 per cent for jail and 38 per cent for prison incarceration ... drug courts did not significantly reduce the average amount of time offenders spent behind bars, suggesting that any benefits realized from a lower incarceration rate are offset by the long sentences imposed on participants when they fail the program.
>
> (Sevigny *et al.* 2013: 416)

Thus, legal commentators have expressed concerns that drug courts are often highly punitive, with a heavy reliance upon sanctions (Clarke and Neuhard 2004). They argue that coercion (and undue influence) is a characteristic of many problem-solving specialist courts where defendants can be pressurised to take the option of pleading guilty and accepting treatment instead of proceeding to trial and hearing the evidence against them, albeit with the overarching threat of imprisonment (Meekins 2006).

More broadly, others have observed that a 'therapeutic' approach to case processing evidenced in some drug courts, reflects judicial engagement in processes of 'social engineering' (Quinn 2009). Hence it follows that the treatment and 'therapeutic' orientation of drug courts raises important questions about power relations and due process. A primary feature of the therapeutic paradigm within the drug court model is the requirement that participants 'see the process as therapeutic and treatment oriented instead of punitive in nature ... [T]he team's focus is on the participant's recovery and law-abiding behavior – not on the merits of the pending case' (Hora *et al.* 1999; Hora and Stalcup 2008). The therapeutic discourse is thus arguably underpinned by the notion that 'change begins with the individual, and is rooted in a narrative of self-esteem, motivation, suffering and finally transformation, which is instrumental for change' (Malkin 2005: 380). The therapeutic paradigm, according to Miller (2009), rejects the protections conferred by the due process model on the basis that they are an impediment to its instrumental or utilitarian objectives of well-being and mental health and instead creates an environment whereby the offender is held responsible for their progress and rehabilitation. Consequently:

> The relationship is not one between peers engaging in free and open dialogue, in which the plurality of each other's values commands respect. Rather, it is a relationship in which one is dominant, dictating the nature of the courtroom reality, and the other subservient, required to learn to accept that reality and speak in the governing language of therapy.
>
> (Miller 2009: 426)

On the other hand, it has been argued that the therapeutic framework in fact envisages an approach that extends beyond the mere *provision* of due process,

Drug courts and domestic violence courts 67

but endeavours for a reduction in adversarialism and a comprehension of and responsive position on different individual circumstances, needs and issues (Freckelton 2007).

Selectivity in sentencing

Drug courts which operate using a judicial model have also been criticised for reproducing the selectivity of the criminal justice system and thus relegating a public health approach (DPA 2011; JPA 2011). In the US particularly, there is some evidence that access to drug courts, and the treatment that they provide, is inequitable for ethnic minorities and economically disadvantaged communities since drug courts are generally used for offenders who have committed low-level offences related to their drug use. This excludes a significant proportion of offenders with serious drug problems. African Americans are less likely to be permitted entry to drug courts because they are more likely to have criminal records associated with their drug use. The rate of arrest for drug-related crimes among African Americans in the US is 238 times that of white offenders. Of the total number of offenders incarcerated for these crimes, African Americans and Latino-Americans make up two-thirds of the imprisoned population. This is despite the fact that these populations use and sell drugs at comparable rates to white Americans. Many US drug courts (particularly federally funded courts) have strict eligibility requirements which mean that because African Americans are more likely to have criminal records associated with their drug use, they are also more likely to be excluded from entry into the drug court (DPA 2011). There is also evidence that African Americans are 30 per cent more likely to be expelled from drug court programmes than white court participants. Economic vulnerability, lack of ethnic minority drug counsellors and culturally acceptable treatment programmes are significant factors here (DPA 2011).

In a recent report on the role of US defence attorneys in problem-solving courts, the National Association of Criminal Defense Lawyers raised a number of serious concerns about the operation of problem-solving courts, including in respect of their differential sentencing practices and treatment access arrangements for minority racial and ethnic groups (NACDL 2009). The report conceptualises the defence attorney's role in narrow terms – rejecting the team participant paradigm and promoting the independent, advocacy role of defence counsel in criminal proceedings. Particular concerns have been raised about the defence counsel's decreased role in providing advice to clients about the legal consequences of the court's treatment regime, and in being able to supply an independent check upon the court's decision-making (Meekins 2006, 2007; Pinard 2006; Quinn 2000, 2008). This has implications for the protection of the defendant's constitutional and due process rights.[2]

As we shall see in the following sections, the potential for drug courts in England and Wales to reproduce selectivity in sentencing is also evident. The issue of criminal justice practitioners 'cherry-picking' cases which are more likely to produce measurable positive outcomes is also more broadly problematic as a

68 *Drug courts and domestic violence courts*

consequence of the Governments' new payment by results approach (previously discussed in Chapter 2). Evidence suggests that 'cherry-picking' of 'easier' and 'less complex' cases has been an issue highlighted in the operation of a number of drug courts in other jurisdictions where some courts have deliberately designed strict entry requirements in order to exclude more difficult cases which have less chance of success. In an age of austerity, problem-solving courts are increasingly required to demonstrate their effectiveness. Therefore it is not surprising that courts are more reluctant to take on complex cases with less chance of success, even though these offenders may be in urgent need of treatment. At present, drug courts in England and Wales do not oversee prolific offenders. This undoubtedly has implications for selectivity in sentencing, as well as more fundamental concerns about the provision and allocation of treatment.[3]

Effectiveness

The drug court model has been adapted and modified to suit certain requirements in different jurisdictions. Therefore, as we have seen, no single drug court model exists. While this is clearly a strength in the respect that the model can be altered to suit the specific characteristics and diversity of particular regions/locales, it also necessarily has consequences for the evaluation of the limits and effectiveness of such courts because general conclusions about outcomes and effectiveness are not empirically valid. The majority of the available evidence is also to be found within the US literature, where drug courts generally restrict drug court participation to non-violent, substance-dependent offenders and will often exclude drug-dealing offenders or individuals with extensive and serious criminal histories and/or serious mental health problems. Moreover, studies which aim to evaluate drug court outcomes encounter a number of methodological difficulties which impact upon their scientific rigour and validity. For example, many previously published studies were conducted on a small scale, without a control group and did not utilise samples and variables that could easily be compared or reproduced (Merrall and Bird 2009). While small-scale studies have been useful in their application to local praxis contexts, their generalisability to other courts is much more limited (Hickert *et al.* 2009). As Eric Miller has argued in the foreword to this book, although we know that drug courts tend to reduce recidivism during the course of the programme, and for two years after the programme ends, the precise factors that deliver 'success' within the drug court model require further examination and study (Rempel *et al.* 2012). Moreover, existing evidence on 'success' in the drug court setting is not currently able to demonstrate that long-term recidivism disappears, nor that participants are cured of addiction, or aggression.

Outside of the US, the evidence base on drug court outcomes also lacks coherence. In Canada, a 2007 review of drug courts found that little was known regarding the success of these courts in contributing to the long-term reduction of drug use and recidivism among drug court participants; and that the cost-effectiveness of these programmes required further study (Werb *et al.* 2007). The researchers concluded that:

Drug courts and domestic violence courts   69

Further funding for DTCs in Canada should be dependent on the implementation of randomized controlled trials that measure the success of these programs in reducing drug use and recidivism in the long term; that measure the impact of DTCs on societal end-points such as rates of crime and incarceration of injection drug users; and that include components to measure the cost-effectiveness of DTCs compared with other interventions aimed at reducing the negative effects of problematic drug use and drug-related crime.

(Werb *et al.* 2007: 12)

A further review of Canadian problem-solving courts, including a review of the evidence on drug courts, published in 2010 found that although problem-solving courts have been proliferating in Canada there remains little knowledge of their measurable effectiveness in reducing crime (Slinger and Roesch 2010).

Yet despite the methodological limitations identified above, there is also a more rigorous and coherent body of empirical work beginning to emerge (particularly in the US but also in Australia) that is starting to more convincingly evidence the positive outcomes of drug courts compared to traditional punitive criminal justice responses. Reductions in levels of recidivism and cost-effectiveness are outcomes that have begun to be associated with the work of drug courts. A recent meta-analysis, which synthesised 154 drug court studies,[4] found that although much of the existing research on drug courts is generally methodologically weak,[5] there is nonetheless sufficient evidence to support the use of adult drug courts (Mitchell *et al.* 2012). The meta-analysis revealed that the effectiveness of drug courts is very much dependent on a range of different factors. The authors concluded that:

This analysis shows there is no simple answer to the question, 'Do drug courts reduce crime?' The answer is – 'It depends'. What it depends on is partly what the court is compared against. Weaker studies which cannot exclude the possibility that more promising offenders find their way to drug courts also find the largest effects. Presumably crucial variables – like how committed the offenders are to succeed, their social and family support, or professional assessments of how well suited they are to a drug court regimen – are rarely available to researchers so cannot be adjusted for. Effects remain even in randomised trials which should eliminate this source of bias, but perhaps partly because these are so rare, pooled results from these trials are not statistically convincing.

Results also vary with another feature of the comparator – the degree to which it is like the drug court it is being compared against. This probably works both ways: the gap between the two may be narrowed because the drug court is unable to fully implement a drug court model, or because the comparator already incorporates features of this model. Both influences may account for the lack of impact of Scottish drug courts in the main UK study to report on recidivism.

70 *Drug courts and domestic violence courts*

The two features found by the featured analysis to be associated with increased drug court effectiveness – seeing offenders at least twice a month and holding out the prospect that success would expunge the original offence – were among the effective ingredients also identified in a major study funded by the US Department of Justice of 23 drug courts.

(Mitchell *et al.* 2012: 70)

A serious effort is now underway to try to formulate a body of scientific evidence which is able to explain the circumstances in which drug courts can offer a genuine and appropriate alternative to traditional case processing. To what extent this largely US-based evidence is of relevance to the UK needs to be considered in light of the currently limited evaluations that have taken place in Britain.

Court-ordered drug treatment in England and Wales

Prior to 2005, court ordered treatment for drug dependency in England and Wales operated largely through the use of Drug Treatment and Testing Orders (DTTOs) which were introduced by the Crime and Disorder Act 1998. The creation of these orders was directly influenced by the development of US drug courts. British politicians, who had travelled to America to observe the operation of specialist courts including drug courts and community courts, were impressed with the problem-solving model that these courts utilised and in particular their efforts to address the link between drug use and crime. Thus the potential for effective drug treatment, operating within the criminal justice system, to result in abstinence from drugs and in turn significant reductions in (especially acquisitive) crime, was extremely appealing (Harman and Paylor 2002). The DTTO was subsequently introduced as a new type of community sentence enabling courts to make an order requiring offenders to undergo treatment either as part of another community order or as a sentence in its own right. These orders differed from existing probation orders as the sentencing court became responsible for checking and monitoring progress and compliance throughout, with sentencers responding to individual progress or problems, including failed urine tests. In policy terms, DTTOs were intended as a 'tougher' probation response to drug-addicted offenders that utilised coercive treatment enforced through the criminal justice system (Bean 2002: 74). In practice, however, there was evidence of significant variation in the standard of supervision provided in different parts of the country, as well as implementation problems associated with multi-agency/partnership working and local treatment availability (Sparrow and McIvor 2013). A number of commentators also expressed concerns that the more limited/less enhanced role that the sentencer occupied in the DTTO review hearings in England might potentially impact upon the effectiveness and measurable outcomes of the review process, relative to the central role of judges in (particularly US) drug courts who have responsibility for a much wider range of processes and sanctions within the drug court's operation (Nolan 2001; Crichton and Fidler 2004). Despite these implementation difficulties, there were nonetheless positive

Drug courts and domestic violence courts 71

reports of reductions in both drug use (Turnbull *et al.* 2000) and recidivism (Hough *et al.* 2003).

Under the Criminal Justice Act 2003, DTTOs were then subsumed within a new generic community order which allows a court to make an order with a drug rehabilitation requirement which can be formulated to be equivalent to (or a less intensive version of) a DTTO. Drug Rehabilitation Requirements (DRRs) became available in April 2005 and combine drug treatment, drug testing and weekly supervision with a probation officer.[6] A DRR can last from between six months to three years and are intended for those offenders who have a history of drug use, who have been unsuccessful in previous attempts to desist from using drugs, who are committed to giving up drugs and who are prepared to fully engage with a programme of court ordered drug treatment. In those circumstances where an individual has been prosecuted for an offence and they have a drug addiction that they are willing to undergo treatment for, Probation may recommend to the court that a DRR is an appropriate sentencing option. Where an order is subsequently imposed by the court, the offender will then agree the terms of their treatment (an individual care/action plan) with Probation and the treatment service provider. The plan sets out the agreed treatment goals including reduction of offending, the level of treatment and testing required at each stage of the order, and identifies the various agencies and/or services that will be involved in the offender's treatment. Treatment includes for example, cognitive behavioural therapy, health education, alternative therapies, activities to improve social skills, and promotion of education, training and employment.

The terms of DRRs vary according to the number of contact hours which offenders are required to attend and these are determined by the nature and seriousness of the offence committed. Less intensive orders will require a lower number of contact hours, usually involving a weekly drug test and meeting with a probation officer, as well as attending a drug treatment agency for a treatment session, while more intensive orders will generally involve at least two weekly drug tests as well as a number of treatment sessions and other contacts with the treatment provider(s) including group sessions. An offender's progress on a DRR will be reviewed monthly by the court. If offenders fail to keep to the agreed terms of their individual treatment plan, they will be returned to court for breach of the order, which often results in a more onerous sentence being imposed. Offenders who successfully complete their DRRs but who have continuing need of treatment support will be offered referral into voluntary treatment services in their locality. Lawyers are absent from DRR review hearings. While the absence of defence lawyers in the process may be viewed as having implications for the protection of defendant's right and procedural protections, James Nolan's study (2009) of the operation of DRRs suggested that this format actually elicited a range of important benefits central to the problem-solving court model, particularly in respect of reducing the formality of proceedings and facilitating improved engagement between judge and offender.

An important difference between the DRR and the old DTTO is that the latter was generally only used for Class A drug users who were at risk of an immediate

72 Drug courts and domestic violence courts

custodial sentence. The DRR is much wider in its availability and is identified as appropriate for a broader range of drug user, making court mandated drug treatment an option for low level persistent offenders, including the homeless (Hollingworth 2008). It has been argued that this in turn raises questions about potential net-widening, the appropriate allocation and management of resources required for these extra cases, and the implications for low level users to come into contact with and be influenced by more serious drug abusers (Sparrow and McIvor 2013). The emphasis upon the identification of lower class drug use is also evident elsewhere through more recent plans for reform. For example, the Rehabilitation of Offenders Bill, currently before Parliament, sets out plans to amend those drug testing requirements which form part of offenders' release on license conditions in the Criminal Justice and Courts Services Act 2000, to include mandatory drug testing for Class B as well as Class A drug use.

The use of DRRs as a component of community orders must however be differentiated from the objectives and operation of drug courts. The introduction of drug courts in England actually pre-dates both the DTTO and DRRs: the first two drug courts were created in West Yorkshire in 1998. However, following the introduction of the DTTO, these two courts were then incorporated within the national DTTO programme. Drug courts then reappeared a number of years later when two dedicated drug court (DDC) pilots were launched in magistrates' courts in Leeds and West London in 2005. The Ministry of Justice commissioned an independent process evaluation of these pilot courts between January 2006 and May 2007. The process evaluation was undertaken by Matrix Knowledge Group in partnership with the Urban Institute and supported by academic researchers from the Universities of Stirling, Sheffield, Cambridge and Kent. It took place over a 17-month period at the two DDC pilot sites and identified a number of significant findings relating to the working practices in the courts. Reflecting similar findings in other jurisdictions such as Scotland and the US, evidence suggested that judicial continuity was central to obtaining reductions in re-offending but that this was often hard to achieve in the English context due to court scheduling constraints. The evaluation further noted the importance of appropriate and high quality judicial training for those sentencers involved in the drug court model. Effective partnership working between the different treatment and support agencies was highlighted as crucial to obtaining positive outcomes in the drug court process. While the evaluation attempted to undertake a cost-benefit analysis to explore the costs of the DDC and the costs to society of drug-misuse offending, as the report of findings acknowledges, 'a robust quantification of impact was not possible because of the difficulties in collecting sufficient data on a control population of offenders. Even if the data had been collected, the relatively low number of offenders seen by the courts over the pilot period, compared to that expected, would have reduced the strength of the statistical basis for assessing the impact of the DDC on drug misuse and offending' (Matrix Knowledge Group 2008: viiii). Thus, the evaluation provided some useful information on qualitative aspects of the two courts' operational processes but was unable to produce any rigorous quantitative data on the statistical viability

Drug courts and domestic violence courts   73

of DCCs in reducing re-offending or on the wider economic implications of DCCs when compared with the associated costs of drug misuse.

It was however intended that the key operational differences and the lessons learned in the evaluation of these initial two pilot courts would then provide data to inform the establishment of additional DDCs. Subsequently, a further four pilots (in Barnsley, Bristol, Cardiff and Salford) started operations in 2009. The principal aims of these drug courts were two-fold: (i) to reduce illicit drug use, and (ii) to reduce re-offending amongst drug-misusing offenders who commit specifically low-level crime to fund their addiction. Unlike other jurisdictions, drug courts in England and Wales do not have dedicated buildings in which they operate but are subsumed within the workings of the main court building. Under the drug courts pilot, sessions were set aside in existing magistrates' courts for dedicated panels of magistrates or particular district judges to sit for sentencing. Offenders who had been convicted of a low-level 'acquisitive' offence, and who were identified as 'drug misusing' could be referred to the DDC pilot for sentencing.[7] Based upon Her Majesty's Courts Service (HMCS)[8] guidelines on the DCC model, the four key dimensions of the drug courts pilots were defined as follows:

- Continuity of judiciary between sentencing, review and breach of community orders with a drug rehabilitation requirement, so that an offender's court hearings took place before the same panel of magistrates or the same district judge throughout their order.
- Training of judicial and court staff, probation, and other stakeholders, such as treatment providers working within the DDC model, alongside awareness raising for all Criminal Justice System partners in the area. The framework stated that such training was likely to include visits and events and the production of guidance on the DDC processes and awareness material.
- Improved partnership working between the court, judiciary and key partner agencies in the area.
- Exclusivity in that the DDC should exclusively handle drug-misusing offenders from sentencing to completion or breach of any order.

(Kerr *et al.* 2011: ii)

Following the creation of the additional DCC pilots in 2009, two further studies were then undertaken which investigated, respectively, the feasibility of conducting a robust impact evaluation of the DDC pilot (Kirby *et al.* 2010) and another empirical process evaluation, this time including the four newly created DDCs. The former was conducted by the National Institute of Economic and Social Research and the Institute for Criminal Policy Research, King's College London. The feasibility study maintained that a full impact assessment was possible but that it would not offer value for money because of the length of time that it would take to complete and the possibility that it may not then find any substantive impact. The researchers concluded as follows:

74 *Drug courts and domestic violence courts*

There were two feasible designs to consider – an RCT [Randomised Control Trial] and a between-area design. For any design it would be difficult to measure a reduction in drug misuse. Running an RCT presents a risk of failure during the randomisation process, as it requires compliance and assistance from a large number of practitioners. The between-area comparison design runs the risk of falsely attributing outcome differences to the DDC when other factors are involved. The between-area comparison seemed the most cost-effective and least risky approach. However, the length of time needed for either approach would be considerable. Given the lack of robust evidence on the likely effect and the small degree of difference between DDCs and non-DDCs, there is a high risk that the sample sizes proposed here would not be large enough to detect a reduction in reoffending if it was less than five percentage points. If the effect was smaller than this, the sample size would need to be increased to identify the impact. This would have time and cost implications.

(Kirby *et al.* 2010: 4)

The second process evaluation (of all six pilot DDCs) was undertaken between 2009 and 2010 (Kerr *et al.* 2011). Although the study was able to capture the practice and processes across the six sites, in common with the previous evaluation of the DCCs in West London and Leeds, it was also not able to provide any rigorous statistical evidence on the DDCs' potential to reduce drug use and associated offending. Quantitative data was collected on descriptive statistics such as social-demographic profiles of offenders but the validity of these data sets was subject to a number of significant limitations, impacting upon their validity and generalisability however.[9]

Nonetheless, the process evaluation provides some useful qualitative evidence on the particular working practices across courts and it found that, overall, the DCC model was viewed by both offenders and court staff as a useful adjunct to the range of existing initiatives for drug addicted offenders. Again, the evaluation highlighted the value of sentencer continuity as a key element of the DCC model 'in providing concrete goals, raising self-esteem and engagement and providing a degree of accountability for offenders about their actions' (Kerr *et al.* 2011: i). It appeared to be easier to achieve continuity with one district judge than with three magistrates sitting on the DDC bench. Vital factors in achieving continuity were identified as judicial commitment to appropriate listing and effective planning of the court rota. In terms of the scalability of the DCC model, the evaluation identified that it would be necessary to provide national standardised training guidelines for magistrates and practitioners involved in the drug court process, as well as clear guidance on how the DDC model should be both theoretically and practically implemented, and therefore how drug court praxis and philosophy can be reconciled within the existing parameters of the criminal justice system. Interestingly, the costs of setting up and running DDCs were viewed as small. This is largely because English and Welsh DCCs do not require separate buildings or additional staff, although the provision of additional

Drug courts and domestic violence courts 75

training would necessitate some additional funding. It is worth observing that in other jurisdictions, some studies have suggested that drug courts are unlikely to result in a reduction in financial and resources pressures on the criminal justice system. On the contrary, drug courts have tended to increase pressures since the creation of drug courts can correspond with an increase in arrests because police are more likely to detain people for minor drug offences (King and Pasquarella 2009). Nonetheless, the English evaluation reported practitioners' views that efficiency savings could potentially accrue in a number of areas, such as the amelioration of existing practices so that drug-misusing offenders are seen on the same day, resulting in treatment provider presence only being required at the one designated court. It is also important to note that empirical evidence from this evaluation suggests that the practices and procedures of drug courts in England have been developed largely ad hoc and without any standardisation of court processes (Kerr *et al.* 2011).

Thus while the administration of both drug courts and DRRs are concerned with monitoring and reviewing compliance with offenders' drug treatment, drug courts are specifically intended to prioritise judicial continuity in subsequent review hearings. Moreover, judges in drug courts are intended to take a more active role in the planning of treatment programmes whereas sentencers overseeing review hearings in magistrates' courts will generally defer to Probation. A number of commentators have observed that the more central role that sentencers are intended to inhabit in the problem-solving court model, may be resisted, or may create tension, with other agencies (most notably, Probation) who are accustomed to having more power in the court process, particularly in terms of advising on appropriate treatment (Nolan 2009; Bean 2004). Nonetheless, recent evidence suggests that sentencers in English drug courts continue to attach a significant level of importance to the advice and interests of other members of the 'problem-solving team' at sentencing. During the DCC evaluation, magistrates reported using information from both Probation and treatment providers to assist them in their sentencing decisions because of the experience and expertise of these organisations relative to their own. One magistrate observed that:

> Sometimes we [the magistrates] are the only amateurs in the whole system … our legal advisers are professional, the solicitors are professional, probation are professional … so I think there is a feeling at some point we have to be guided by the professionals.
>
> (Kerr *et al.* 2011: 11)

In a similar vein, another sentencer noted that: 'From a magistrate's point of view, it can be quite difficult because we have to learn how informal to be … it's all unwritten rules … because we are breaking new ground with this' (Kerr *et al.* 2011: 12). These findings suggest that specialist judicial training for drug (and other problem-solving) court judges is a vital component of the DCC model. Without tailored and specialised training, sentencers are not able to take on the 'enhanced' role that the problem-solving model envisages. Although Nolan has

76 *Drug courts and domestic violence courts*

identified the 'strength of Probation' in playing a very prominent role in the development and operation of English drug courts (2009: 50), it is likely that the strength and power of Probation will be significantly impacted upon in light of recent reforms that many see as essentially the 'privatisation' of the Probation service in England and Wales.

Moreover, although the *formal* objectives of drug courts and DRRs are different, in practice sentencers in DRR review hearings often engage techniques traditionally associated with drug court judges. For example, in the course of my own research, magistrates reported to me that:

> Many of us like to engage with the offender and see how they think it is going as well. It is usually obvious to the bench that the offender is finding it difficult or that they are making good progress purely from the look of them ... eyes no longer sunken, good skin colour and bright eyes etc.

Magistrates observe that engagement and encouragement during the review process including 'congratulating on good progress' and 'commiserating on poor progress', is important even when it takes place with an offender whose progress they have not reviewed before, because it helps to demonstrate to offenders that the court 'cares about his progress' and 'encourages them to keep going'. Interestingly, it was not generally viewed as particularly problematic from the perspective of magistrates interviewed as part of my research, that there is a lack of continuity in the sentencer reviewing the progress on the DRR. This of course runs contrary to much of the evidence on sentencer continuity within the problem-solving domain but does, I think, also serve to highlight that even when a problem-solving approach has not been adopted either wholesale or formally, it can still be the case that aspects of such an approach are being practiced, whether explicitly as part of a conceived 'problem-solving' rationale, or indeed simply as part of the routine function of sentencers who see value and merit in engaging and encouraging offenders' progress. Previous empirical work on DTTO and DRR review processes revealed that the effectiveness of these hearings can be constrained by the operational realities of sentencing and court work in England and Wales (McSweeney *et al.* 2008). Nolan (2009: 48) for example, has argued that 'because lay magistrates serve in panels of three on a rotating basis, DTTOs and DRRs often lack the kind of continuity and close personal interaction that is at the very heart of the American drug court model'. While it is certainly the case that sentencer continuity is an issue for DTTOs and DRRs, it is important to acknowledge that many magistrates do try to engage with offenders in ways which could technically be recognised as 'problem-solving'. However, these interactions would undoubtedly be made more effective if judicial continuity could be established. That magistrates *already* can be seen to engage with offenders in problem-solving ways in traditional magistrates' courts as well as for DTTOs, holds promise for the establishment of a streamlined problem-solving approach, if the issue of court listing can be addressed.

Drug courts and domestic violence courts   77

A further area of interest here is the number of review hearings that come before the courts, and their associated cost implications. Under the Criminal Justice Act 2003, review hearings only need to be held in those circumstances where a DRR is imposed for over 12 months or, in the case of DRRs imposed for under 12 months, where the court specifically requests a review hearing(s). Where an offender is assessed at sentence of being at a high or very high risk of harm, for example where the individual is a prolific offender and/or has an OASys score of 100 or above, then statutory guidance indicates that it is good practice for reviews to be scheduled. Research on US drug courts suggests that review hearings are expensive and time/resource intensive and therefore ought to be targeted appropriately at those offenders who are high-risk and are most likely to benefit from such monitoring processes (Marlowe *et al.* 2005). This very much overlaps with magistrates' current observations on the impact of cost savings/pressures and court closures on the scheduling of DRR reviews. Many note the reduction in DRR sittings (usually from one day a week to half a day) and that 'DRR courts' are being 'run down' due to 'budget reasons'. In places like Cornwall, positive discussions have been had about the introduction of drug review courts but no action has been taken primarily because of funding issues. Drug courts are dependent on timely and adequate funding (Guzman 2012). For example, in Scotland there have been problems in guaranteeing sufficient funding to ensure high quality treatment services. At present, there are limited resources and capacity to create and develop drug courts. Critics argue that this has important consequences for the work of existing courts who are likely to prioritise cases where people are more likely to successfully complete treatment. While there is some evidence of this in the US, there is not so much evidence of this in the drug courts in England at present.

Intermediate sanctions for non-compliance

One of the central criticisms that has been made of drug courts in England is that intermediate sanctions, including 'short sharp shock' custodial periods, are not available to sentencers in the same way that they are commonly deployed in other jurisdictions (Nolan 2009). As a consequence, it has been argued that this has largely circumscribed the effectiveness of English drug courts, because they instead operate more like 'an extended type of probation order' with the options available to drug courts being limited to the imposition of more onerous requirements, or revocation and re-sentencing (Bean 2004: 131). On the other hand, McSweeney *et al.* (2008), citing a report of the National Institute for Health and Clinical Excellence (2007), have argued that evidence suggests that the use of incentive-based approaches towards affecting behaviour change, are likely to prove more effective than punishment-oriented approaches. Moreover, they observe that:

> The system of incentives used to encourage behaviour change as part of contingency management arrangements that has been applied successfully

78 *Drug courts and domestic violence courts*

in different drug treatment settings (including clinic privileges, vouchers, monetary incentives and award draws) seems politically incompatible with treatment delivered in a criminal justice context.

(McSweeney *et al.* 2008: 48)

The availability of short-term 'punitive' sanctions (particularly the availability of short custodial terms) is a crucial element of the debate on the drug court model, but it also extends to broader arguments about re-offending and the efficacy of magistrates' courts use of custody for those subject to community supervision requirements following short-term prison sentences.

Much of the criminological/criminal justice literature and empirical scholarship has identified the substantial use of short custodial terms by the courts in England and Wales; and the higher rates of re-offending associated with their use when compared with sentences served in the community. For example, recent evidence suggests that community sentences are 8.3 per cent more effective in reducing re-offending rates (Ministry of Justice 2011a). Custodial sentences of less than 12 months were less effective at reducing re-offending in England and Wales by between 5 and 9 percentage points, than both community orders and suspended sentence orders in 2008 (Ministry of Justice, 2011a).[10] Consequently, it has been a central concern of prison reformers that there should be a move towards reduction in the magistrates' courts use of short custodial terms and correspondingly greater use of community sentences. They argue that community sentences offer a more effective penalty against offending which involve a measure of restitution to the community; and they have lower rates of re-offending, both in volume of offending and seriousness of offences (Howard League for Penal Reform 2012). The debate on community sentencing is also salient in the context of court budgets and resources, and the need to free up court time for more serious offences. For example, when cases involving street-drinking are taken to court, they are generally dealt with by way of conditional discharge as magistrates do not wish to impose a more serious penalty for what is, essentially, a low-level offence. These types of offences may well be better addressed outside of the court system, either by way of fixed penalty notice (issued by the police) or through the use of a Neighbourhood Justice Panel (see Chapter 6).

Here it is important to consider the consequences for offenders who are subject to a community order in England and Wales and who breach the terms of their order. When offenders breach the conditions of a community order, such as missing an appointment with their Probation officer, they are expected to explain their reasons for the breach. In those instances where their explanation is not satisfactory, they will likely receive a warning. If a subsequent breach occurs, Probation has little choice but to return the offender to court where the court is not able to give a further warning to the offender or a fine but will instead look to altering or creating more onerous conditions of supervision or it may impose a considerable custodial term upon the offender. Phil Bowen (2013) has recently made the case that these arrangements are unsatisfactory because they potentially

Drug courts and domestic violence courts 79

result in serious ramifications for technical breaches of orders; they fail to recognise that offenders' routes out of crime are not linear; and as a consequence they can result in offenders' treatment and support needs being neglected while they are in custody undermining their opportunities for rehabilitation.

He observes that:

> Under our present arrangements, breaches of community supervision rules – missed appointments, positive drug tests etc. – are often met initially with mercy, and then with severe and sometimes damaging consequences. The mercy is to be found in probation officers trying their best to keep an offender in compliance on a community order, recognising that the path out of crime is often a series of two-steps forward with one step back. But when a probation officer gives an offender a second chance and then that offender breaches the rules again, they often have no option but to take the offender back to court. There, the offender is either faced with an adjustment of their community supervision (which can often be viewed as 'getting away' with it) or they can be met with substantial doses of prison – often for months and sometimes for years. This means our system is geared to applying the ultimate sanction – deprivation of liberty for extended periods – as the first and only sanction to what can be just a series of technical infractions. Offenders left in this position often have no route back out into community support until the end of their sentence.

Importantly, this argument has some support from magistrates themselves, who of course recognise that offenders' pathways to desistance are not linear and do indeed often follow the 'two-steps forward, one step back' trajectory that Bowen, as well as many criminal justice researchers, have previously identified (see for example, Maruna 2011). One magistrate who participated in my fieldwork, for example, highlighted the primacy of Probation in having sufficient discretion in being able to determine when an offender ought to be returned to court:

> Why not a third chance or a fourth, or fifth ... alcohol and drug addiction 'patients' ... may trip up and fall back into a short period of repetitive behaviour, only to pick themselves up again to continue on the straight and narrow ... Who better than Probation to judge when enough is enough and let them decide when it is time to apply to the courts for more onerous punishment. It is not only ... a matter of justice being served but also the social aspect.

However, Probation can also be inconsistent in its approach to returning offenders to court. Breaches are technically given for the second breach of conditions but always following at least two other non-appearances. Offenders can be returned to court in circumstances when there have been many late shows and a scattering of acceptable absences, together with other non-compliant issues that are not commented on in any reports. Therefore, Probation's decision to return an offender to court is often (but far from always) subjective.

80 *Drug courts and domestic violence courts*

The more controversial corollary of Bowen's argument of course, is that courts should be enabled to use short periods of custody as a sanction for failure to comply with community orders. This stands in opposition to the case made by those who advocate a movement away from 'punitive' sanctions to the use of 'treatment' oriented 'incentives' to encourage behaviour change, especially for those offenders with drug and alcohol addictions (Sweeney *et al.* 2008). However, the effectiveness of systems which prioritise rewards *as well as* punishments to promote reduced drug use has been highlighted in a broad range of international literature (see for example Burdon *et al.* 2001; Griffith *et al.* 2000; Higgins *et al.* 1999; Turnbull *et al.* 2000; McIvor 2006). The international evidence also suggests that it is important for courts to see offenders frequently enough to apply penalties swiftly and sensitively in response to the offender's progress (Hawken and Kleiman 2009; BOCSAR 2008; Freeman 2001). It appears that a combination of sanctions and rewards are more likely to influence behaviour than an approach which relies only on the revocation of a community sentence and termination of treatment programmes as a type of 'all or nothing' approach. This approach is reflected in the work of the Glasgow drug courts for example, where the emphasis has been on the court actively seeking to minimise infractions and to avoid recourse to custody by motivating offenders and adjusting their treatment appropriately (McIvor 2010).

It follows then that a valuable dimension to the work of English drug courts ought to be the availability of incentives together with short-term intermediate sanctions, with revocation of DRRs an option of last resort. As we have seen thus far, these options are not currently available to sentencers in DDCs. An interesting recent development in this area is, however, now underway in England and Wales. The Offender Rehabilitation Bill, currently going through Parliament, proposes new powers under section 4 for magistrates to impose a two week return to custody (or fine/'supervision default order') for any offender who breaches their new supervision period, following a sentence of less than 12 months in prison. If these types of interim sanctions could be extended for use as punishments attached to DRRs, this would potentially help to address some of those existing criticisms of DRR and drug court operation. It may be that the courts would not seek to make considerable use of these powers. For example, in Scotland the lack of formal sanctions available to the courts short of revocation was rectified by the Criminal Justice (Scotland) Act 2003, which provided drug courts with the power to impose short-term prison sentences, although evidence suggested that the Scottish courts did not make substantial use of these powers (McIvor *et al.* 2006). Yet it must be borne in mind that a central critique of the drug court model has been the potential for such courts to result in drug court participants spending more time in prison than they would have if they had been processed through the ordinary court system. This is clearly an issue of salience in the context of the proposed introduction of intermediate custodial punishments for drug court participants and therefore must be carefully assessed against the potential benefits of the proposed introduction of additional intermediate sanctions. If expensive sentence failure and imprisonment are to be

Drug courts and domestic violence courts   81

avoided, it would be essential that such adjustments were made before offenders got to the point where their breaches led the court to revoke the drug court order and re-sentence for the original offence.

Domestic violence courts

Domestic violence (DV), also referred to as 'intimate partner violence' (IPV), remains a very significant problem in modern society. DV against women is a global public health and human rights concern. Although DV is not only perpetrated in heterosexual relationships by men against women (Cook 2009; Rothman *et al.* 2011; Ard and Makadon 2011), research identifies that DV is experienced much more commonly by women than by men. Evidence from the World Health Organisation's (WHO) *Multi-Country Study on Women's Health and Domestic Violence* documented the widespread and global nature of DV (Garcia-Moreno *et al.* 2006). There is also a corresponding body of literature which identifies the broad range of physical, mental, sexual and reproductive health consequences for victims of DV (see for example Ellsberg *et al.* 2008). In England and Wales, two women are killed each week by their partner or ex-partner and collectively, nearly 1 million women experience at least one incident of domestic abuse each year (Home Office 2010c). Victims of DV are more likely to experience repeat victimisation than victims of any other types of crime (Home Office 2010c). Moreover, DV is a multifaceted socio-legal problem, which spans criminal, civil and family law simultaneously (Dalley 2013). Historically however, in Britain and internationally there have been relatively low reporting rates for DV. This has in part been attributed to perceptions that the police and courts are typically unhelpful to victims (Gover *et al.* 2007).

In an effort to address these difficulties, the introduction of specialist domestic violence courts (SDVCs) began in the US and Canada during the 1980s and early 1990s. In common with the introduction of drug courts, the development of SDVCs in these countries operated according to a range of different models, although with SDVCs some courts have only jurisdiction for civil or criminal cases, while other courts have powers to hear both civil and criminal matters (Tutty *et al.* 2008). Typically, domestic violence courts are victim-focussed, with an emphasis on risk reduction and victim safety (Stewart 2011). Some problem-solving family violence courts in the US utilise an approach to judicial monitoring of offenders which is based upon the principle of deterrence and the court's coercive powers. If offenders fail to comply with the terms of the programme, the court will take remedial action, including the use of (re)imprisonment (King and Batagol 2010). Yet others use monitoring as a motivational tool to try to promote change in an offender's behaviour, and to enhance victim safety. These courts may invoke judicial praise and the lifting of restrictions as rewards and may encourage engagement and participation in rehabilitation. Although King and Batagol (2010) note that in the US, the rationale for domestic violence courts is different to drug courts. In drug courts, offenders are usually non-violent and willing to engage in rehabilitation programmes, whereas in domestic

82 Drug courts and domestic violence courts

violence courts, there will have been violent behaviour perpetrated by the offender and both parties are often reluctant to attend. It should be further acknowledged that US courts operate in a different legal framework to the UK. Not only is there no equivalent human rights legislation preventing the hearing of criminal charges after civil findings have been made, but the plea bargaining system means that there are in practice very few trials.

There is significant agreement among criminal justice professionals and victim advocates that the legal response to DV should include both criminal sanctions against perpetrators of criminal offences and civil legal remedies in the form of enforceable protection orders and victim compensation (Stewart 2011). Given the historical context of relatively high levels of domestic violence compared with low reporting rates and evidence of victim dissatisfaction with existing criminal justice processes, it has followed that SDVCs have been developed with an explicit focus on the victim, and the way that the court process may itself serve to ameliorate some of these existing difficulties, while prioritising victim safety, through increased victim inclusion and support. Although treatment of offenders is a common component within SDVCs, these courts differ somewhat from other types of problem-solving court because their primary focus has tended not to be on reducing re-offending per se, but in ensuring the court process is oriented around the victim. However, as Stewart (2005, 2011) and others (see for example Tutty *et al.* 2008) have identified, there has in recent years been evidence of a shift away from the emphasis on victims in SDVCs, towards an emphasis on offenders and in particular, prioritising reducing levels of recidivism. A common theme in the evaluative literature on domestic violence courts is that SDVCs are particularly important and useful with regard to enhanced judicial understanding of domestic violence issues, perpetrator accountability and more comprehensive support for victims at an early stage (Cook *et al.* 2005; Kelitz 2001). In England and Wales, there is the existence of broad support for the SDVC approach. In the US, SDVCs have evolved further over the years and now extend to incorporate Integrated Domestic Violence Courts (IDVCs). These integrated specialist courts are intended to reflect the fact that a common feature of DV cases across jurisdictions is that they often end up before multiple judges in multiple courthouses. The IDVC approach is therefore intended to streamline the process by bringing together families with overlapping criminal and civil DV cases before a single judge (Aldrich and Kluger 2010). Although there is no single model, IDVCs are generally administered using a centralised intake system; a dedicated judiciary: 'one family one judge' or 'one family one judicial team'; and dedicated courtrooms (Hester *et al.* 2008: 4). However, it is important to recognise that, despite evidence of the potential benefits of the specialised judicial approach to domestic violence, there is not an uncritical acceptance of the appropriateness of these particular approaches to domestic violence cases. Other researchers have observed the way in which this trend towards a general acceptance of SDVC as an appropriate forum to resolve domestic violence cases appears to be judicially led (Hennessy 2008). This is especially relevant in the context of a paucity of evidence to support the efficacy of resource-intensive perpetrator treatment (Stewart 2011). As yet there have been few evaluations specifically of IDVCs in the US although there is a growing literature on the effectiveness of perpetrator treatment and judicial monitoring (Kleinhesselink and Mosher 2003; Labriola *et al.* 2005; Mansky 2004; Mazur and Aldrich 2003).

Specialist domestic violence courts in England and Wales

Although the first specialist domestic violence court in Britain was established in Leeds in 1999, SDVCs did not begin to proliferate until the mid-2000s. The implementation of SDVCs generally occurred in response to dissatisfaction with the treatment of DV cases in the criminal justice system, which had tended to address the criminality of DV through protection order systems. In England and Wales, SDVCs combine criminal and civil settings and are intended to have increased judicial consistency over orders as well as potentially reduced court administration. All SDVCs are designed to incorporate multi-agency working in their approach to DV cases so that magistrates, court staff, support services, police and other criminal justice agencies work collaboratively in partnership to reduce risk and support victims. In the English context, in some ways it may be more appropriate to think of SDVCs as 'systems' rather than courts because, like English drug courts, they do not have dedicated buildings in which they operate but are subsumed within the workings of the main court building (Home Office 2008).

In the same way that US drug courts had significantly influenced British political intentions to transplant concepts for DDCs over to England and Wales, American innovation in domestic violence court specialisation was also of fundamental importance to their creation in the UK. Practitioners had travelled to the US to observe the functioning and administration of American domestic violence courts and used their experiences to inform the development of SDVCs in England and Wales upon their return. By 2003, four further SDVCs had been set up in Cardiff, Derby, West London and Wolverhampton. These SDVCs were criminal courts at magistrates' level where cases involving domestic violence are clustered together or fast-tracked, and handled by specially trained court staff, magistrates, the Crown Prosecution Service (CPS), and Police. The White Paper *Safety and Justice* (2003) reiterated the Government's commitment to considering whether specialist domestic violence courts would offer more effective protection for victims and resulted in a significant broadening of SDVC activity across the UK with the introduction of a further 23 SDVCs (Matczak *et al.* 2011).

Research carried out between November 2003 and January 2004 then evaluated the five models of SDVC or Fast Track Systems (FTS) operating at the magistrates' courts in Cardiff, Derby, Leeds, West London and Wolverhampton (Cook *et al.* 2004). Although the five courts were at different stages of their development, the study findings suggested three areas in which there were 'notable and positive benefits' associated with the work of Specialist Domestic Violence Courts and Fast Track Systems (Cook *et al.* 2004: 4). These were

84   *Drug courts and domestic violence courts*

identified as enhanced effectiveness of court and support services for victims; greater ease of advocacy and information-sharing; and improvements in victim participation, satisfaction and public confidence in the criminal justice system. Specifically, the lack of links with civil courts and problems of information sharing were noted. Again, reflecting parallel developments in the creation of DDCs, the study found that the administration of SDVCs were modified to suit local conditions and lacked standardisation in their court processes. Subsequently, in 2006, a National Resource Manual outlining the recommended core components of an SDVC was published to aid consistency of service delivery in SDVCs. These key components are summarised as follows:

Component One: Multi-agency partnerships with protocols
Effective multi-agency partnerships are based on a clear understanding of responsibilities and co-ordination of partner contribution, outlined in a protocol.

Component Two: Multi-agency risk assessment and risk management procedures for victims, perpetrators and children
Individual agencies within SDVCs should have risk assessment tools including a Multi-Agency Risk Assessment Conference panel (MARAC).

Component Three: Identification of cases
SDVCs should work to a common definition. All agencies are required to have identification systems in place that link across cases.

Component Four: Specialist Domestic Violence Support Services
The provision of specialist services is critical for supporting the victims and essential to the effective working of the SDVCs.

Component Five: Trained and Dedicated Criminal Justice Staff
The training of staff in the specialised nature of DV is an important element in the success of SDVCs.

Component Six: Court Listing Considerations
Adopting a particular listing practice within an SDVC enables all agencies to adapt and focus their resources to maximum effect. Fast tracking or cluster courts are encouraged.

Component Seven: Equality and Diversity Issues
SDVCs need to address good practice in relation to a range of equality and diversity issues covering at least ethnicity, gender, disability and sexuality.

Component Eight: Data Collection and Monitoring
Quantitative data collection is recommended for all SDVC agencies, to monitor the SDVC performance.

Component Nine: Court Facilities
Separate entrances, waiting facilities and special measures facilities are encouraged.

Component Ten: Children's Services
The leadership role of the Director of Children's Services covers all children in their locality, including those in DV circumstances.

Component Eleven: Community-based Perpetrator Programmes
Programmes for suitable male perpetrators currently supervised by the probation service are provided throughout the National Probation Service in England and Wales. There are community-based perpetrator programmes being run outside the CJS.

(Home Office 2008: Appendix B)

There then followed further expansion in the number of SDVCs, with the creation of another 23 SDVCs which were subject to a review undertaken in 2007, using official data from the Crown Prosecution Service (CPS) (CPS, 2008). For the purpose of the review, SDVCs were measured against 2005–2008 Criminal Justice System (CJS) Public Service Agreements (PSAs). Measures of success were identified as: bringing more perpetrators to justice; improving the support, safety and satisfaction of victims; and increasing public confidence in CJS (CPS 2008). The review found evidence of increased successful prosecution outcomes in DV cases with more courts achieving higher levels of successful DV prosecution outcomes in comparison with their areas and fewer cases being discontinued (CPS 2008). There was also evidence to suggest that the perception of agencies and victims outside of the CJS is that performance was improving (CPS 2008). The number of SDVCs steadily increased to a peak of 141 courts across England and Wales in 2010 (Home Office 2010a). Despite the announcement of government plans to further develop the SDVC system (Home Office 2011), cost cutting following the global economic downturn resulted in the start of significant court closures, reducing the number of SDVCs to a current total of 127.

Thus the overarching goals of SDVCs are to increase rates of conviction, to reduce harm to victims and to increase confidence in the criminal justice system. While Burton (2006) observed some of the successes of the first seven domestic violence courts in England and Wales in striving to achieve these outcomes, she nonetheless argued that more effective interventions in DV cases required greater involvement of the judiciary in on-going monitoring of the defendant's compliance with court ordered perpetrator programmes. Indeed, although SDVCs were inspired by the US model, their development has not continued to be informed by the refinement of DV court processes in the US (Bowen and Whitehead 2013). In fact, the post-sentence arrangements that are often used in the US model have not been incorporated to any significant degree in England. There is thus an absence of review hearings in almost all domestic violence courts in the UK, meaning there is reduced opportunity for interaction between

86   *Drug courts and domestic violence courts*

magistrate and offender (Nolan 2009: 60). This is in spite of significant evidence identifying the potential effectiveness of these practices (Cissner *et al.* 2013). In the US, research has found that dedicated listing sessions for DV were useful not only because they enabled the allocation of specially trained judges and prosecutors but also because they enhanced the provision of specialist support services to victims of DV, from both within and outside the criminal justice system. This enhanced support resulted in the provision of better information to the prosecution but it also had the important consequence of improving victim retention in the court process (Newmark *et al.* 2001). This is particularly important in view of evidence that suggests that in England, victims and witnesses are often dissatisfied with the court process and withdraw their commitment from prosecutions, including their willingness to act as witnesses, because of their loss of confidence in the court process (Donoghue 2012).

Across the existing 127 SDVCs, it appears that the most effective working arrangements are in those courts where victims are referred quickly after arrest to support services which provide important safety advice and keep them up to date with the progress of their case (Bowen and Whitehead 2013). Many magistrates have reported to me their strong support for the work and continued existence of SDVCs, and they have identified many of the 'practical benefits' of holding courts specifically for cases involving DV. The ability to list cases as priority and the availability of a Probation officer throughout the day were identified as especially constructive developments of the SDVC format. However at the same time, there is also very significant concern about the way that economic constraints will impact upon the functioning of SDVCs, with a number of magistrates around the country reporting that SDVC work has ceased due to budget cuts, while others suggest that the operation of SDVCs will be 'greatly affected' by changes to Legal Aid.

Statistical evidence appears to support improvements in reductions in the rate of DV, for example, the *Violence against Women and Girls Crime Report 2011–12* noted that:

> Between 2005–6 and 2011–12 attrition rates have fallen as the proportion of successful outcomes has risen from 60 per cent to 73 per cent over this six year period. Ten areas improved their prosecution outcomes in the last year and the volume of defendants prosecuted decreased over the last year by 3.6 per cent to 79 268.

> (CPS 2012)

In addition, the number of convictions in SDVCs has increased from 30 000 in 2005–2006 to 58 000 in 2011–2012. However, at present, there is insufficient evidence to support the conclusion that SDVCs have resulted in a clear reduction in domestic violence as well as improved outcomes for victims overall. A useful illustration of the difficulties in substantiating claims about the work of DV courts is provided by evidence from Croydon, South London. A sustained focus upon obtaining reductions in DV in Croydon has been evident since the 1990s

(Hester *et al.* 2008). A Family Justice Centre was established in 2005, to provide a holistic response to violence against women, and a pilot Integrated Domestic Violence Court (IDVC) was established in October 2006. Based upon the US approach, the Croydon IDVC was intended as a logical extension of the existing SDVC which also incorporated specially trained personnel, but which differed from the SDVC model in that the IDVC was not a new criminal court jurisdiction but instead brought together both criminal and civil elements relating to the same events, parties and families. Thus the IDVC pilot was intended to bring together cases with a criminal element and concurrent Children Act or civil injunction proceedings at magistrates' and Family Proceedings Court level (Hester *et al.* 2008).

An evaluation of the pilot was undertaken between 2006 and 2007 which aimed to 'establish baseline data against which to evaluate the IDVC; to provide a 'snapshot' of the progress of the new court after 12 months; to consider any differences between the IDVC and a 'typical' (non-specialist) court in their take-up and implementation of the new measures of the DVCV Act; and to identify emerging issues and offer recommendations for policy and good practice' (Hester *et al.* 2008: 16). The IDVC evaluation found that there were significant problems regarding victim safety in that some victims were provided with special measures in relation to criminal charges (such as giving evidence behind a screen), while the same safety measures did not apply to victims in relation to family matters (Hester *et al.* 2008). The evaluation also identified perceived difficulties in the IDVC outcomes and the potential irreconcilability of some of the practices used by the court, with the aims of the IDVC model. For example, it was reported that a victim 'situated behind a screen during the criminal case, where her ex-partner was found guilty of assault, had no such protection during the child contact hearings where she had to sit on the same bench as her ex-partner and was reduced to tears as he attempted to communicate with her. Despite the perpetrator's denial of his criminally violent behaviour and the victim/survivor's fear for her own and the child's safety, the judge in this case expressed strongly that contact should be occurring, and increasing, and that the parents should put aside their differences for the sake of the child' (Hester 2011: 849).

Despite the introduction of the IDVC as well as the creation of The Family Justice Centre in 2005, there has been a 13.4 per cent increase in DV in Croydon in the past year. There were 1043 reported cases of 'violence with injury' in 2012–2013, which was an increase from 903 in 2011–2012, according to official figures (Ministry of Justice 2013). In total, there were more than 6000 allegations of domestic abuse in Croydon in the past year. However, there have been significant cuts in budgets since 2008 and The Family Justice Centre has in the past three years lost vital services, including court accompaniment, safety planning, support groups and childcare. There is a lack of empirical data on the direct effects of budget cuts on the functioning of these innovations but, as I have already alluded to in Chapter 2, economic decline has placed (sometimes severe) pressures upon criminal justice budgets which undoubtedly affect the extent to which initiatives are able to demonstrate measurable results and outcomes.

88 Drug courts and domestic violence courts

Yet there is also cause for some optimism that despite these challenges, new locally conceived and locally driven innovations continue to appear. In response to some of the overlapping issues evident in SDVCs, there has been developing interest in the creation of Family Drug and Alcohol Courts (FDACs), which aim to support families affected by drug and alcohol abuse. The first pilot Family Drug and Alcohol Court (FDAC) was set up at the Inner London Family Proceedings Court in 2007. The FDAC defines itself as a problem-solving court that aims to break the inter-generational cycle of harm associated with parental substance misuse. The main key differences from ordinary proceedings were identified as: 'judicial continuity – FDAC has two dedicated District Judges; frequent non-lawyer review hearings in which the judges encourage and motivate parents to turn their lives around; a multi-disciplinary specialist team attached to the court, providing speedy expert assessment, support to parents, links to relevant local services and parent mentors who have overcome similar difficulties in the past; quick access to a dedicated team of children's guardians; and a rapid and co-ordinated treatment intervention' (Harwin *et al.* 2011: 2). In the same way as other types of problem-solving court, participation is voluntary and families can choose not to be involved in the FDAC and instead have their case heard in the usual family proceedings court.

Parental substance misuse is a serious social problem and is a key factor in around a third of long-term cases in children's services in some areas and it is a major risk factor for poor educational performance and substance misuse in children as well as offending in adults, and child mistreatment (Harwin *et al.* 2011). The FDAC model was specifically adopted from the model used widely in the US in existing family treatment drug courts. These US courts have been 'showing promising results with a higher number of cases where parents and children were able to remain together safely, and with swifter alternative placement decisions for children if parents were unable to address their substance misuse successfully. The catalysts for the FDAC pilot were the encouraging evidence from the USA and concerns about the response to parental substance misuse through ordinary care proceedings in England: poor coordination of adult and children's services; late interventions to protect children; delays in reaching decisions in court; and soaring costs of proceedings, linked to the cost of expert evidence (Harwin *et al.* 2011: 1). The pilot evaluation found a number of very positive results such as more parents controlling their substance misuse, a higher rate of family reunification, more parents engaged in treatment and other services, a more constructive use of court time, as well as cost savings for local authorities and potential savings for courts and the Legal Services Commission (Bambrough *et al.* 2013). The two most significant findings probably relate to family reunification – at the time of the final court order, 39 per cent of FDAC mothers were reunited with their children compared to 21 per cent of the comparison group in ordinary care proceedings; and potential cost savings through shorter care placements (estimated to cost £4000 per child less), shorter court hearings, less need for legal representatives at hearings (saving local authorities £682 per family) and fewer contested cases. Following the success in London of

Drug courts and domestic violence courts 89

the FDAC, in August 2012, a new Family Drug and Alcohol Court was set up in Gloucestershire with a £2 million budget. These developments in FDACs are important because they demonstrate that, despite the impact of budget constraints, changes of government and evidence of lack of success in some areas, problem-solving justice is not a 'spent force'. In fact, in some areas there is more interest, more determination and more optimism about the adoption of problem-solving approaches than perhaps at any time before in England and Wales. The demands that crime and substance misuse in particular place upon health, welfare and criminal justice services mean that practitioners (and some politicians too) are increasingly coming to see problem-solving as a viable approach. In this context, another area which has recently being considered for court specialisation is cases of sexual violence.

Specialist sexual violence courts (SVCs)

Recent statistics published by the Ministry of Justice, the Home Office and the Office for National Statistics (Ministry of Justice *et al.* 2013) indicate that while criminal justice responses to sexual violence have improved, there remain fundamental barriers to justice for victims of sexual abuse. In particular, the length of time that sexual offence cases take to complete is very significant and impacts upon satisfaction and confidence in the courts and criminal justice system more broadly. For rape cases, the average length of time from report to completion is 675 days (Ministry of Justice *et al.* 2013). For all sexual offence cases, this reduces to 496 days, which is considerably longer than the average length of time for criminal cases overall (154 days) (Ministry of Justice *et al.* 2013). Victims' experiences of the trial process, including long delays between report and completion of cases, results in their dissatisfaction with the police and court system and may also deter victims from seeking justice through the criminal justice system (Daly 2011).

In response to these existing problems in the administration of sexual offence cases, the London Mayor's Office for Policing and Crime (MOPAC) have announced their intention to create a specialist sexual violence court (SVC) to buttress the existing work of SDVCs in London (MOPAC 2013; GLA 2012). Although the details of how the SVC will operate are yet to be made clear, it appears that the court will be modelled on and operate in a similar way to SDVCs and with the provision of specialist training to DJs/magistrates. Planning and development for the creation of the SVC is at an early stage, however MOPAC's recent consultation strategy on violence against women and girls draws upon data on the operation and outcomes of sexual violence courts in South Africa. The document notes that:

> In South Africa, specialist sexual violence courts have increased conviction rates and reduced delays. Over the five-year period from 2001–2006 conviction rates rose by 9 per cent. In fact, between 2008/9 the sexual offences courts achieved an average conviction rate of 66.7 per cent. This may also

90   Drug courts and domestic violence courts

be linked to the reduced turnaround time from investigation to prosecution, from up to five years, to less than six months. MOPAC is already committed to delivering one key goal in the Mayor's Police and Crime Plan, namely the ambition to have a speedier criminal justice process, with the goal to reduce delays in the criminal justice system by 20 per cent by cutting the time taken between and offence being committed and the case concluding in court.

(MOPAC 2013: 31)

While there is the potential for the creation of SVCs to address some of the established legal and court practice-based issues which have historically negatively impacted upon victims' participation in the trial process, data on conviction rates and reduced delays in courts operating in other jurisdictions needs to be treated with considerable caution. Criminal justice policy transfer is notoriously complex and evidence of effectiveness in outcomes in one jurisdiction does not translate to efficacy in another, particularly when comparing countries as culturally and demographically different to England as South Africa. Much evidence demonstrates that simple linear comparisons between one and jurisdiction and another are not valid (Newburn 2002). So, for example, while the problem-solving court model has been adopted internationally, we see significant variation in how the court model has been adapted in different criminal justice jurisdictions and, moreover, in the types of outcomes that are achieved and how they can be measured. The implication from the MOPAC strategy document appears to be the assertion that because there has been reduced delay in South African courts, similar outcomes would translate in the English system. Of course, we cannot assume that this would be the case. Not only do specialist courts tend to require significant 'bedding in' time but their functioning is also determined by a range of local/national policies, politics and organisational cultures (Newburn 2002). Moreover, other research undertaken on South African specialist courts suggests that legal requirements will often take precedence over victims' justice needs (Walker and Louw 2003, 2005a, 2005b).

There are also jurisdictional difficulties in attempting to apply examples of positive outcomes in DVCs to SVCs (Daly 2011). In England, DVCs are located in magistrates' courts whereas cases involving serious sexual violence such as rape can only be heard in the Crown Court. Thus proposals for a specialised sexual violence court will need to consider whether the court would operate for less serious sexual offences in the magistrates' jurisdiction or for all types of sexual offences (Daly 2011). There may also potentially be scope for the creation of SVCs in both magistrates' and Crown Courts where magistrates' courts would hear pleas to offences under its legal jurisdiction, and the Crown Court would operate using more specialised approaches during the adjudication and sentencing process (Daly 2011).

There has been some considerable Parliamentary support for the introduction of specialised judicial forums for sexual violence in England. In particular, the administration of child sexual abuse cases has been identified as likely to benefit

Drug courts and domestic violence courts   91

from court specialisation. A recent Report of the Home Affairs Select Committee stated that:

> We ... recommend that the Ministry of Justice introduce specialist courts (similar to the domestic violence courts currently in existence) for child sexual abuse or sexual offences as a whole. We do not mean that new buildings or new bureaucracies should be created, merely that in each region, one court room should be designated as the preferred court for the most serious child sexual exploitation cases. This court room should be selected on the basis that it has the most up to date technology and appropriate access and waiting facilities. For each region a team of specialist child sexual exploitation judges, prosecutors, police, witness support and ushers should be identified, trained and linked into the local Multi Agency Safeguarding Hub and Local Safeguarding Children's Board teams. We believe that at the moment there are training initiatives in the police, CPS, judiciary and so on. There is a lot of will at the top of these organisations and that is to be commended but there is still inconsistent application on the ground. Victims do not experience the will at the top of the organisation, they experience the reality on the ground. In order to ensure that the most serious cases are guaranteed the most experienced whole court team delivering the best practice, we believe specialist whole court teams in court rooms equipped with the necessary technology are the answer. We will write to the Ministry of Justice requesting periodic updates on this piece of work and will revisit the issue in eighteen months time.
>
> (House of Commons 2013 at para 94)

However, proposals for the introduction of SVCs have been met with considerable resistance from the judiciary, who remain sceptical of such proposed court specialisation on the basis of its implications for cost and efficiency. The previous head of the judiciary in England and Wales (Lord Judge was succeeded by Lord Thomas in October 2013), the Lord Chief Justice, argued that the Home Affairs Select Committee's proposals for specialist courts would result in increased cost and longer waiting times. Lord Judge expressed his view in a letter to the Chair of the Home Affairs Select Committee Keith Vaz MP, that he did

> not agree that specialist courts will materially improve the position. It goes without saying that all of those involved in the process should be trained appropriately, but there are likely to be unintended adverse consequences if this proposal is taken forward. Restricting the available venues to a few specialist centres is likely to lead to far greater waiting times because of the limited number of court rooms, judges and staff. Additionally, these courts are likely to prove expensive to set up and run. Instead ... the training of advocates and the additional training of the core group of judges, will in my view deliver exactly the same outcome as a specialist court.
>
> (Lord Judge 2013: 4)

92 *Drug courts and domestic violence courts*

Subsequently, changes have been made to the way that judges are selected to sit on serious sexual violence cases, with these judges now intended to receive bespoke training on how to conduct trials with significantly vulnerable witnesses. Indeed, throughout this chapter we can observe government and policy interest in tackling the overlapping issues of substance misuse and domestic/sexual violence, which together place major demands on health, welfare and criminal justice services. These efforts to create a more collaborative and 'crosscutting' approach have had mixed results. It is important to recognise that SDVCs cannot be said to operate as problem-solving courts since they lack some of the distinctive features of the problem-solving approach, most notably, sentencer continuity. Yet they nonetheless represent innovative attempts to 'test' new approaches to important social problems, and although they are yet to embed true problem-solving frameworks, represent a promising direction of travel in the problem-solving domain.

Notes

1 However, unlike many US drug courts, the Scottish drug courts were specifically targeted at repeat offenders whose offending was assessed as being directly related to their dependence on or propensity to use drugs and who were at immediate risk of receiving a custodial sentence.

2 *See* Brown v State, 971 A.2d 932 (Md. 2009). The Petitioner had argued that the Baltimore City Adult Felony Drug Treatment Court lacked fundamental jurisdiction and that the imposition of a 35-day jail sentence for violating a drug court rule followed by the subsequent violation of probation for the same act after the sanction of 35 days had been served, violated double jeopardy rules. In his Petition for Writ of Certiorari, the Petitioner argued that:

> All of these problem-solving courts, including the one involved in the case at bar, have 'team' meetings prior to any review hearing in open court. In these meetings the team discusses whether or not sanctions should be imposed, reports on poor behavior and non-compliance with the rules. Further, each team member votes on the sanction. All of this is done in the absence of the defendant/participant/client. Maryland has long recognized the right of a criminal defendant to be present at all stages of a trial ... As the United States Supreme Court observed, the right of a criminal defendant to be present at every stage of trial is scarcely less important to the accused than the right of trial itself.... The right to be present at trial is a common law right guaranteed by Article 5 of the Maryland Declaration of Rights, and is also to some extent protected by the Fourteenth Amendment to the United States Constitution, and is guaranteed by compliance Maryland Rule [4–231]. Yet, the participant is excluded from meetings where his or her with drug court rules is discussed. In short, these courts allow the judge to participate in legislating the entire problem-solving program, supervising the execution of the program, and then adjudicating whether or not participants within the program have violated the very rules the judge designed, all in clear violation of the Separation of Powers Doctrine.

The Appeal was dismissed by the Court on the grounds that (1) the Petitioner's argument on what constituted 'fundamental jurisdiction' was flawed, and (2) that the double jeopardy claim was not properly preserved for review, Brown v State, 971 A.2d at 936–7.

Drug courts and domestic violence courts 93

3 However, at a recent symposium in London in September 2013 (Better Courts: Cutting Crime Through Court Innovation), the Chairman of the Magistrates' Association, Richard Monkhouse, argued that drug review courts should be extended to include prolific offenders.

4 The majority of studies used in the analysis were based on US drug courts. Four of the remaining evaluations examined adult drug courts in Australia; two evaluations were of Canadian drug courts; one evaluation assessed a juvenile drug court in New Zealand; and another examined an adult drug court in Guam (Mitchell *et al.* 2011).

5 Of the 154 studies used in the meta-analysis, only 8 studies had randomly allocated offenders to drug courts versus alternative judicial procedures, whereas the majority of studies selected comparison groups using procedures which were not free from researcher bias, therefore impacting upon the validity and reliability of the study findings.

6 Despite DTTOs being phased out from 2005, a number of magistrates who were interviewed for this book continue to refer to drug rehabilitation requirements in community orders by their old name (DTTO) rather than as DRRs.

7 It is important to note that offenders' entry into the drug court pilot process was not rigidly defined which meant that offenders could enter the DDC at varying stages in the different pilot court process, as a consequence of particular processes in operation at that court, or due to other conflicting processes and systems operating irrespective of the DDC. Some drug court participants entered the DDC court at their first court appearance, while others did not enter it until their first review as they were seen in a non-DDC before that (Kerr *et al.* 2011).

8 Her Majesty's Courts Service (HMCS) merged with the Tribunals Service to become Her Majesty's Courts and Tribunals Service (HMCTS) on 1 April 2011.

9 The researchers note that the quantitative analyses detailed in the report of findings

> should be only used in a descriptive way, i.e. as background information providing a context to the study. Any attempts to generalise the findings to a wider population of offenders warrant a number of caveats. Firstly, the representativeness of the data collected in the tracker was not formally assessed and it would be very difficult to assess how typical, in a statistical sense, the analysed sample of offenders was. Second, a large portion of information was missing, and the authors had no information about the processes behind this data unavailability (i.e. whether data were missing at random or not), which prevented application of statistical methods that could counteract this effect. Finally, in most of the cases the sample size was too low for the observed differences to be significant according to standard criteria.
>
> (Kerr *et al.* 2011: 41)

10 A quarter of offenders on community orders or on license in 2008–2009 did not complete their sentence due to breaking the conditions of that order or license (Ministry of Justice 2010b).

5   Community courts and mental health courts

Problem-solving courts emphasise the explicit incorporation of the community into the judicial process as a way of improving the functioning of the criminal justice system and 'empowering' local communities. No courts emphasise this aspect of their work more than community courts. However, many critics of problem-solving courts suggest that the 'therapeutic' rationale that these courts deploy is most problematic of all when applied to community courts, and, in view of the contested nature of the term 'community' (Young 2002) gives rise to concerns about 'who decides what is "therapeutic", in which circumstances and for whom?' (Petrila 1993: 881) Community courts are 'neighbourhood-focussed', problem-solving courts that prioritise the delivery of local justice to solve local problems. The first US community court opened in 1993 in New York City and since then there have developed many variations of community courts internationally; where they have been introduced in South Africa, Australia and Canada. Community courts can be understood as a development in community justice. Over the last decade in particular, there has been growing interest in the new concept of 'community justice' (Berman and Feinblatt 2005; McNeill and Whyte 2007; Simon 2002). In response to claims that the criminal justice system pays insufficient attention to the everyday consequences of crime and disorder upon citizens and neighbourhoods, community justice practices and innovations have developed that explicitly include the community in their processes and set the enhancement of community quality of life as a goal (Karp and Clear 2000). Examples of recent community justice initiatives include community crime prevention, community policing, community courts, sentencing circles, citizen reparative boards and restorative justice sanctioning systems. Community justice innovations 'share a common core in that they address community-level outcomes by focussing on short and long-term problem solving, restoring victims and communities, strengthening normative standards and effectively reintegrating offenders' (Karp and Clear 2000: 323).

In England and Wales, over the last decade, much effort has been devoted to the generation of community justice innovations. In 2009, the government sought to formalise its disparate range of community justice innovations around a clear framework. The Green Paper *Engaging Communities in Criminal Justice* (2009) set out the following eight key principles of community justice:

Community courts and mental health courts 95

1 Courts connecting to the community. There should be significant liaison between the courts and the local community so that the community is able to put forward its views, and the court has a view of the wider context of the crime.

2 Justice is seen to be done. Better information about the criminal justice services so that local people have an opportunity to put forward their views on the way offending is tackled. Compliance with the court's orders or other penalties should be seen and recognised by the community.

3 Cases handled robustly and speedily. Harnessing the combined potential of a range of agencies working together, meaning increased speed and ensuring offenders begin sentences promptly.

4 Strong independent judiciary. Enabling the judiciary to lead the problem-solving approach and maintain oversight over offenders' progress after sentence.

5 Solving problems and finding solutions. Making use of a range of available service providers in order to tackle the underlying causes of offending. Problem-solving can operate both at the community also when dealing with individual offenders at court.

6 Working together. A team approach to decision-making and dealing with offenders. Ensuring that a range of agencies, necessary for problem-solving, is available to the court, delivering an end-to-end service to offenders, victims and the community.

7 Repairing harm and raising confidence. Seeking the views of the community on what projects should be carried out by offenders on unpaid work. These unpaid work projects should then be badged once completed so the community can see what has been achieved.

8 Reintegrating offenders and building communities. Improving social bonds and cohesion within the community. Developing pathways to support the reintegration of offenders back in to their community.

Community justice is therefore viewed as a method of addressing the problems of offending in a local area by engaging with the local community, making the court more responsive to local people and working in partnership with criminal justice agencies, support groups and the local community.

In instrumental terms, community courts are politically appealing because they appear to relieve punitive pressures on the criminal justice system by shifting responsibility for law enforcement (including recidivism and sentence compliance) to the courts while seemingly minimising governmental accountability for a range of institutional shortcomings in the areas of health care, education, housing, and employment. As we have seen in previous chapters, in this way, the creation of specialised problem-solving forums might be understood as an attempt to correct the flaws/failures of social service systems (Meekins 2006; Dorf 2003). The fundamental socio-economic, cultural and structural problems that contribute to and facilitate (particularly low-level) local crime and disorder

96   *Community courts and mental health courts*

are invariably deeply entrenched (Bursik 1988; Jennings *et al.* 2012). Complex processes addressing the roots of crime require sustained political attention and the investment of resources over an extended period of time, synthesised with efforts to inculcate norms of social and civic responsibility which, as empirical research suggests, can be very difficult to achieve and often lack durability (Fung 2004). However, in order for communities to be resilient and socially cohesive, evidence indicates that there must be minimum standards of trust and reciprocity among residents and it is precisely these elements that are undermined by local crime and disorder (Carr 2003). Problem-solving courts are designed to take place in a context of 'community empowerment', where prosecution and punishment of offenders are designed to rid communities of their social problems and to engage citizens in the dynamics of social control and regulation. Here the aim is to increase 'community' participation in crime reduction, with a residual goal being to improve relations with residents in the neighbourhood in which formal control operates. Community courts may therefore, in the absence of a commitment to long-term sustainable strategies, hold some promise as short/medium term initiatives for the recovery and regeneration of high-crime communities through the operation of problem-solving courts as locations in which the community can engage in processes of capacity building and self-accounting (Ali *et al.* 2011; de Souza Briggs 2008).

Community courts in England and Wales

As we have seen, the concept of community justice originated in the United States and was first demonstrated by the Red Hook Community Justice Centre, Brooklyn, New York. In the early 2000s, the Lord Chief Justice and the Home Secretary both separately visited the Centre and resolved to create something similar in the UK (McKenna 2007). The subsequent March 2003 Home Office White Paper *Respect and Responsibility – Taking a Stand Against Anti-Social Behaviour* contained a commitment to establish a community justice centre in England and Wales. The first Community Justice Centre opened in England and Wales in September 2005. The North Liverpool Community Justice Centre (NLCJC) was established in a disused school building, and brought together the magistrates' court, youth court and Crown court with other criminal justice agencies as well as a range of problem-solving services such as drug and alcohol treatment. Collectively, these were intended to operate as a 'one-stop-shop' for tackling offending in the local area (McKenna 2007: i). The NLCJC covered four local authority wards with a total population of 65 000 residents. The Centre operated as a hub for a range of different community resources including Citizens Advice, probation and drug-treatment officers. One judge presided over all cases in order to provide consistency in decision-making and enhance accountability through continuity.[1] The Centre combined court process with wider community resource provision and aimed to enhance working relationships between criminal justice agencies while more closely involving the local community in the criminal justice system. Among the Centre's distinguishing

Community courts and mental health courts 97

features were: the application of a problem-solving approach to criminal cases; a dedicated circuit judge who presides over all cases/offender reviews; co-location of the relevant criminal justice agencies (police, probation, Youth Offending Services, prosecution and court services); and the provision of a range of services available to the community (including legal/financial advice and support services for housing, addiction and so forth). A Community Engagement Team (CET) also worked proactively to engage with the community and there were established mechanisms for the local community to identify the types of crime and disorder that were causing concern, as well as providing information about opportunities for useful reparation to the community through the unpaid work requirements of community orders (Clinks 2011). The specific objectives of the NLCJC were to:

- reduce low-level offending and anti-social behaviour;
- reduce fear of crime and increase public confidence in the criminal justice system (CJS);
- increase compliance with community sentences;
- increase victims' and witnesses' satisfaction with the CJS;
- increase the involvement of the community in the CJS; and
- reduce the time from arrest to sentence.

(McKenna 2007: i)

The NLCJC, as the first, and most highly developed, example of a community justice court in the UK, was also initially a showcase for government plans for problem-solving and community justice more broadly (Mair and Millings 2011). Following the establishment of the NLCJC, twelve other Community Justice Initiatives were subsequently introduced but these adopted different models to that of the North Liverpool Community Justice Centre. The NLCJC was the only pilot model that was closely based on the Brooklyn Red Hook Community Centre in that it operated from a specially designated building (separate to an existing court) and housed other criminal justice agencies as well as problem-solving agencies on the same site (Booth *et al.* 2012). Other models, such as the Salford Community Justice Initiative, were delivered from existing courts and/or did not feature co-location of problem-solving services. Most also did not prioritise sentencer continuity and so did not follow the single judge model. As we have seen with drug and domestic violence courts, this was also the case for the establishment of these courts too which similarly do not operate as separate court jurisdictions and are housed in the same buildings as existing courts.

In order to have their case processed by a community court in England, a defendant must have indicated a guilty plea (Brown and Payne 2007). Those defendants who comply with the orders of the community court avoid a criminal conviction. In March 2006, the judge at the Liverpool Community Justice Centre was given special legislative powers under the Community Order (Review by Specified Courts in Liverpool and Salford) Order 2006. These facilitate the monitoring of those who have appeared before the community court whilst they

98   *Community courts and mental health courts*

complete their court orders. The judge may make an order, commonly referred to as a review order, for the defendant to reappear before the court to review their progress and to address any relevant issues which may have arisen since his/her last court appearance. Defendants who plead not guilty and are referred to the regular court for hearing, are referred back to the community court for sentencing upon a guilty verdict. In those cases where a person is given a custodial sentence, staff at community courts will maintain contact with the offender whilst he/she is in prison and a support package will be developed prior to the offender's release. Upon release, the offender will return to the community justice centre where housing may have been organised for him/her, information on benefits will be provided and other support services can also be put in place.

The first process evaluation of the NLCJC was undertaken between 2005 and 2007 (McKenna 2007). The evaluation used qualitative research methods, namely a survey and in-depth interviews with offenders; peer research with members of the community; in-depth interviews with staff and agencies; and on-going research with victims and witnesses (McKenna 2007: 3). In addition, the evaluation also used management information that had been collated on the Management Information System (MIS). The research produced tentative results suggesting that there was increased efficiency in NLCJC court proceedings when compared to the national average. There was also evidence from interviews with staff and offenders that participants in the NJCJC were generally positive about their experiences in the court and that they felt the problem-solving approach could have a positive impact on improving compliance with court orders and reducing re-offending. Given that the NJCJC was only created in 2005, the report of findings rightly observes that 'the full impact of the NLCJC across many of its objectives may take years to assess as the Centre develops and embeds itself in the local community' (McKenna 2007: vii). Nonetheless, it observed early evidence 'that the Centre is making progress towards many of its original objectives, and that much has been learnt about new models for delivering community justice' (McKenna 2007: vii). The limits of this initial evaluation are clear: there was no quantitative analysis of re-offending conducted; the NJCJC had only been in operation for a short period of time; and assertions made about positive outcomes had no inherent validity or generalisability.

In an effort to provide some rigorous statistical data on the substantive outcomes of the NLCJC, an initial evaluation of reconviction rates was conducted on offenders who were sentenced at the NLCJC and Salford Community Justice Initiative in 2006 to assess the impact of community justice on re-offending (Jolliffe and Farrington 2009). Analysis showed that there was no statistically significant difference between offenders sentenced at the Community Justice courts and those sentenced in the research comparison group: 37 per cent of offenders in the comparison group (Manchester) were reconvicted within one year, compared with the community justice initiative (CJI) areas of North Liverpool (38.7 per cent) and Salford (38.3 per cent). Therefore, those in Salford and North Liverpool were as likely to be reconvicted as those in Manchester (the comparison

Community courts and mental health courts 99

group). However, the evaluation did find that the breach rates of those sentenced in the Community Justice Initiatives were significantly higher than those in the comparison group. It is possible that this may have been attributable to increased scrutiny of this group. While the statistical evidence was unable to demonstrate positive outcomes in terms of re-offending rates specifically, the researchers observed that measures of success in community justice initiatives are dependent upon:

> many factors, not least the importance of having strong links with the local communities to support offenders both in and out of court, and increased confidence in the Criminal Justice System. New initiatives and ways of working take time to become embedded within the community, and this is true of CJIs. Therefore, results from this study, which were based on the experiences of offenders who passed through CJIs in their first year of operation, should be seen as tentative. Once greater numbers of offenders have passed through the Community Justice courts, and the changes initiated have become deeply embedded, this, along with data on specific interventions and types of offence on reconviction, could provide more robust evidence on the impact of Community Justice Initiatives. Community Justice does not have reducing re-offending as its sole objective; it also involves strategies for working more closely with the community and increasing confidence in the Criminal Justice System.
>
> (Joliffe and Farrington 2009: 3)

These are important caveats to the measurement of positive outcomes in community justice initiatives such as the NLCJC, particularly because of the 'bedding in' time required by such initiatives, together with the importance of going beyond narrow indicators of success such as reoffending rates which tend to be favoured by politicians. With this in mind, it was unfortunate in the Government's subsequent 2010 Green Paper, *Breaking the Cycle: Effective Punishment, Rehabilitation and Sentencing of Offenders*, that although enhanced community engagement with and involvement in the criminal justice process was identified as an important objective of policymakers, the Paper also asserted that there was a 'prohibitive cost' associated with the NLCJC and that there was a paucity of evidence for its impact on reducing re-offending (Ministry of Justice 2010b).

In July 2012, the Government published another analysis of re-offending rates and efficiency in court processes in the NLCJC (Booth *et al.* 2012). Again, it found that there was 'no evidence that the NLCJC is any more effective in reducing re-offending than other courts. Offenders receiving a court order at NLCJC were more likely to breach the conditions of their order than offenders receiving court orders elsewhere' (Booth *et al.* 2012: iii). There was also no evidence to suggest that offending behaviour generally had improved more in the North Liverpool area than elsewhere. In terms of efficiency, although there was some evidence that the NLCJC operated more speedily than other courts, there was also

100 *Community courts and mental health courts*

evidence of inefficiency, including a higher proportion of 'cracked trials' than elsewhere.

A year later in July 2013, the Government announced a six week public consultation on the proposed closure of the NLCJC. A statement written by the Minister for Victims and Courts noted that the workload had fallen, leaving the Centre underused and that '[i]n the light of current and future financial constraints it is increasingly difficult to justify the on-going operation of [the Centre]' (Ministry of Justice 2013d). Moreover, the Ministry of Justice argued that the Centre was expensive with an operating cost of £980 000 in 2012–2013 with 'no evidence that it has or will deliver results on re-offending levels' and it does not deliver value for money for the taxpayer (Ministry of Justice 2013d).[2] The Liverpool Community Centre cost £5.2 million to set up in 2005, with an additional £1.8 million annual running costs. Evidence on the operation of the Centre indicated serious limitations to it being able to quantitatively justify the contribution that it had made to the objectives set for community justice (Mair and Millings 2011). Although there was some qualitative data to suggest that the Centre could have been judged to be 'doing well' in buttressing community justice objectives, in statistical terms, the Centre was 'unable to *demonstrate* effectiveness', particularly in terms of recidivism rates (Mair and Millings 2011: 5).

In an attempt to avoid the proposed closure of the Centre, the local Police and Crime Commissioner (PCC), Jane Kennedy, argued that the Government's consultation was ill-timed because the announcement was made as Parliament went into recess, which made it difficult for politicians to take account of the views of many local stakeholders (BBC News 2013). She has also raised broader concerns that closure of the Centre would impact negatively on the work of the police because the work that had been undertaken so far with prolific offenders would lose focus, and she argued that it would necessarily be problematic to transfer the workload of the Centre to the local magistrates' court (Sefton court) because of the two different styles of court cultures (BBC News 2013). Sadly, on 22 October 2013, Parliamentary Under-Secretary for Justice, Shailesh Vara, announced that the Lord Chancellor had decided the proposed closure of the court should proceed, with the majority of the court's work being transferred to Sefton Magistrates' Court. The closure of the NLCJC is very unfortunate: it was an innovation that was supported by many exceptionally dedicated professionals who were determined to bring a more 'community focussed' and 'therapeutic' approach to the court system when compared to traditional case processing. However, one of the main problems with the Centre was that it was an initiative that was introduced 'top-down' by central government, as a stand-alone pilot example of a community justice centre. Attempts to evaluate a single court sitting with a single judge, and to use this court as an illustrative policy example are problematic for a number of reasons.

Aside from the fact that the Government evaluations did not examine the various additional outcomes underpinning community justice such as courts connecting to the local community; justice being seen to be done; having a strong independent judiciary and raising confidence within the community (Booth *et al.*

Community courts and mental health courts   101

2012: 28), the studies were undertaken far too soon and with unrealistic expectations from government. The 2012 evaluation maintained that 'sufficient time has elapsed to establish working practices and develop the necessary working relationships within the NLCJC' (Booth *et al.* 2012: 3). However, the methodology used in this most recent evaluation study to assess the impact of the NLCJC on re-offending, used data on 'offenders who were sentenced at the NLCJC between 1 January 2007 and 31 December 2009' (Booth *et al.* 2012: 4). Given that the Centre was only established in September 2005, some of the data used was less than two years old. This is undoubtedly insufficient time; not only for substantive practices to be embedded and ameliorated but for measurable outcomes to be determined. Moreover, the official studies of reconviction rates tell us far from the whole story about the operation of the NLCJC: not only in terms of additional community justice outcomes, but also with regard to the climate of fiscal austerity in which the Centre has had to operate. Reductions in criminal justice budgets have resulted in cuts to local treatment and support services for example, which are likely to impact upon recidivism levels. The irony is, of course, that while the NLCJC has closed, government discourse on community justice has proliferated with renewed vigour and is exemplified in its 'Big Society' agenda; its commitment to localism; and in numerous policy documents proposing plans for greater community engagement in justice processes (Ministry of Justice 2011, 2012a, 2012b).

However, although the closure of the NLCJC is lamentable, there is still cause for some optimism. One of the community justice initiatives introduced following the establishment of the NLCJC was the Plymouth Community Justice Court which was set up in May 2007. The CJC operates one day a week as a CJSSS (Criminal Justice – Simple, Speedy, Summary) court, focussing mainly on low-level offences. Cases that may potentially benefit from a problem-solving approach are identified from case listing by police and probation and a list of suitable cases is then given to magistrates (Auburn *et al.* 2013). At the hearing, magistrates then engage with offenders to identify relevant issues and the case is potentially referred for a problem-solving meeting. At the problem-solving meeting, police and a third sector organisation, Community Advice and Support Service (CASS), are involved in problem identification, advice and signposting of relevant services. Notably, lawyers are not involved in the problem-solving meeting. At sentencing, police give an oral report to the bench on issues raised at the meeting and referrals made to other agencies, and the sentence is then based on the outcome of the problem-solving meeting but in accordance with statutory sentencing guidelines (Auburn *et al.* 2013). Follow-up on problem-solving cases is provided by CASS which is a charity project that offers advice, signposting and friendly guidance to people who are at court for low-level offences.[3] CASS typically works with clients for an average of a few months but contact ranges from one-off advice to clients, to on-going work up to two years. The service offers information and referral on to other agencies to address issues such as housing, financial problems and mental health issues. According to CASS the success of problem-solving is very much a result of magistrates being well-trained in this specialist area (Livingstone 2013)

102 *Community courts and mental health courts*

The Plymouth CJC initially possessed two important features that differed from the operation of a traditional magistrates' court. The community was directly involved in identifying the types of criminality or anti-social behaviour/ quality of life crimes which were to be targeted by police and they were involved in identifying work which offenders could undertake to make reparation to the community. In addition, the court uses problem-solving meetings involving the offender, probation, police and treatment/support services to understand the offender's behaviour and these discussions then form the basis of the court's rationale for sentencing of the offender. While the Plymouth CJC originally incorporated these two features, it now only possesses the latter feature. Previously, the Plymouth CJC was limited to cases occurring in two deprived neighbourhoods of Plymouth. However, practitioners felt that this was unfair as it had meant that only some had access to problem-solving and so the CJC was opened to cases across the city. This meant that a lot of the local community work that had previously occurred in the two neighbourhoods fell by the wayside as it was difficult to do the same intensity of community work across the whole city. Now the main distinctive feature of the CJC is the problem-solving meeting itself (involving police and the third sector agency, CASS) and the involvement of police and probation before the meeting, where they identify potential cases for problem-solving. This is a very significant change as it means that the explicit practice of incorporating community engagement is no longer a central feature of the CJC.

An independent study of the Plymouth Community Justice Court, funded by the Economic and Social Research Council is currently being undertaken by researchers at the University of Plymouth, which runs from August 2012 to August 2014. The purpose of the study is to develop an understanding of the effectiveness of the court by tracking cases and examining re-offending data; providing evidence on how the CJC operates, how problem-solving meetings function, and on what basis decisions are made; and it will provide evidence on how communities respond to the CJC and what sort of confidence they express in its procedures. Interim findings from the study suggest that positive developments are indeed occurring in the operation of the Plymouth CJC but that that the longevity and sustainability of the problem-solving approach is likely to be limited by a number of factors. The researchers have observed that:

> While a core group of magistrates, police, probation staff and the Third Sector CASS team members have shown a dedicated commitment to maintaining the community court ... in practice embedding community justice and more 'therapeutic' practices has been constrained by a number of factors including the challenges of practicing problem-solving justice within a summary justice context and the impact of ever diminishing resources. Inconsistent practices mean that there is a 'lottery' justice of sorts, with defendants receiving differential treatment dependant on which court they are in or whether the magistrates before them are skilled in engagement.
>
> (Hanley-Santos *et al.* 2013).

Community courts and mental health courts   103

Two highly significant issues in the administration of the CJC appear to be related to magistrate engagement/training and problems in court listing which, as we have seen thus far, are recurrent inadequacies evident in the attempted adoption of a problem-solving approach in other courts in England and Wales.

Another salient area of interest is the extent to which the Plymouth CJC embodies a therapeutic jurisprudence approach to the treatment of cases. According to their interim findings, researchers at Plymouth CJC have observed that although it has not yet been clearly articulated, in theory, the sentencing of the CJC is intended to be moving in the direction of therapeutic jurisprudence. If this is borne out in the final report of findings, this will be an interesting development in Plymouth's adoption of the problem-solving model. Previously, James Nolan (2009) had observed that therapeutic jurisprudence, as a theoretical basis for either problem-solving courts, or their sentencing practices in England and Wales, had explicitly *not* been adopted. Existing problem-solving courts, such as community courts and their associated judicial officers, had preferred the language of 'problem-solving' rather than therapeutic jurisprudence, both in their theoretical frameworks and in their day-to-day praxis. As such, Nolan contended that 'British community courts differ from American courts in [an] important respect: no reference is ever made to therapeutic jurisprudence. It is never discussed by court officials, nor is it mentioned in court or government documents on community courts' (Nolan 2009: 69). While the researchers at Plymouth CJC observe that therapeutic jurisprudence has never been clearly articulated as a goal of the CJC, they note that the theory behind the CJC's administration is intended to be 'moving in this direction' (Gilling *et al.* 2013). This would be somewhat of a change in emphasis from the (theoretical) frameworks of a number of other problem-solving courts in England and Wales. The final report of study findings will thus be an important piece of research and will hopefully provide useful evidence with which to inform the development of other community justice initiatives and will go some way to 'filling in the gaps' about existing knowledge of how community courts are evolving in England – and the distance they still have to go in achieving their stated objectives. This is particularly the case in terms of some of the problems associated with community engagement. The difficulties experienced in making community engagement a central feature of the CJC in Plymouth can be understood in the context of existing research literature, which exemplifies some of the distinct challenges that this aspect of problem-solving justice poses for courts in England and Wales, which will now be considered in more detail.

Conceptualising community engagement and its outcomes

In England and Wales, the development of community justice initiatives represents an attempt not simply to address the limitations of traditional magistrates' courts in responding to the underlying causes of criminality but also, through specifically prioritising 'community engagement', it reflects a broader effort by successive governments to try to ameliorate social/community cohesion,

104 Community courts and mental health courts

diminish anxieties about crime and enhance the legitimacy of the lower courts. Despite the obvious challenges it poses, community courts emphasise the central importance of community engagement with the courts to improving community 'quality of life'. Although government evaluations did not seek to measure community engagement or community satisfaction with the North Liverpool Community Justice Centre (NLCJC), it is also important to note that the NLCJC's attempts to function as a community justice innovation were not undertaken without difficulty. We can see that this difficulty has also been evident in the work of the Plymouth CJC. It will be important for future community justice projects in Britain to recognise the obstacles that these courts have encountered in trying to inculcate community engagement into the court framework. The findings from the study of the Plymouth CJC are currently at an interim stage. However, we do know more about the barriers that affected the development of community engagement at the NLCJC.

Community engagement was a fundamental objective and a pervasive aspect of the work of the NLCJC and a substantial amount of staff time was allocated to activities aimed at informing the community about the work of the Centre and in trying to engage residents in various ways (Mair and Millings 2011). As we have seen thus far, the unique and enhanced role of the court judge is of crucial importance in process(es) of engagement. In particular, the personal qualities of the judge, such as their ability to communicate effectively with offenders, and their dedication, skills in and commitment to problem-solving have been identified as especially salient to the effective functioning of the court, but they are also very difficult replicate. This is particularly reflected in the fact that, although he retired before the closure of the NLCJC was announced, the court's single judge, Judge Fletcher, was exceptionally well-regarded and admired for his proactive, 'therapeutic' (his words) approach to cases. Yet despite his enthusiasm for the problem-solving approach, this did not transfer to judicial attitudes in magistrates' courts more widely (Donoghue 2012). Moreover, while research suggested that members of the community served by the Centre were generally supportive of its work, there were concerns about how well known the Centre was across the community as a whole (Mair and Millings 2011). A significant tension between the Centre as a criminal justice agency on the one hand and a general community resource on the other, was identified (Mair and Millings 2011).

The problems experienced in North Liverpool dovetail very similar difficulties that have been evidenced in courts operating with problem-solving principles in other jurisdictions. Empirical research suggests that the mere presence of a problem-solving court in a community or neighbourhood is not enough to generate its own legitimacy or to reassure the community about 'Government' (Fagin and Malkin, 2003: 937). For example, evidence on the Red Hook Community Justice Centre (RHCJC) in New York demonstrates that while over 70 per cent of Red Hook residents know about the RHCJC, and those who are aware of it generally approve of what it does, the most common assumption that defendants and residents articulated about why the Court is in Red Hook, is that the lower criminal

Community courts and mental health courts   105

courts are overburdened and not that the Court's primary motivating factor is Red Hook's public good (Lanni 2005).

Government policy on mainstreaming problem-solving justice assumes that the problem-solving court model will strengthen the relationship between the lower courts and residents, and build legitimacy by addressing local crime and disorder problems. However, community engagement must be conceptualised in terms of what it is intended to achieve in and for these (particularly high crime) neighbourhoods. Numerous policy documents and guidance argue that community engagement in the functions of the lower courts is important to ameliorate social/community cohesion, diminish anxieties about crime and enhance the legitimacy of the lower courts (see for example Cabinet Office 2009; Ministry of Justice 2012b). Thus if the purpose of community engagement in problem-solving processes is to promote social cohesion and to improve the resilience of local areas, then the current approach to problem-solving in England and Wales must engage more systematically with the available literature which indicates the limits as well as the strengths of problem-solving justice. For example, empirical research suggests that in some high-crime areas operating with problem-solving courts, residents continue to attribute many of their problems to unsatisfactory responses by government agencies, agencies that residents feel could have made an immediate difference, most significantly the police and the housing authority (Fagan and Malkin 2003; Brown and Payne 2007). Moreover, a substantial body of scholarship documents the difficulties associated with attempting to enlist the community in local processes of engagement, particularly as it is often attempted in poor neighbourhoods (Crawford 1997; Carr *et al.* 2007). Research suggests that efforts to enlist residents in active forms of engagement are challenged by the existence of social exclusion and concentrated poverty (Brown and Payne 2007). The reasons speak to the complexities of creating a new legal institution in a neighbourhood operating with strong deficits of social capital, social cohesion and collective efficacy. These limitations are considered further in the next chapter. While it is not my purpose to suggest that these sort of challenges in any way invalidate the work of community courts, it is important for the development of future innovations that they are paid close attention.

A further particular issue which my research has highlighted is the failure of government to really think through how 'community engagement' will operate as a distinctive aspect of magistrates' competences. In England and Wales, one of the key distinguishing features of problem-solving courts is intended to be the training of magistrates and court staff in 'local issues and concerns' to ensure that, in their decision-making, the judiciary are 'fully aware of what matters to the local community' (Cabinet Office 2009: 14). While successive governments have acknowledged the importance of magistrates' training and the need for the provision of awareness sessions and support in assisting the bench to successfully engage with communities, the training provided to magistrates to assist them in fulfilling the responsibilities and obligations of their 'enhanced' role as problem-solvers has been inadequate. Although in 2008, HMCS and the Judicial

106   *Community courts and mental health courts*

Studies Board (JSB) jointly created training materials to support magistrates in their community engagement activity, this training has not been systematically implemented and problem-solving and community engagement do not yet form part of the standard training for newly appointed magistrates. In addition, the Government has also provided little direction on how 'community engagement' in problem-solving processes should be conceptualised or undertaken by the courts. Despite its localism agenda (see Localism Act 2011) magistrates' courts are, paradoxically, subject to central administration (see Courts Act 2003). As a consequence, magistrates lack the powers to develop and introduce specific community engagement practices, rules and initiatives in local courts. Thus the limited direction by the Government assumes greater significance because the lower courts are centrally administered.

The failure of policymakers to actively determine how the new competences that they are asking magistrates to develop should be inculcated is also problematic in view of the existence of a significant body of legal scholarship which illustrates the difficulties of trying to engage 'the community' in judicial processes (Crawford 1997; Berman 2004). Although community engagement is identified as integral to problem-solving court processes, in practice the enhancement of community participation in judicial practices is extremely limited. Evidence suggests that problem-solving courts exemplify near-total reliance on experts (the judge and social welfare professionals) in sanctioning decisions and in almost all other aspects of the court process. Some commentators have argued that there is seldom any opportunity for meaningful citizen participation in any of the court's practices (Lanni 2005). In contrast, other forums which have tried to inculcate community participation such as neighbourhood/community prosecution and sentencing circles are rarely composed of a representative sample of the relevant community. Such mechanisms of community participation often fail to foster meaningful popular participation as they are prone to being dominated by a vocal and active minority who are not genuinely representative of the community (Fagan and Malkin 2003).

Moreover, if community engagement with the courts is intended to ensure that the judiciary are 'fully aware of what matters to the local community', then policymakers would do well to consider the limitations exemplified by other recent attempts to increase community engagement with court processes in England and Wales. For example, Community Impact Statements (CISs) were introduced by the previous Labour administration in 2009 and are designed to give an indication of the impact that particular types of offending have had upon the local community. The CIS is intended to be used in criminal proceedings to provide information to the Crown Prosecution Service and the courts, allowing them to reflect upon 'community concerns' when they consider imposing a sentence on an offender. Since their introduction, CISs are rarely, if ever, used by courts. This suggests 'a tokenistic, 'tick-box' approach to community engagement, where the introduction of 'tools' to involve local residents in the justice process is used to provide legitimacy to new supposedly community justice-oriented initiatives' (Donoghue 2012: 604). Nonetheless, the Coalition

Community courts and mental health courts 107

government has recently announced plans to complement the CIS with a new Community Harm Statement (CHS) for use in the county court. The CHS will provide:

> A recognised template to present evidence of harm on communities to court in a consistent way ... For example, it can show judges the impact that anti-social behaviour is having on a whole community, to balance alongside considerations of the rights of the perpetrator.
>
> (Home Office 2012: 20)

The limitations of the existing CIS however, as a tool for enhancing community engagement with the courts has not been acknowledged.

Considerable effort has been made in recent years to try to prioritise community engagement as a central part of the lower courts' function and criminal justice policies are clearly aspiring to more systematic and consistent engagement between courts and communities (Department for Communities and Local Government 2006, 2008). However, evidence suggests that levels of engagement with local communities in England and Wales are very limited (Jarvis *et al.* 2011). There are a number of (largely practical) explanations for this. Magistrates participate in and actively contribute to the day-to-day life of communities through, for example, the use of local shops and businesses, school Parent Teacher Associations (PTAs), sporting and arts organisations, and they use these avenues to disseminate information about the work that they do. Yet, there is evidence that some magistrates feel uncomfortable about and untrained for undertaking the kinds of tasks that are now being asked of them, in neighbourhoods that many will not have visited before (Ames *et al.* 2011). Not all magistrates serve on the bench nearest to where they live and so are not always familiar with certain areas or comfortable visiting them (although no data currently exists on the distance between magistrates' homes and the court(s) in which they preside).

There has also been an emphasis from central government upon trying to ensure better engagement with 'hard to reach' groups (Cabinet Office 2009; Home Office 2004). These groups include (but are not limited to) racial/ethnic/religious minorities, gypsy/traveller populations, the lesbian/gay/bi-sexual and transgender (LGBT) community and social housing residents. Amongst the problems that have been experienced in trying to prioritise engagement with 'hard to reach' groups is a lack of agreed definition about what constitutes 'hard to reach groups' which has in turn led to magistrates being concerned about whether they are insured to visit certain groups and areas, and if requisite health and safety checks have been carried out to ensure that magistrates are safe. Similarly, as a result of criminal justice spending cutbacks, there is no longer a separate budget for community engagement. Thus if there is an expectation that magistrates should undertake more visits and engagement activities, there is simultaneously less money available to cover expenses. It has been reported that this has led to problems with budget holders about what expenses can be claimed for and how much money is available for 'engagement' activities.

108　*Community courts and mental health courts*

Despite these problems, there is evidence that formal, adequately resourced community engagement initiatives can be successful. The Magistrates in the Community (MIC) project that operates in England and Wales has demonstrated successful outcomes in involving the community in the work of the lower courts (Magistrates' Assocation 2011). However, community engagement initiatives can be problematic to implement and often lack durability. Ultimately, the key challenge for the Government in seeking to enhance community engagement with the lower courts as part of problem-solving justice is to transform a legal institution which functions as a court, into a court which also functions as a community institution.

Mental health courts

Official statistics and empirical studies in Britain and internationally suggest that there are now more people with mental health problems in prison than ever before (Bradley 2009). In Europe, estimates suggest that up to 40 per cent of prisoners suffer from a type of mental illness (UNODC 2008). Moreover, high levels of *severe* mental illness are consistently reported in prisons in many countries globally (Fazel and Seewald 2012). In the US in 2006, for example, 56 per cent of state prisoners and 64 per cent of jail inmates reported treatment for severe mental illness (Pycroft 2012). However, estimates vary for the prevalence of serious mental illnesses among all people entering jails, with one recent study estimating this at 16.9 per cent (14.5 per cent of men and 31 per cent of women) (Steadman *et al.* 2009). In New South Wales, Australia, 80 per cent of the prison population have some type of mental health problem, compared with 31 per cent of the general population (Pycroft 2012). Thus prisoners have significantly higher rates of mental health problems than the general public. Much of the literature within criminology and psychology has argued that people with mental illnesses are often repeatedly processed through the criminal justice system involving a cycle of courtrooms and prisons that they contend are ill-equipped to address the complex needs of these individuals and, in particular, to provide them with adequate treatment (Almquist and Dodd 2009; Skeem *et al.* 2011). As a response to these concerns, specialist mental health courts (MHCs) have begun to be developed as a means to divert this particular category of offender from the 'revolving door' of repeated appearances in court.

In common with the other types of problem-solving courts discussed within this text, the cross-jurisdictional spread of MHCs has largely been influenced by US court innovation in the mental health domain. The first MHCs originated in the US, in Indiana and Florida in 1997 (Johnston 2011). By 2009, more than 250 MHCs were in existence in 43 states in America (Almquist and Dodd 2009). Again, in common with the development of problem-solving practices more generally, MHCs have been subject to changes and refinement in their processes according to (amongst other factors) funding priorities, local policies and organisational arrangements. Even though the US has led the way with the creation and development of MHCs, there remains a very strong tendency towards idiosyncrasy in these courts (Erickson *et al.* 2006).[4] Generally, MHCs operate as specialist criminal courts for offenders with mental health problems (Griffin *et al.* 2002). It has been suggested that these courts are less adversarial and more informal than traditional criminal courts (Petrila 2003). The aim is diversion from prison into community-based mental health and substance use treatment in order to reduce the prevalence of offenders with mental health illnesses repeatedly processed through the criminal justice system. Judges will usually have received some degree of specialist training and may have voluntarily elected to sit in these courts. In the US, the operation of mental health courts is often underpinned by principles of therapeutic jurisprudence (Berman and Feinblatt 2005). In the same way as drug courts, MHCs operate pre-sentence where entry into drug court is part of diversion from the traditional criminal process, or post-plea where drug court participation is a condition of deferred sentence or probation. While Nolan (2009) noted that MHCs predominantly include defendants who have committed low-level offences such as petty theft and disorderly conduct, Redlich *et al.* (2005) observed an increasing acceptance of felony versus misdemeanant defendants into MHC programmes.

A point of difference with other problem-solving courts such as drug courts and community courts – that include defendants who have committed similar offences, is that for entry into MHCs, participants must have a demonstrable mental illness which has directly contributed to their offence (Nolan 2009). Moreover, in the same way that entry into drug courts is deemed to be voluntary, individuals' participation in MHCs is intended to be of their own volition. However, once they have elected to participate, they must comply with the orders of the court. In this way, MHCs have been described as practising a form of 'voluntary' coercion (James 2010). The court can mandate that MHC participants must take certain prescribed medications, attend treatment, support meetings or appointments and attend periodic review hearings (Redlich 2013). Failure to comply with court orders can result in a range of sanctions, including increased judicial and community supervision, community-based sanctions and the use of short periods of custody (Redlich 2013), although some courts make use of rewards and incentives (such as certificates and gift cards) as well as sanctions (Callahan *et al.* 2013). Successful participation in, and completion of, MHC programmes can then lead to charges or convictions being removed from the individual's record (Redlich 2013). However, although enrolment in MHCs is intended to be 'voluntary', very little is known about this aspect of the courts (Redlich *et al.* 2010). A number of commentators have argued that the use of 'euphemistic' language such as 'therapeutic' and 'treatment oriented' serves to mask the fundamentally punitive nature of the courts and facilitates the justification of incarceration on the basis of therapeutic rationale (Nolan 2009). Researchers have also questioned the 'voluntary' nature of mentally ill offenders' participation in the MHC process. A US study undertaken with 200 MHC participants in two separate courts found that although all participants reported that they had chosen to enrol in the court, at the same time they also stated that they did not realise that the court was voluntary and that they did not know the

110   *Community courts and mental health courts*

requirements of the court prior to entering. A number of participants were also found to have impairments in legal competence (Redlich *et al.* 2010).

Effectiveness

While the structure and function of MHCs has been extensively discussed (Goldkamp and Irons-Guynn 2000; Watson *et al.* 2001), there is a much smaller body of work documenting their substantive outcomes and effectiveness. One of the reasons for this is that many mental health courts operate at a local level with small budgets and so it can be difficult for them to find the necessary resources to collect and analyse data (Steadman 2005). The consequence of this has been somewhat of a 'catch-22' situation, in that many courts are therefore unable to statistically demonstrate effective outcomes and so are unlikely to attract further additional funding from policymakers to ameliorate and build on existing good practices (Steadman 2005). Mental health courts are also a relatively new criminal justice innovation and so there is inevitably a lack of significant formal work on long-term outcomes associated with these programmes. Of those studies that have been conducted, most do not track participants beyond 12 months after programme participation, which means that findings on the long-term impact of participating in a mental health court are limited (Almquist and Dodd 2009). In other international jurisdictions too, there have been calls for improved research techniques in the field of mental health courts (Schneider 2010).

While sanctions and incentives are considered crucial to the functioning of MHCs, there is scant empirical evidence to support or refute their use, and there are no agreed terms to define what they are (Callahan *et al.* 2013). For example, a recent study of four MHCs in the US found that the factors associated with receiving a jail sanction are recent drug use, substance use diagnosis and drug arrests; being viewed as less compliant with court conditions, receiving more bench warrants and having more in-custody hearings; and MHC programme termination (Callahan *et al.* 2013). However, the development of a more rigorous evidence base which is capable of identifying which MHC participants are more likely to follow court orders and avoid sanctions, as well as those who have difficulty adhering to court conditions, is clearly important to improving understandings of how MHCs work in practice and how their different approaches to sanction and rewards variously influence offenders and impact upon recidivism. Moreover, there is also little research on what 'treatment' is actually provided by mental health courts, including how the treatment models differ in impacting reductions in re-offending (Luskin 2013).

There is nonetheless a small but growing body of research on the effectiveness of mental health court programmes. This suggests that mental health court participation is associated with positive outcomes in several categories (Almquist and Dodd 2009; Steadman *et al.* 2005). These include reductions in rates of recidivism, increased treatment engagement and efficiency savings (Almquist and Dodd 2009). Findings of a recent meta-analysis (Sarteschi *et al.* 2011) suggest that MHCs are an effective intervention – in certain circumstances.

Community courts and mental health courts   111

However, the majority of the studies used in the analysis were not methodologically strong and come burdened with many of the limitations evident in empirical evaluations of other problem-solving courts such as lack of a control group, small sample size and selection bias. Therefore the conclusions of this review must be treated with some caution and claims about the generalisable effectiveness of MHCs should be understood as limited. However, a scientifically rigorous prospective multisite study on mental health courts, with treatment and control groups, recently sought to determine if participation in a MHC is associated with more favourable criminal justice outcomes than processing through the regular criminal court system. It aimed to identify defendants for whom the courts produced the most favourable criminal justice outcomes (Steadman *et al.* 2011). It found positive evidence that MHCs lower post treatment arrest rates and days of incarceration. Factors that the researchers found were associated with better outcomes among the MHC participants include treatment at baseline, not using illegal substances and a diagnosis of bipolar disorder rather than schizophrenia or depression.

While existing research appears to support the idea that MHCs are more effective than the traditional court system in responding to mentally disordered offenders, and that MHCs may produce positive outcomes for their participants and for the public including cost savings, so far research has been unable to determine with any degree of certainty '*why* some individuals do well in mental health courts and others do not, or *why* certain programs seem to be more effective than others' (Almquist and Dodd 2009). Hence there is clear requirement for further work in this area that utilises methodologically sound scientific approaches to determine whether MHCs are able to deliver successes in re-offending rates and cost savings, as well as wider improvements in public health and benefits to society (Wolff and Pogorzelski 2005).

Mental health courts (MHCs) in England and Wales

Offenders with mental health problems typically present a range of complex health and justice needs, including problems accessing secure housing, poor educational and social skills, difficulty obtaining employment, substance misuse and poverty, and inadequate treatment and support (Winstone and Pakes 2012). Evidence also indicates that imprisonment is frequently both an ineffective and inappropriate disposal for offenders with mental illnesses because custody does not offer adequate support and treatment services and can exacerbate mental health problems leading to increased vulnerability and risk of self-harm including suicide (Bradley 2009). It is not surprising therefore, that my research found very considerable support among the judiciary in England and Wales for the creation of mental health courts. Mental health was an area identified by magistrates 'perhaps more than any other within the courts system', which many sentencers in England and Wales believed 'would benefit from some form of court specialisation'. This is in part a consequence of the sentencing options available to magistrates, which are sometimes viewed by them as an impediment to the

112   *Community courts and mental health courts*

delivery of appropriate treatment to mentally ill offenders. For example, one magistrate mentioned:

> there was a case ... in regard to a man who believed that he was involved in a relationship with a horse. The matter came to court because he was caught having sex with the horse. However, this man brought the horse gifts and in his mind was in a relationship! Despite all of this he was sentenced to a custodial sentence without any mental health treatment. He patently had lots of issues – as revealed in the full pre-sentence report produced by probation with the assistance of a medical assessment.

The existence of these types of case has led some magistrates to suggest that 'sentencing options should be reviewed so that appropriate treatment can be given [to offenders with mental illness]'. An important caveat identified by sentencers is that MHCs must be able to 'provide an appropriate framework so that those indicating mental health issues did actually have diagnosed mental health issues. Some people do have issues but they are simply undiagnosed until they come to the attention of the courts'. Such a framework is a central feature of MHCs and, as the evaluation of the pilot MHCs in England demonstrated (see below), a diagnosed mental illness was required for participation in the programme.

However, somewhat paradoxically given the high number of incarcerated offenders with mental health problems, the Government in England and Wales has historically supported a diversionary approach to offenders with mental health problems, and policy and practice developments in health and criminal justice over the last two decades have gone some way to creating a more receptive context for implementing a diversionary approach.[5] This diversionary approach has incorporated:

> A process of decision-making, which results in mentally disordered offenders being diverted away from the criminal justice system to the health and social care sectors. Diversion may occur at any stage of the criminal justice process: before arrest, after proceedings have been initiated, in place of prosecution, or when a case is being considered by the courts.
>
> (Bradley 2009: 16)

Yet, in a recent government-sponsored review of services for mentally disordered offenders in England and Wales, undertaken by Lord Bradley, it is clear that the lack of a standardised nationally guided approach has meant that implementation has been inconsistent (Bradley 2009).

In December 2007, Lord Bradley was asked to carry out a review of how more offenders with severe mental health problems could be diverted away from prison and into more appropriate facilities. The subsequent report of findings, *The Bradley Report* (2009), highlighted gaps in the provision of services to offenders with mental health problems and suggested the creation and development of new

Community courts and mental health courts 113

innovations which might more successfully address these problems in a targeted and effective way. In particular, the Report identified concerns about the quality of current assessment practices undertaken by police and the CPS in determining whether a criminal justice outcome (versus diversion to health and social services) should be pursued, as well as the availability to police of evidence on detainees' previous contact with services. The Report recommended that Local Safer Neighbourhood Teams should play a key role in identifying and supporting people in the community with mental health problems or learning disabilities who may be involved in low-level offending or anti-social behaviour by establishing local contacts and partnerships and developing referral pathways. It stipulated that community support officers and police officers should link with local mental health services to develop joint training packages for mental health awareness and learning disability issues. The Report also recommended that the Crown Prosecution Service should review the use of conditional cautions for individuals with mental health problems or learning disabilities and issue guidance to advise relevant agencies.

Mental health court pilot

In 2009, the issues identified in *The Bradley Report* were reflected in the objectives of the first Mental Health Court pilot in England and Wales, which sought to evaluate whether the MHC model could contribute to a range of policy objectives for this particular group of offenders with complex needs. Offenders suffering from mental illness have typically received 'decades of patchy provision for complex needs', which has been further exacerbated by weak engagement with statutory and clinical support and a failure to establish meaningful professional relationships between practitioners and offenders (Winstone and Pakes 2012: 135). A primary objective of the pilot MHC therefore was to assess whether reductions in re-offending could be achieved through more effective offender engagement with statutory, health and third sector (charitable) services but there was also an emphasis on evaluating whether increased offender engagement with these services could lead to improved health outcomes. The pilot also aimed to test whether community sentences tailored specifically to the needs of this particular offender category could be a viable alternative to a short prison sentence. This is particularly significant in view of evidence which indicates that short custodial terms have little impact on recidivism for these individuals because the mental health support that they receive while incarcerated is often of a poorer quality than mainstream mental health support services provide, and periods of custody can disrupt difficult to establish community links (Bradley 2009).

The Mental Health Court (MHC) model was piloted at magistrates' courts in Stratford (London) and Brighton (Sussex) in 2009. The Stratford MHC was set up under section 178 of the Criminal Justice Act 2003 and the Brighton MHC operated within regular magistrates' court provisions. The pilot was intended to facilitate the identification of offenders with mental health issues that could then be considered during sentencing. This process was facilitated, where appropriate,

114 *Community courts and mental health courts*

through the use of community orders with requirements specifically tailored to address the mental health issues impacting on offenders' behaviour. The court (or Probation) was then involved in regular review of the offender's compliance with the terms of the orders. Although both MHCs operated as part of existing magistrates' courts, there were some differences between the models that reflected local policies and resource arrangements. One obvious difference was in terms of costs associated with the provision of treatment and support services. In the Stratford MHC, participants were directed into mainstream statutory services and arrangements were negotiated with providers to ensure that participants received the appropriate services. In Brighton however, the MHC referred participants to a wide range of non-statutory community based services and the costs for this were met by the Probation area. Despite the different arrangements for the use of statutory and third sector services, the costs associated with these services were felt by staff and MHC participants to be prohibitive at times.

An official evaluation of the pilot, undertaken on behalf of the Ministry of Justice, analysed 547 cases that came before the courts between January 2009 and January 2010, together with cost information for the same 12-month period. The evaluation also included interviews with criminal justice practitioners involved in the operation of the MHCs, as well as offenders on community orders. During the course of the evaluation period, the cases of more than 4 000 defendants due to appear at the courts were proactively screened through the use of paper-based evidence such as medical documentation. Face-to-face interviews or assessments were not used. Of those defendants who were proactively screened, 547 individuals were identified as requiring a formal mental health assessment, of which 394 were completed. From the initial screening of the 547 individuals, 181 (33 per cent) were found to have no mental health needs. Individuals had the right to decline the opportunity for mental health assessment and to have their case dealt with through normal court procedures, and this accounted for why some of the assessments did not take place. Otherwise, assessments did not generally take place due to the unavailability of MHCP. Offenders were eligible for entry into the MHC following a conviction and where the offender's mental health needs were deemed to be manageable on a community order. Importantly, offenders were not eligible to participate in the MHC if they possessed primary need regarding substance misuse. Individuals could be included in the MHC if there was a *dual diagnosis* of mental health and substance misuse issues however. In those cases where substance misuse was the primary diagnosis, offenders would be directed to the relevant services.

The summary conclusions of the evaluation found that the MHC model facilitated improved multi-agency collaborations in responding to offenders with mental health problems (Winstone and Pakes 2010). These innovative collaborations helped to address the needs of offenders that would otherwise likely 'have gone unmet' (Winstone and Pakes 2010: v). Improved outcomes were also a result of early consultation at senior management level, which was facilitated by the MHC model. Crucially, it was reported that any wider implementation of MHCs 'would require significant changes, supported at a national level, in the current patterns of multi-agency information sharing and data collection' (Winstone and Pakes 2010: v). It was also noted that a significant limitation of the MHC pilot was that it excluded certain groups. The evaluation recommended that these exclusions ought to be further investigated to determine whether their removal would permit wider access to services offered by the MHCs. It should also be noted that some of the emerging issues in MHC praxis highlighted in the international literature, appear to some degree at least, replicated. For example, it was reported that the majority of participants in the MHC pilot 'were not fully aware' that they were being supported by a specialist MHC team while going through the court process (Winstone and Pakes 2012: 142). That so many participants found the experience of the court process 'overwhelming' is not surprising given the health issues including 'anxiety and mental confusion' that many are likely to be experiencing during the court process (Winstone and Pakes 2012: 142). However, these observations also link in with emerging empirical findings in the US which suggest that MHC participants may not realise that the court is voluntary and do not understand the requirements of the court prior to entering (Redlich *et al.* 2010). This would seem to suggest that greater efforts ought to be made to communicate the voluntary nature of the courts to MHC participants and to make clear the requirements of the court before and during the court process.

Scalability

The evaluation of the two pilot MHCs in England found that going to scale with the MHC model across the country would require a number of core requirements to be present: the availability of a Mental Health Court Practitioner (MHCP) daily at court; the prior establishment of multi-agency agreements for information exchange and to identify and agree the priorities of collaborating agencies; a comprehensive screening and assessment of defendants for mental health issues; tailored use of community orders for offenders; court review of the effectiveness of community orders; involvement of the MHCP post-sentence; increased training for practitioners and stakeholders; and identification of, and engagement with, local resources for signposting and referral of defendants to appropriate support services (Winstone and Pakes 2010: v).

The potential scalability of MHCs in England and Wales, outlined in the pilot evaluation, needs to be considered in light of a number of political and economic dimensions. First, court innovation in the diversion of mentally disordered offenders must be understood in the context of the limited progress that has been made in this area over the last twenty years (see for example a previous government-sponsored review undertaken by Reed 1992). Although the *Bradley Report* set out comprehensive plans for future service development, a lack of firm direction by central government has previously led to patchy and slow advances in achieving agreed goals (James 2010: 247). *The Bradley Report* argued that one of the most significant problems associated with previous policy development in the domain of mental health and criminal justice has been the

116   *Community courts and mental health courts*

piecemeal and uncoordinated approach that has been taken by government departments, agencies and third sector organisations, who have worked independently of one another and who have generally tended to focus on one aspect of the system at a time. Consequently, there has to date been no clear, strategic national focus for the development and delivery of policy in this area. The lack of a centralised strategy on the diversion of offenders with mental health problems away from prison has meant that innovations (such as MHCs) have developed locally and on a small scale. Across the range of different schemes, of which MHCs are but one, the aims and objectives display variation and inconsistency, as well as a lack of rigorous empirical data on the impact of these services on mental health outcomes, value for money, or on reducing re-offending rates (Bradley 2009).

While the evaluation of the English MHCs provides information about the characteristics that might potentially make their operation effective, much more needs to be known about the various elements and functions which would contribute to reductions in recidivism for any significant investment of national resources. A lack of national investment in MHCs is not necessarily fatal to their incorporation into the criminal justice landscape since there is evidence that innovations have been created despite a lack of national investment. This is especially true since the operation of MHCs does not incorporate a new client group and therefore efforts to make better use of existing resources in responding to mentally disordered offenders may potentially raise the possibility of cost savings for the criminal justice system, although this would obviously require further empirical study and scientific evaluation. The current emphasis on payment by results will likely have significant consequences for the way that the independent and voluntary sector contributes to treatment and support. It may also be the case that, given the overlap between mental health issues and drug use, MHCs are better subsumed within the drug court model (or vice versa). An important finding from the pilot evaluation was that many professionals expressed concern that individuals were excluded from the MHC when substance misuse was identified as the primary need. Given the high prevalence of dual diagnosis (mental health problems combined with drug and/or alcohol problems) in offenders, careful consideration must be given as to how both issues can successfully be dealt with in drug and mental health courts. It has also been suggested that the holistic approach of domestic violence and community courts may better address the typically multiple needs of offenders. In the US, an increasing number of courts are 'dual-diagnosis' and therefore although these courts may identify in name as MHCs, they focus on clients who have mental health issues *as well as* substance abuse issues. There is not necessarily a requirement that eligibility be restricted to only those with co-occurring problems and the 'dual diagnosis' orientation of these courts means that they accept nearly all referrals (Redlich *et al.* 2005: 531).

An independent Commission was set up to carry out a five-year review of *The Bradley Report* and which aims to document how some of the Report's recommendations can be implemented following the major changes that have taken place in health and criminal justice services since 2009. The final Report is due for publication in 2014. However, the significant political and fiscal changes that have occurred since the initial Report was commissioned in 2007 undoubtedly mean that the Report's very substantial number of recommendations, and the extent of their potential implementation, need to be (re-)considered in this new climate. For example, although many magistrates take the view that mental health courts would be an excellent innovation, it has been argued elsewhere that the MHC model is unlikely to be embedded in Britain because of the availability of mental health law and diversion mechanisms which 'enable more directly interventionist solutions to be adopted' (James 2010: 246). Despite concerns about the 'punitive' nature of some MHC models, particularly in the US, proponents have argued that MHCs have actually been instrumental in bringing our attention to the plight of mentally disordered accused (Schneider 2009). Although they undoubtedly have associated limitations and current models have associated challenges for practitioners to address, they nonetheless represent a commitment to a more therapeutic approach to mental health issues within the criminal justice system in order to try to reduce the unnecessary criminalisation of those with mental illness. What is unfortunate is that mentally disordered offenders are perhaps a group more than any other within criminal justice that would benefit from problem-solving courts. Yet at the same time, they seem to be the least likely to receive the potential benefits of the problem-solving approach, at least for the time being.

Notes

1 A single judge hears all non-trial summary and most either-way offences committed within the designated catchment area (adult and youth). A team of magistrates hear summary trials (McKenna 2007: i).
2 Shortly after the opening of the North Liverpool Community Justice Centre, an attempt was made to try to achieve a similar approach without the additional resources that had been assigned in North Liverpool. Consequently, other community justice initiatives, such as the community court in Salford, are delivered in the same building as the traditional magistrates' court, with little opportunity for co-location of staff and services, and without a single judge presiding over the court. The 'stripped down' Centre in Salford has running costs of only £100 000 a year. This has meant challenges for court administrators in listing cases in a way that ensures continuity of sentencer at successive review hearings.
3 CASS is currently based in both Plymouth and Cornwall.
4 As Alison Redlich (2013: 147) has observed, it quite aptly describes the operation of the courts to say that: 'If you've seen one mental health court ... you've seen one mental health court'.
5 For example, offenders are now recognised as part of a socially excluded population.

6 Neighbourhood justice panels

Innovation in victim-offender mediation first began to attract interest during the 1970s and 1980s. However, it was not until the development of restorative experiments taking place in Australia and New Zealand during the 1990s that practices of victim-offender mediation, and particularly the concept of restorative justice, received worldwide academic attention and policy interest (Braithwaite 1989). Restorative justice (RJ) has been discussed elsewhere in this text and so there is no need to revisit the concept in detail here, however it is useful to bear in mind that restorative models aim to incentivise a new design that prioritises engaging communities in localised justice processes, which are grounded in both parochial and private controls (Schiff *et al.* 2011). Neighbourhood Justice Panels (NJPs) are an example of restorative justice oriented innovations, which operate using a highly localised restorative decision-making model that seeks to engage victims, offenders, families and the wider community as resources in developing a more effective response to local, generally low-level crime problems. NJPs can be located along the continuum of non-adversarial restorative decision-making practices and forums that have developed over the last twenty years (Bazemore and Griffiths 1997). They are heavily reliant on community volunteers and operate as a form of diversion from formal court processes. Although 'NJPs' is currently the term in operation for these restorative panels in England and Wales, elsewhere similar types of restorative forums exist by other names such as neighbourhood accountability boards, reparative/citizen boards or community accountability boards.

Restorative reparation schemes employing victim-offender mediation were first introduced in England at the end of the 1970s and by 1990 there were 14 such schemes in operation in various localities across the country (Marshall 1991). In the US, the first restorative panels originated in 1994 in Great Falls (Montana) and Boise (Idaho) and these were then followed shortly afterwards by panels in the counties of San Bernardino and Sacramento, California (Schiff *et al.* 2011). In 1996, as part of a large, cross-national study of victim/offender mediation involving analysis of programmes in the US, Canada and England, researchers found evidence that victim/offender mediation projects in England were producing positive results for victim and offender satisfaction and perceptions of fairness in the justice system's response when compared with victims and offenders who were referred to the programmes but never participated (Umbreit and Roberts 1996). The study also reported findings that victims who participated in the programmes were less fearful of being re-victimised (Umbreit and Roberts 1996). By the mid-1990s, restorative practices were evident in the US, Canada, England, Wales, Australia, New Zealand, Scotland, Japan and Germany (Galaway and Hudson 1996).

Interest in restorative programmes has continued apace and there are now a broad range of different types of restorative panels operating in many jurisdictions across the globe. One of the most well-known examples in the US is the Vermont Neighborhood Accountability Board (NAB) which was established after citizens argued that they could respond to non-violent offenders in the community better than the criminal justice system (Schiff *et al.* 2011; Karp *et al.* 2004). In countries such as South Africa (Froestad and Shearing 2007) and Northern Ireland (Erikkson 2009), where variations of NJPs exist, these models have been developed locally with significant support from a range of stakeholders. Moreover, the use of restorative practices has been implemented for both adult and young offenders. In Scotland, the Children's Hearing System adopts a fundamentally restorative approach to youth justice which utilises Children's Hearing Panels rather than formal court processes for responding to offending by children and young people (McVie 2011; Crawford and Newburn 2003), and in England and Wales, Youth Offender Panels are restorative in nature (Gelsthorpe and Morris 2002).[1] Internationally too, other jurisdictions operate with restorative justice programmes for young offenders. Most notably, in Canada, following the enactment of the Youth Criminal Justice Act 2003, restorative Youth Justice Committees were introduced to respond to cases involving low-level youth criminality (Hillian *et al.* 2004). The restorative approaches to youth justice in Canada and in Britain are different to the restorative programmes in the US, however, because they have embedded national frameworks to implement restorative justice initiatives.

Despite the interest that has developed internationally in restorative panels over the last few decades, there is at present a rather limited body of research evidence available on the impact of neighbourhood panels. Some detailed analysis has however been undertaken in the US, especially on Reparative Boards in Arizona and Vermont (Rodriguez 2005; Karp 2001). These studies have tended to suggest that neighbourhood panels can be a useful innovation but that they come burdened with a range of practical and conceptual difficulties, many of which were discussed in the previous chapter on community courts and community engagement, such as ensuring genuine and representative 'community' or volunteer participation; issues of adequate training and retention; and limited victim participation. However, before we go on to examine the implementation of NJPs in England and Wales, we must first consider the broader diversionary context in which these innovations have developed.

120 *Neighbourhood justice panels*

Diversion and out of court disposals in England and Wales

The creation of NJPs in England and Wales can be located within the wider context of diversion from the criminal process and the growth of out of court disposals. Out of court sanctions include cautions, reprimands, fixed penalty fines and restorative justice projects. It is also important to understand the creation of out of court disposals as premised upon the objective of achieving reductions in police bureaucracy. According to the Ministry of Justice, out-of-court disposals allow the police to deal quickly and proportionately with low-level, often first-time offending which does not merit prosecution at court. This is intended to allow the police to spend more time on frontline duties and tackling serious crime. Since 2003, the number of out-of-court disposals administered each year increased by 135 per cent from 241 000 in 2003 to 567 000 in 2008, peaking in 2007 at 626 000 (Ministry of Justice 2010c). Although over the last five years the number of out of court disposals issued by the police has dropped by 42 per cent, out-of-court disposals still account for one third of all offences brought to justice in England and Wales, and so there remains concern that the substantial growth in the use of out-of-court disposals has led to significant inconsistencies in their use, in particular for persistent and more serious offending.

Media interest in, and criticism of, the use of out of court disposals has often focussed upon those instances when police cautions have been used for offences which are indictable only (such as rape and serious assault).[2] The potential problematic implications of out of court disposals for victims is clear – for example, there is no provision for the assessment or consideration of a victim impact statement; there is no imposition of the victim surcharge for a police caution and no opportunity for the imposition of financial recompense for injury or for criminal damage; something which the courts *must* consider. However, there are also significant implications for defendants. Issuing a police caution is dependent on the accused admitting his or her guilt. This raises concerns about equivocal pleas – something which a court is not allowed to accept. In a speech in 2011, the Lord Chief Justice Lord Judge expressed concern about whether the convenience of avoiding the court process altogether may lead an offender to admit to something for which he or she would have a defence (Judge, 2011). Thus it may be the case that some suspects prefer to make a false admission and accept a caution in order to avoid 'going to court'. There is also a broad lack of consistency in the use of out of court disposals across police force areas, as well as no supervisory mechanism, which is troubling. While a caution requires an admission of guilt and is recorded on the Police National Computer (PNC), penalty notices for disorder do not require an admission of guilt and paying the PND involves neither an official finding nor an acceptance of guilt.

According to magistrates, out of court disposals cause more discussion and debate than almost any other subject in retiring rooms up and down the country, from those who think that magistrates should be involved in administering cautions, to those who believe that this is entirely inappropriate and that magistrates should only pass sentence in a formal court setting. There are also those who think that magistrates *could* be involved in the administration of out of court sanctions but only in clearly defined circumstances, with some happy for that to take place in non-court-room settings.[3] To what extent magistrates do eventually become involved in the use of out of court disposals will become more apparent as the Government's plans to reform the role of magistrates progresses (Ministry of Justice 2013b). Given the concerns that have been raised about the continued existence of the lay magistracy, it seems evident that the role of magistrates is likely to need to have to evolve to remain relevant and sustainable. Whether this reformed role will involve new responsibilities such as the administration of out of court disposals including cautions remains to be seen – there is much concern among the magistracy about whether any future plans for them to scrutinise out of court disposals will operate prospectively or retrospectively. In June 2013, the Senior Presiding Judge, Lord Justice Gross, published brief guidance for magistrates on the scrutiny of out of court disposals. This noted that Lord Justice Gross:

> Supports, in principle, magistrates' involvement in retrospective arrangements to scrutinise the decisions of police forces in dealing with offenders through the use of out of court disposals to enhance consistency, transparency, and public confidence ... [but that] scrutiny will always be retrospective and will not involve magistrates endorsing, rescinding, or otherwise changing individual out of court disposals in any way.
>
> (Judiciary of England and Wales 2013b: 1)

However, as the drive towards efficiency savings continues apace, reflected in court closures and increasing centralisation, the government is placing new emphasis upon the need for the magistracy to improve efficiency in the delivery of summary justice, which may require them to become further involved in summary processes (Ministry of Justice 2013b). As part of the current consultation on the role of the magistracy, the Government is considering whether magistrates could become involved in the work of neighbourhood justice panels.

Justice panels

Neighbourhood Justice Panels (NJPs) (also known as Community Justice Panels or Neighbourhood Resolution Panels) are an alternative disposal for first-time, low-level offences that would normally attract a Reprimand or Final Warning for young offenders or a Caution for adults. They can involve both criminal and anti-social incidents and can be referred from sources including police and housing agencies/registered social landlords. They bring together the wrongdoer and harmed person, along with supporters, to discuss what has happened, how it has affected them and how all parties can move forward. Outcomes usually involve some form of reparation on behalf of the wrongdoer, to make good for

122   *Neighbourhood justice panels*

the harm caused. The Panels only work with offenders who have admitted their guilt and only in those circumstances where the victim consents to be involved. The introduction of NJPs are collectively about reducing delay in the criminal process, 'dealing with crime on a shoestring' and giving the victim a greater 'voice' in the criminal justice system.

Research suggests that for wrongdoers, the main motivation for participating in Panels is the opportunity to avoid criminal proceedings since neighbourhood justice panels do not result in a criminal record (Clamp and Paterson 2011; Meadows *et al.* 2010). Neighbourhood Justice Panels are based on the premise that by giving the community and those directly involved in an incident of crime or anti-social behaviour more control over its resolution, this will result in a more effective way of preventing neighbourhood disputes and low-level offending from escalating and progressing to more serious and persistent criminal activity. Additionally, it has been argued, that increased contact between members of the community and the resolution of conflicts' within the area in which it takes place will help to reduce perceptions of increased crime and improve feelings of safety and community cohesion by involving communities in community based restorative justice.

The first NJPs in England were set up in 2005 in Chard and Ilminster (Somerset). Their introduction was a direct consequence of local courthouse closures in the area: magistrates' courts had recently been removed from the locality and residents felt frustrated by a perceived lack of local justice (Meadows *et al.* 2010). Although neighbourhood justice panels generally deal with lower level criminality, it was in fact two high profile murders in the local area that acted as the catalyst for the introduction of the NJP in Somerset. Publicity surrounding the murders served to reinforce existing local concerns about crime levels in the area and a perception that, because the nearest magistrates' court was 18 miles away, access to justice had become detached from and inaccessible to residents. The local newspaper subsequently ran a campaign called 'Bring Justice Home' to try to get the local magistrates' court, which had closed the previous year, reopened (Clamp and Paterson 2011). When it was decided reopening the court was not feasible, the community turned to the restorative justice model as an alternative method for dealing with a variety of offences in the community while at the same time involving residents and victims in the process. The development of the NJP occurred 'bottom-up', with the initial idea of a panel originating at the local level. This involved collaborations with various agencies and the creation of a steering group to take the idea forward to central Government to seek funding for the initiative, which was in turn granted by the Home Office's Anti-Social Behaviour Unit (Mirsky 2006). Local volunteers from the community were then recruited to sit on the Panel, alongside police officers and Police Community Support Officer (PCSOs). According to Clamp and Paterson (2011), outcomes have to date been very positive with recent figures indicating that some 330 cases have been dealt with by the Panel, which has resulted in a reduction in police administration time by 75 per cent, and a recidivism rate for participants of 5 per cent.

Neighbourhood justice panels 123

Following this initial success, NJPs were then officially trialled in Sheffield, Manchester and Somerset. The Ministry of Justice reported evaluations of these pilots found low re-offending rates of between 3 and 5 per cent and victim satisfaction rates of over 90 per cent (Ministry of Justice 2012b). Although there was evidence of low numbers of referrals to the schemes at the outset, as well as some other implementation problems and resistance by some police officers to the new more 'informal' arrangements, there were a number of positive outcomes from the pilots including reduced delay in processing low level cases (Meadows *et al.* 2010). In October 2012, the Government's announcement that they would be testing the panels in an additional 15 areas came as part of the introduction of the new 'Swift and Sure Justice' policy aimed at substantially increasing the number of flexible criminal justice pilot schemes across England and Wales.[4] These measures included the extension of magistrates' courts opening hours and maximising the use of video links.

The 'Swift and Sure Justice' policy reforms, which were set out in a government White Paper in July 2012, were in part a response to the English riots of 2011. During the period of the riots, magistrates' courts across England opened for longer, some through the night, to deal with the large volume of people being processed through the criminal justice system. In addition, the policy reforms were also a response to long-standing concerns about delays in the criminal justice system. The average length of time between an offence taking place and a sentence being passed is five months, despite the fact that most cases do not have to go to trial or are uncontested. With neighbourhood panels, a case can go from referral to panel in two to three weeks. Cost is also another significant factor. In Somerset, the basic cost for police and the CPS of taking a criminal damage case through court is £612, yet through the panel it costs £163.50. Thus it is important to recognise that the potential for NJPs to offer a more 'flexible' approach to the delivery which might significantly reduce both cost and delays in the resolution of cases, is likely to be particularly politically appealing characteristics of the panels.

While only the 15 identified test areas will form the basis of the government evaluation, other areas across the country have also been encouraged to set up their own panels. According to the government White Paper *Swift and Sure Justice*, NJPs 'involve community representatives and use restorative justice techniques to get a firm and early grip on offending, preventing problems escalating unnecessarily' (Ministry of Justice 2012a: 7). Some examples of cases that have been taken to a panel include neighbour disputes, criminal damage and assault. However, the operation of the panels varies according to the different locales in which they operate. Some panels will only hear cases involving adult (over the age of 18) victims and offenders, while panels in other areas will accept referrals for cases involving young people and children. In Kirklees, West Yorkshire, for example, the panel will only accept cases with adult victims and perpetrators and those which involve thefts (under £100); criminal damage (under £300); a number of public order offences; anti-social behaviour; and neighbour disputes. However, in Salford the NJP has dealt with a number of

124 *Neighbourhood justice panels*

cases involving young people and children as part of its restorative approach to youth justice. One case involved criminal damage: two 12 year-old boys had deliberately damaged the children's play area in their local park using a cigarette lighter, whilst they were playing truant from school. A local police community support officer (PCSO) witnessed the incident and they were apprehended. The case was referred to the NJP where it was agreed that the boys would undertake a tidy up in the park each Monday for the six-week summer holiday period. Both boys also agreed to undertake a session with the fire service and 'Prison! Me! No Way!' scheme. In another case involving adult victims and perpetrators, the NJP was used to resolve a long-standing neighbour dispute that had culminated in one neighbour assaulting the other. The two parties attended the panel and reached a resolution where they agreed not to shout abuse at each other and to stay away from one another. The panel in Trafford can also deal with low-level criminal offences that have already received (or will receive) a formal out-of-court disposal. In these types of cases, it is intended that the work of the Panel will complement the existing disposal by agreeing for additional reparative activity to be undertaken by the offender.

In Swindon, the Panel consists of 23 local volunteers and it meets weekly to hear cases of anti-social behaviour and low-level criminality. Of the 15 pilot sites operating with NJPs, the Panel in Swindon has heard over 60 per cent of cases across the total number of test areas. The Swindon NJP has been viewed as very successful by local residents and in the first 12 months since it began operating, there was a 36 per cent recorded fall in anti-social behaviour in the area. Although data is not yet able to evidence a clear correlation between a drop in disorder and the work of the Panel, there are many local positive reports about the NJP's work and there are now plans to extend the work of the NJP across Wiltshire. That NJPs appear to be quicker, cheaper and more effective ways of delivering summary justice for low level offences is at the core of their appeal for the Government, and in many ways for communities themselves. We can observe the way that, again, the issues highlighted at the start of this book interlock in the Government's developing approach to criminal justice and low-level offending in particular:

> Through our plans for re-conceiving summary justice...; strengthening the restorative element in sentencing; ensuring all community sentences contain a punitive element; and building on the strengths of restorative justice in communities through the development of Neighbourhood Justice Panels, we are at the start of a process of ensuring that justice is sure: that it has an impact on offenders and forces them to face up to their actions. Too often, the system reacts to the life experiences of offenders rather than shaping them. Sure justice requires that punishment becomes an immediate, not remote, concern for those who would commit crime.
>
> (Ministry of Justice 2012a: 35)

It is worth observing that empirical work on the operation of magistrates' courts during the English riots suggests that they appeared to some to be delivering closer to a form of 'conveyor belt' justice (Newburn 2012). Although the Ministry of Justice (2010a: 68) states that NJPs aim to 'bring the CJS [criminal justice system] closer to communities and increase transparency and visibility and in turn increase confidence', NJPs must nonetheless be careful that reduced delay does not impact negatively upon or indeed compromise principles of due process in the delivery of justice. Moreover, there has been no formal statistical evaluation of the impact on re-offending to date so any claims about recidivism are preliminary. The introduction of NJPs has in part occurred as a response to the closure of magistrates' courthouses. In this way, they may offer another opportunity or an alternative avenue for the delivery of local justice that is potentially cheaper; and potentially more effective, than the formal court system. However, their creation also undoubtedly provokes further issues around fairness in the delivery of justice.

Role of magistrates in NJPs

One of the most important and controversial aspects of the Government's plans to incorporate the use of restorative panels more widely into the justice process, which has been alluded to in brief terms in official policy documents, is that magistrates may be expected to be involved in the operation of NJPs. However, exactly what role they might play remains unclear. The Minister for Policing and Criminal Justice,[5] explained in the *Swift and Sure Justice* White Paper:

> The lay magistracy is one of the most important assets in our criminal justice system and we should greatly value their role. I want to give magistrates new roles and responsibilities, including to oversee the use of out-of-court disposals and support the new Neighbourhood Justice Panels. This enhanced role for magistrates will also help deliver sure justice as part of our ambition to create a system that grips offenders at an early stage.
>
> (Ministry of Justice 2012a: 3)

The Paper goes on to note that:

> Magistrates are the key link between the criminal justice system, and the communities it serves. We have used this review as an opportunity to investigate more fundamental reforms to the way in which magistrates deal with low-level offences in ways which apply a more local approach, are swifter, and involve less cost and bureaucracy ... By promoting the involvement of magistrates as members of the community we are looking both to benefit from their skills and experience and also to build a further bridge between local communities and the formal criminal justice system.
>
> (Ministry of Justice 2012a: 38–9)

This was then followed by a speech on *Reforming the Role of Magistrates*, given by the Minister for Policing and Criminal Justice on 14 August 2013, in which

126 *Neighbourhood justice panels*

he explained that the Government was currently 'exploring new roles for magistrates in cutting crime locally, for example by scrutinising the police's use of out of court disposals (such as cautions)', and in engaging with the local community through community justice oriented initiatives (Ministry of Justice 2013b). Whether the Government intends that magistrates are actually going to be directly involved in the operation of NJPs remains unclear and the Minister for Policing and Criminal Justice is currently seeking views from the magistracy on the development of their role as part of a national consultation process.

In the course of my research, it became apparent that the majority of magistrates have, at present, limited knowledge about the workings of the justice panels. This is in part a consequence of the lack of a standardised model for neighbourhood panels which operate differently across individual locales, and the fact that NJPs are a relatively recent innovation. However, there were also a significant number who articulated a range of concerns about the creation and development of the panels, and the role that magistrates may be expected to adopt to support their administration. There is also strong resistance from within the magistracy to changes in the judicial role which would require them to be involved in local justice panels. My previously published ESRC-funded research has highlighted some of the areas of contentiousness around the judicial role in magistrates' courts more generally, in the context of the recent emphasis upon community justice and problem-solving (Donoghue, 2012).

However, in the context of NJPs specifically, magistrates perceive a tension between processes of 'formal' and 'informal' summary justice. The formal rules and procedures of the magistrates' courts are identified by sentencers as important safeguards in the delivery of an equitable and procedurally fair system of justice and which are not, some believe, reflected in the work of the other informal modes of dispute resolution that are becoming more prevalent in the summary justice system. On this point, one magistrate reported to me that:

> the problem with the system of introducing local justice panels is that, on one hand, you have the magistrates' court system which is bound by the rules of the legal system, court procedure and what some magistrates see as the increasingly restrictive sentencing guidelines. On the other hand you have referral panels and local justice panels which because they are not part of the formal justice system, appear to operate outside any legal constraints and can impose whatever solution they want.

Similarly, the previous Lord Chief Justice recently argued that the arrangements by which neighbourhood justice panels are created, the ways in which they work, and their jurisdiction and powers need to be very carefully examined so as to ensure that they are either directly linked to the magistrates court system or directly linked to the police out of court disposal system, thus avoiding the possibility of three separate levels of summary justice (Judge, 2011). Moreover, magistrates observe that it is not unusual to see defendants in both the adult and

Neighbourhood justice panels   127

youth courts pleading guilty to crimes they 'clearly don't think they have committed in order to get a quick-fix solution that gets them out of the court as quickly as possible'. Another magistrate noted that:

Balancing the rights of the offender against the rights of their victims is a difficult task that has been carried out in the past by the judiciary acting within the constraints of the law and court procedure. We need to consider to what extent those same constraints exist for local justice boards and to what extent they could be invoked as a legal way for local communities to gang up on those that misbehave.

There was evidence of some frustration among magistrates between what they perceived as the appropriate and principled restrictions placed upon the operation of magistrates' courts, and the more 'ad hoc', 'unconventional' and pragmatic way that referral and local justice panels operate. One magistrate used the following example to illustrate their concerns in this regard:

This is exemplified by a case that I met in the youth court the other day. He was a bit of a local tearaway that had finally run out of cautions and final warnings and had appeared in court for his first offence/conviction. The bench, as the defence solicitors love to point out to us these days, was legally obliged to impose a referral order and send him to the first group of 'local, trained volunteers' for them to impose a suitable solution to his behaviour. The trouble was that whilst the bench was trying to sort out a suitable date for his first appointment, we discovered that he already had an extensive career of nuisance behaviour on the estate on which he lived. The problem with fixing a time/date for his appointment was that whatever local justice system was working in the area had already imposed a 12 hour curfew on him that was being controlled and monitored by a local PCSO [police community support officer]. A restriction on somebody's liberty is a pretty serious matter in the magistrates' court and we cannot impose it without pre-sentence reports etc. and there is a limit to the length of time for which it can be imposed. Not so on the estate in [information removed] where whole groups of young people had been more or less permanently denied the right to go outdoors after 6.00 pm.

This is a good example of where some of the tensions lie in creating separate tiers or forums for the delivery of summary justice, and how they reconcile, or are perhaps failing to reconcile, in practice. It raises the issue of how diversionary approaches function at different levels and in different forums of summary justice and in what circumstances diversion from the judicial system is appropriate. As the example demonstrates, while justice panels operate as a form of diversion from the formal court process, thereby preventing offenders from receiving a criminal record for what are often minor criminal offences, the use of such diversionary measures may mean that an individual could subsequently

128 *Neighbourhood justice panels*

appear in the magistrates' court having good character (no criminal record) when they have been repeatedly engaging in criminal or sub-criminal behaviour in their community for months or potentially years. Diversion will not always be appropriate and greater discussion needs to be had about the circumstances where, even though the offences are technically minor in nature, the use of informal resolution panels is not appropriate. This is an issue that has received particular attention in the context of the use of out of court disposals such as fixed penalty notices (FPNs) where it has been argued that the increased use of this disposal is undermining the court of first response, and is also inappropriate as a sanction for certain criminal offences. Much of the government's emphasis on the creation of NJPs has been as a way of tackling anti-social behaviour (ASB) more efficiently and effectively. Many cases of ASB concern repeated acts of nuisance behaviour (often coupled with aggressive attitudes towards neighbours) over a prolonged period of time, and which are often perpetrated by a small number of individuals in neighbourhoods. To what extent NJPs are the appropriate forum for dealing effectively with the effects of this type of cumulative criminal or sub-criminal behaviour is similarly a matter of contention amongst magistrates.

Moreover, in the context of the creation of NJPs, magistrates often referred to the responsibility carried by magistrates' courts in the preservation and protection of the rights of the individuals that appear before them; particularly with regard to the court's duties towards young people and children under the Children and Young Persons Act 2008. It will be important to ensure that locally developed and administered justice panels maintain similar protections for the rights of those (both adult and youth) who are brought before them in order that they are seen to be accountable and transparent in their approach to cases. The magistrate in the above example, for instance, said that they felt that:

> the parents of young people may well put their children at risk of not getting the help and support they really need in their desperation to avoid their children getting a criminal record or in their desperation to appease the neighbours that they have to live with.

Thus, greater thought needs to be given to the reconciliation of the creation of justice panels as an adjunct to the existing court system.

Although magistrates have raised a number of important concerns about the introduction of NJPs, others have also given thought to what their role in the panels could potentially consist of. This could mean for example, possibly chairing the meetings. One magistrate mentioned that they were

> convinced that ... it would be of an advantage to have a mixture of JPs and lay persons on the panels. You only have to look at any newspaper or listen to friends' conversations, to realise that the general public have very little understanding of the process of law.

Magistrate involvement in the work of the panels is viewed by some sentencers as potentially facilitating an important oversight function to ensure that:

- The process is fair to both the victim and offender.
- The rights of the offenders are properly protected;
- The solutions are fair and proportionate;
- Local residents don't use the system to 'harangue or humiliate offenders' or turn it into 'something of a kangaroo court';
- Correct decisions are made about whether the offender should be put into the court system (in the same way that the magistrates' court commits to the Crown Court) rather than dealt with outside of it.

The possibility of magistrates' providing an oversight and accountability mechanism in the operation of NJPs, in a similar way to how they may provide retrospective scrutiny for out of court disposals, appears to be the most likely involvement that they will undertake. NJPs are an important criminal justice innovation with a realistic prospect of reducing resource demands on the police as well as potentially reducing recidivism, particularly for low-level offenders. However, in planning for their wider implementation across the country, it will be important to consider and pay attention to the following issues: levels of community participation and how this is reflected in different diverse communities in both urban and rural areas; the extent of police and other agency 'buy in' to the process; and to what extent provision is made for accountability and transparency mechanisms (judicial or otherwise). It may be worth thinking about expanding the remit of panels to include referrals from the court which may further reduce the pressures on the limited resources of the criminal justice system and result in a more balanced approach to offenders and victims.

Pre-sentencing restorative justice

As part of the government's criminal justice reforms, the courts have been conferred new powers to defer sentencing to enable processes of restorative justice (RJ) to be undertaken. Part two of the Crime and Courts Act, which received Royal Assent on 25 April 2013, creates a statutory framework for RJ in the courts in England and Wales. The new legislative provisions allow the courts to defer at the pre-sentence stage in order for the victim and offender to be offered RJ at the earliest opportunity. The legislation sets out the detailed provisions as amendments to the Powers of Criminal Courts (Sentencing) Act 2000 as follows:

Part 2 Deferring the passing of sentence to allow for restorative justice
5   After section 1 of the Powers of Criminal Courts (Sentencing) Act 2000 (court's power to defer passing of sentence) insert—
'1ZA Undertakings to participate in restorative justice activities
(1) Without prejudice to the generality of paragraph (b) of section 1(3),

130 *Neighbourhood justice panels*

the requirements that may be imposed under that paragraph include restorative justice requirements.

(2) Any reference in this section to a restorative justice requirement is to a requirement to participate in an activity—

(a) where the participants consist of, or include, the offender and one or more of the victims,

(b) which aims to maximise the offender's awareness of the impact of the offending concerned on the victims, and

(c) which gives an opportunity to a victim or victims to talk about, or by other means express experience of, the offending and its impact.

(3) Imposition under section 1(3)(b) of a restorative justice requirement requires, in addition to the offender's consent and undertaking under section 1(3), the consent of every other person who would be a participant in the activity concerned.

(4) For the purposes of subsection (3), a supervisor appointed under section 1A(2) does not count as a proposed participant.

(5) Where a restorative justice requirement is imposed under section 1(3)(b), the duty under section 1(5) (to give copies of order) extends to every person who would be a participant in the activity concerned.

(6) In a case where there is such a restorative justice requirement, a person running the activity concerned must in doing that have regard to any guidance that is issued, with a view to encouraging good practice in connection with such an activity, by the Secretary of State.

(7) In this section "victim" means a victim of, or other person affected by, the offending concerned.'

Proponents have argued that these provisions are the most significant development for restorative justice in England and Wales since legislation introducing referral order panels to the youth justice system in 1999 (RJC 2013). Yet there has been a mixed reaction to these reforms from sentencers. Some magistrates view the provisions as usefully providing magistrates with an alternative sentencing option that may hold some promise in reducing the impact of crime. Yet there is a range of clearly problematic issues associated with Schedule 2 implementation, which it appears, have been paid little attention by government and policymakers to date. In particular, issues around cost and training seem likely to have a significant impact on the extent to which this alternative sentencing option is used. Some magistrates were concerned at the extra work that pre-sentencing RJ might require of magistrates in overseeing these decisions, pointing out that 'this may not be acceptable to the HMCTS under the present financial restraints'. Another magistrate in the West Midlands argued that:

the overriding principle should be around justice and not cost. That must be drummed into all parties involved in the process and the victim should be of

Neighbourhood justice panels   131

paramount importance – I am not 100 per cent convinced that element comes across in the schedule. Training would be beneficial for all magistrates to ensure consistency of deployment.

There has to date been no training or guidance issued to magistrates about this element of the Act, and many magistrates have stated that they feel that this will fundamentally impact upon the extent to which the provisions are used in court. Without adequate training, magistrates do not feel comfortable in using the new provisions, and they have expressed their confusion at the way the sentencing option would work in practice. A magistrate in the South West described their concerns to me as follows:

> The question here is whether the participation in the restorative justice would mean that the offender is spared the punishment. If not, then it would mean delaying the inevitable and bringing the offender back for another court appearance. If so, where would the decision be made to revoke the punishment? Will the offender return to court with a recommendation from the local justice panel; would the decision be made by the probation service or would it be made by the bench? If the last, once again this means another unnecessary return appearance in court.... The alarming aspect of this approach is to say that the court would be obliged to undertake restorative justice before deciding what level of sentence to apply and that the outcome of that restorative justice would have an impact on the level of that sentence.
>
> The practical implications are enormous. Someone held on conditional bail before the trial not to contact the victim, once convicted would be released on bail (conditional or unconditional?) to go and meet the victim to discuss the impact of the offence and the punishment imposed may or may not depend on how the meeting goes. The bench would be obliged by this legislation to remove the protection to the victim provided by the bail conditions.
>
> If someone is on remand before a trial because they may not appear because of the likely outcome of the case or to protect the victims, would have to be granted bail on conviction so that RJ could take place.
>
> In simple terms, the terms [of the Schedule] would have a fairly large impact on the work of the court and none of it would be good – just adding unnecessary complication to a system that works at the moment.

Other magistrates felt that deferring sentence was not useful, especially when magistrates could easily make an RJ element within a community order, a process which one magistrate observed that their bench in the South East had been undertaking 'for many years'. While magistrates displayed a range of opinions about the new provisions, what became very clearly apparent was that, without the provision of training and guidance (both to bring magistrates' attention to its introduction as well as to help provide information about how it will

132 *Neighbourhood justice panels*

work in practice), pre-sentencing RJ will not occur. It would be a great shame if this reform failed to get off the ground especially because evidence suggests that pre-sentence RJ can be a more effective route to dealing with offenders, diverting them away from the formal court process. It provides the judiciary with better information to inform sentencing and can be introduced without causing delay in court proceedings. However, the very limited amount of money that is currently available to fund magistrates' training, as well as the centralised nature of the courts' administration, means that without serious effort made to prioritise training and guidance, pre-sentencing RJ will likely be limited to those courts (and those magistrates) who take a special and pro-active interest in restorative practices. Clamp and Paterson (2011) argue that one of the main reasons for the lack of development in RJ in England relative to other jurisdictions across Europe is the continuing overriding influence of punitive mentalities towards those who offend in England. Lately, however, there appears to be increasing support for the introduction of NJPs: some of this support may appear to be based more on economic pragmatism than on an ideologically driven desire to reduce the 'punitive' capacity of the conventional system, and it may also be understood as a response to local courthouse closures and community demands for the re-establishment of 'local justice'. Either way, a new space has opened up wherein there is a genuine opportunity to drive restorative community-based innovations such as NJPs forward in England and Wales. On the other hand, other initiatives such as pre-sentence RJ, which require both judicial commitment and additional training, appear less likely to have any significant impact in the near future.

Notes

1 Although recent research has identified some significant tensions between the aspirations of restorative justice and the reality of current practice in the English system (Newbury 2011).
2 In September 2013, the Justice Secretary Chris Grayling, announced reforms that will remove the availability of cautions being issued for serious offences such as rape, manslaughter and robbery.
3 An important and interesting issue that has been highlighted in my research is that a number of magistrates have reported that they have observed circumstances where a pattern of relatively minor offences – most often shoplifting – are only being tried in court when the defendant requires an interpreter. This is because clearly if a suspect cannot speak English, it is not possible for a police officer to deal with a matter on the spot. Magistrates have expressed concern that this may indicate that police cautions are often only being made available to those who speak English. If so, they suggest that this would potentially raise issues of racial discrimination.
4 The fifteen areas in which NJPs are currently being trialled are in Barnsley (South Yorkshire), Broadland (Norfolk), Halton (Cheshire), Islington (London), Kirklees (West Yorkshire), Lambeth (London), Manchester, North Wales, Salford (Greater Manchester), Staffordshire, Stockport (Greater Manchester), Swindon (Wiltshire), Trafford (Greater Manchester), Wakefield (West Yorkshire) and Wigan (Greater Manchester).
5 Nick Herbert served as Minister for Policing and Criminal Justice from May 2010. On 4 September 2012 he was replaced by Damian Green.

7 Problem-solving and court specialisation

Prospects and pitfalls

Practices that might loosely or informally be characterised as 'problem-solving' in nature have been evident in the work of magistrates in England and Wales for many years, for example in the exercise of their discretion, the speeches that they give on sentencing and the way that they engage with offenders in the lower court system. However, as many magistrates have observed, the notion of problem-solving has come to feature much more prominently in the business of the courts in recent years. Attempts have been made to formalise and extend existing practices, to situate them with specialist courts and to prioritise community engagement by firmly placing magistrates at the 'centre of their communities' (Ministry of Justice 2013b). In this regard, we have observed the way that the judicial role is altered in problem-solving courts. In the traditional role, judicial decision-making is grounded in adherence to precedent and the court's historical development of fact, while the 'transformed' or 'enhanced' judicial function in problem-solving courts is intended to reorient the judicial role (Miller 2009). Judges subsequently participate in more subjective processes of evaluating and monitoring offenders; they function as a member of the problem-solving court 'team' through collaborative meetings and discussions with other agencies; and they are expected to try to establish more meaningful interactions with offenders, as well as participating in processes which will enhance community engagement with the courts.

One of the most fundamental problems associated with the development of problem-solving justice has been the potential impact of the enhanced judicial role upon judicial independence. Judicial independence is a fundamental tenet of the rule of law as part of the system of accountability that ensures that no branch of government dominates, and independence as a separate branch of government is essential if courts are to discharge their responsibility impartially. Consequently, achieving an optimal balance between judicial independence and accountability and thus ensuring that judges are autonomous when interpreting and applying the law but also that judges are not so detached as to undermine public confidence in the courts, has been a perennial policy struggle (Department for Constitutional Affairs 2005a, 2005b; Cabinet Office 2009). The enhanced judicial role in problem-solving courts requires both increased and less formal levels of interaction between judges and offenders, as well as judicial collaboration with other

134 *Problem-solving and court specialisation*

government agencies and the broader community, all of which have the potential to impact upon judicial independence. That judges should apply the law impartially to all is at the forefront of these concerns. As one magistrate pointed out to me: 'The oath makes it quite clear … "to do right to all manner of people … according to the laws and usages of the realm". I think that phrase defines accurately the role and function of the judiciary'. However, *it is* possible to remain devoted to the principles of unbiased, detached adjudication conducted by third party neutrals while at the same time valuing decision-makers who understand community issues and who are engaged in substantive processes of 'truth seeking' through engagement with local communities. Community engagement need not undermine judicial independence and indeed, it should be seen as a fundamental aspect of magistrates' competences, in their role as representatives of the communities that they serve. Being clear about what community engagement can and cannot achieve, as well as setting clear boundaries about the purpose(s) of engagement activities is important in managing resident expectations and guarding against judicial conflicts of interest however.

While problem-solving courts have proliferated over the last two decades, advocates have pressed further for broader acceptance and integration of problem-solving justice in criminal case processing (Becker and Corrigan 2003). Although court specialisation in England and Wales began under New Labour and was then further developed throughout the Labour administration's terms in office, the coalition Government has since committed to embedding a problem-solving approach in the magistrates' courts while emphasising the value and importance of enhanced community engagement with the courts as a vehicle to facilitate problem-solving objectives. Similarly, the Magistrates' Association has identified the development of a mainstreamed problem-solving approach as a strategic priority for the lower courts. The creation of specialist courts and a streamlined problem-solving approach in magistrates' courts can be understood as a response to a range of institutional gaps in the adequate provision of welfare services that have been partly responsible for the 'revolving door' phenomena of the presence of repeat offenders in the lower courts. Court specialisation and problem-solving justice hold promise as (initially) short/medium term initiatives to harness social cohesion and community resilience by more effectively responding to local dimensions of crime and disorder.

Consequently, over the last 15 years, a range of problem-solving court types have been introduced: drug courts, domestic violence courts, community courts and mental health courts. Yet as we have seen, although demonstrating potential, these efforts have not been wholly successful. Each has associated challenges. One of the central criticisms that has been made of drug courts in England is that intermediate sanctions are not available to sentencers in the same way that they are commonly deployed in other jurisdictions. As a consequence, this has largely circumscribed the effectiveness of English drug courts, because instead they operate more to facilitate the existence of what approximates an extended probation order. It is likely that a combination of sanctions and rewards are more likely to influence behaviour than an approach which relies only on the

Problem-solving and court specialisation   135

revocation of a community sentence and termination of treatment programmes as a type of 'all or nothing' approach. Intermediate sanctions could potentially be introduced by extending existing legislative proposals which introduce short penalties for supervision orders. Moreover, drug courts in England and Wales do not oversee prolific offenders. This undoubtedly has implications for selectivity in sentencing, as well as more fundamental concerns about the provision and allocation of treatment. Domestic violence courts in England have failed to demonstrate measurable impacts in re-offending, although new locally conceived and locally driven innovations continue to emerge and there is also developing interest in the creation of Family Drug and Alcohol Courts. However, SDVCs are not really problem-solving courts. They cannot be said to operate as true problem-solving courts since they lack some of the distinctive features of the problem-solving approach, most notably, sentencer continuity.

One of the main problems identified with the development of community courts and justice centres has been that they have been implemented centrally and, in the case of North Liverpool, as a stand alone pilot example of a community justice centre. In conversations that I have had with practitioners, the LCJC has sadly been described by some as 'a spectacular failure'. Yet the failure is most perceptibly a consequence of its inability to ameliorate practice and generate data quickly enough to ensure its continued survival. Given the problems associated with its evaluation as well as some of the difficulties associated with the implementation of community engagement into the Centre's processes, the forthcoming study of the Plymouth community justice centre will be very important. This will hopefully be able to provide specific information on 'best practice' to inform the development of community justice centres and courts. Finally, the roll out of a national programme of mental health courts, while largely supported by magistrates and criminal justice professionals, is circumscribed by a number of political and economic dimensions, including limited resources and lack of empirical evidence to support going to scale.

While financial cutbacks to criminal justice and court budgets have reduced the ambit of local justice through the closure of magistrates' courts, there have also been innovative responses from local communities. Somewhat ironically, the introduction of NJPs has in part occurred as a response to the closure of magistrates' courthouses, and in this way, they may offer another opportunity or an alternative avenue for the delivery of local justice which is potentially cheaper – and potentially more effective, than the formal court system. The possibility of magistrates providing an oversight and accountability mechanism in the operation of NJPs, in a similar way to how they may provide retrospective scrutiny for out of court disposals, appears to be the most likely involvement that they will undertake in these new forums. NJPs are an important new criminal justice innovation with a realistic prospect of reducing resource demands on the police as well as potentially reducing recidivism, particularly for low-level offenders. However, some thought must be given to how they are conceptualised within the existing system of summary justice. Much less likely to materialise, is the wholesale introduction of pre-sentence RJ. This is not particularly a consequence of a

136 *Problem-solving and court specialisation*

lack of support for RJ, although some magistrates are indeed sceptical, it is an issue of training. Without the provision of training and guidance (both to bring magistrates' attention to its introduction as well as to help provide information about how it will work in practice), pre-sentencing RJ will not occur. The very limited amount of money that is currently available to fund magistrates' training, as well as the centralised nature of the courts' administration, means that without serious effort made to prioritise training and guidance, pre-sentencing RJ will likely be limited to those courts (and those magistrates) who take a special and pro-active interest in restorative practices.

Mainstreaming problem-solving justice

In the course of this book I have sought to illustrate some of the main over-arching barriers and challenges that presently exist to the realisation of problem-solving objectives and these are worthy of some further elaboration here. Magistrates' courts in England and Wales, as currently constituted, are ill equipped to achieve problem-solving objectives/goals; not because magistrates lack competence but because problem-solving has been introduced centrally, resulting in the expansion of magistrates' responsibilities in the absence of the necessary training for the bench and other members of the court team. Government policy documents and guidance have previously referred to magistrates' 'training' in a rather simplistic and tokenistic way and without any detail of what this training should entail and how it should be undertaken (Department for Constitutional Affairs 2005a, 2005b; Cabinet Office 2009). Moreover, despite the existence of a significant body of legal scholarship which illustrates the difficulties of trying to inculcate 'the community' into judicial processes (Fagan and Malkin 2003; Carr *et al.* 2007), Government has provided little direction on how 'community engagement' in problem-solving processes should take place or, more broadly, be conceptualised within the existing framework of criminal court adjudication. Problem-solving courts are useful to politicians because they allow them to pass responsibility for law enforcement to the courts but if problem-solving justice is to achieve their stated objectives of reducing re-offending, enhancing social/community cohesion and enhancing the legitimacy of the lower courts, then politicians must go beyond simply introducing specialisations or legislating new powers; they must actively determine how the new competences that they are asking magistrates to develop are to be inculcated in order for sentencers to exercise these powers effectively.

At present, there is no formal system in place to ensure that an offender appears before the same judge for every court hearing related to their case. That there is so little continuity of judges means that the bench may not necessarily be aware of the complexities of a case and will not likely be able to develop any meaningful working relationship with those individuals involved, including victims and witnesses who are also a key part of the problem-solving approach. A formal system of court procedure should be implemented that allows judges to reserve or be automatically given cases which they have previously heard, in order to create consistency in the relationship between the judge and offender. It is an important and necessary change that, if undertaken consistently in the lower court system in England and Wales, would provide one route to more systematically embedding problem-solving justice. While such a change is not comparable in scale to the introduction of a network of community courts (as originally proposed by the previous Labour government), it is clear that current economic constraints mean that policymakers must consider how they can begin to achieve 'more, with less' resources. Substantive changes in court procedures are one way to help try to secure the longevity and sustainability of problem-solving justice in the current climate of fiscal austerity. Cost and efficiency are big problems for the courts however. Penny Derbyshire, in her comprehensive study of the courts in England and Wales (2011: 446), has reported on the 'chaotic' management of cases in the lower courts as a result of understaffing and the failure to establish satisfactory IT systems. She has also observed the severely underfunded nature of the agencies serving the courts that resulted in poor or inadequate case preparation or presentation, delays, adjournments and a cumulative waste of resources. Indeed, problems of cost and efficiency percolate through the entire court system in England and Wales.[1] And while problem-solving has been raised in government policy documents, as well as in publications of the Magistrates' Association, again there is yet to be collective agreement (among policymakers and the professionals who work within the criminal justice system) on a common approach to take forward. This again highlights the difficulty in attempting to progress a problem-solving approach in England and Wales, when some of the most fundamental aspects of the model are still being debated by the Government, courts and practitioners.

Government emphasis on 'mainstreaming' problem-solving in the magistrates courts, as opposed to necessarily creating new specialised judicial forums, can in part be understood as a response to the current financial climate in which reduced and limited budgets are available to finance what are perceived to be resource-intensive projects such as specialist courts. However, it is not the case that problem-solving courts are no longer being created. For example, we have seen the creation of a new Family Drug and Alcohol Court in Gloucestershire in August 2012 following the documented success of the Family Drug and Alcohol Court in London (see Harwin *et al.* 2011). 'Mainstreaming' problem-solving is more appealing to the Government because it aims to achieve similar outcomes/ objectives as specialist courts but ostensibly appears not to require the same investment of resources. As a result, the requirement for empirical justification of effectiveness in *existing* problem-solving courts in England and Wales becomes even more salient if specialised court forums are to be able to survive and attract continued investment and support from Government. Problem-solving courts that are unable to provide data evidencing that they are cost-effective and, most importantly in the political context, that they are impacting upon re-offending rates, will be less likely to receive continued investment and support from government, especially when mainstreaming problem-solving in the magistrates' courts is an overarching policy objective.

138 *Problem-solving and court specialisation*

Yet effective 'streamlining' of problem-solving justice in all magistrates' courts requires significant investment of resources to achieve successful outcomes. For community engagement to take place, there needs to be investments in communication arrangements by the local court and police and the community requires representative structures to facilitate effective communication. Instead, the onus is largely being placed upon magistrates to ameliorate problem-solving processes and facilitate effective engagement with local neighbourhoods. This is, in effect, setting the magistracy up for failure. Without broader recognition of the challenges that problem-solving processes face in their attempts to re-legitimate legal institutions at the local level and, without a commitment to clearly defined expectations for community engagement combined with appropriate investment of resources, judicial training and support; attempts to mainstream a problem-solving approach in magistrates' courts will find it hard to generate successful outcomes.

Encouragingly, magistrates report that different manifestations of what they identify as 'problem-solving practices' are being used far more than they were ten years ago but they observe that these types of innovative practices are limited by the resources of probation and other agencies, as well as the significant cost implications. Clearly what is viewed as 'problem-solving' is widely interpreted by magistrates, and operates largely ad hoc.[2] Unfortunately, magistrates also report that there is evidence that 'even openly successful problem-solving courts are being shut or curtailed, without any consultation, and mostly due to cost, not effectiveness'. In addition, a significant barrier to local courts developing their own practices and rules has been the broader issue of court centralisation, which has made it much more difficult for magistrates to introduce effective practices into their own courts. In order for local courts to administer problem-solving justice effectively, magistrates must be empowered to introduce innovative new practices into their own courts: this has been virtually impossible for magistrates to undertake since the courts have been nationally administered following the implementation of the Courts Act 2003. There is therefore a clear incongruity between the localism emphasis placed on the development of problem-solving justice in all magistrates' courts – which relies upon the local delivery of solutions to neighbourhood crime problems – and the national administration of magistrates' courts which creates fundamental barriers to the delivery of 'local' court justice.

Other scholars have identified the important characteristics of individual judges that are essential to the success of problem-solving justice (Chase and Hora 2000; Freiberg 2003). It follows that the judiciary must be supportive of a problem-solving approach; motivated; and properly trained (McIvor 2009). Consequently, the level of engagement with problem-solving justice in the courts in England and Wales is largely contingent upon the attitudes and willingness of individual judges. Given the reluctance and scepticism of many lower court judges who hear the vast majority of criminal cases in England and Wales, opportunities for the substantive and sustainable development of problem-solving justice are heavily constrained unless there is a change in thinking by judicial officers together with a concomitant

Problem-solving and court specialisation 139

acceptance that the traditional role of judicial officers is evolving to meet the needs of the communities they serve. Problem-solving courts possess a strong comparative advantage in procedural justice over large, fractured and impersonal centralised courts (Berman and Fox 2010). In addition, community engagement in solving local problems of crime and disorder is an 'engine for legitimacy' (Fagin and Malkin, 2003: 950) which is 'central to the concept of leveraging felt justice into social control, and to engaging citizens in partnership with police to enforce social norms and laws' (Fagin and Malkin, 2003: 951). The Government aspires to imbricate these aspects of problem-solving courts through mainstreaming problem solving justice in the magistrates' courts. Existing research illustrates the challenges that problem-solving courts face in their attempts to create unique institutions to re-legitimate legal institutions at the local level. Therefore, the expectations for problem-solving justice in the magistrates' courts need to be made clear in order to assess how far they are realised by the courts. Consequently, attempts to successfully embed problem-solving justice in the magistrates' courts in England and Wales will not be realised until the Government actively determines how the new competences it is asking magistrates to develop are to be inculcated and until much more significant efforts are made to conceptualise problem-solving justice as part of the existing framework of criminal court adjudication.

James Nolan (2009: 49) has observed that: 'adjusting drug courts to a British context has necessarily involved suiting the program to fit a system in which the lay magistracy is a central and defining feature'. At the time of Nolan's writing, there were more than 30 000 lay magistrates in England and Wales. Following court closures, budget cutbacks and difficulties in recruitment, this number has now fallen significantly to 23 500 lay magistrates. With the increasing professionalisation of the magistracy and debates about their continued existence within the summary justice system in England and Wales, this could have profound effects for the way that problem-solving justice may be inculcated in the magistrates' court process. Another important aspect of Nolan's (and others, see for example Bean 2004) analysis of drug courts in England and Wales has been the 'strength of Probation', which is identified as playing a very prominent role in the development and operation of drug courts (2009: 50). However, it is likely that the strength and power of Probation will be significantly impacted upon in light of recent reforms that many see as essentially the 'privatisation' of the Probation service in England and Wales. The Probation service, traditionally a locally based servant of the court, is being divided into 21 package areas, in order to suit the needs of 'prime providers'. Many probation practitioners have described this as the 'death of probation'. Moreover, the government's adoption of the PbR model appears likely to undermine opportunities for the delivery of local justice, particularly by restricting the ability of decision-makers in local areas to determine how money is best spent and failing to include a range of local providers in consultation and decision-making as to the purposes and services delivered by new providers locally.

The most important factors now limiting problem-solving justice relate to cost (especially in a climate of austerity); and the role of the lay magistracy.

140 *Problem-solving and court specialisation*

At the annual Hamlyn lecture, held at the University of Leeds in November 2012, Labour MP and former Home Secretary under Tony Blair, The Right Honourable Jack Straw spoke about the future of the criminal courts in England and Wales following Auld's *Review of the Criminal Courts of England and Wales*. He identified two principle barriers to the prospects for problem-solving courts and the inculcation of community justice principles into the lower courts system in England and Wales: cost and a lack of judicial continuity in the management of offenders. He argued that case listing in the magistrates' courts is a 'major problem' that may only be solved by 'root and branch changes' to the lay magistracy and magistrates' courts. He added that although he was one of the ministers under the Labour government who had attempted to introduce problem-solving courts to the criminal justice system in England and Wales, he also felt that 'there are things you can do as an MP, and things you cannot' and commented that he had felt that for problem-solving to be successful, it would have required changes to the magistracy which would have been very unpopular with lay magistrates. In the current climate, with the continued existence of a lay magistracy potentially in doubt, and the Government undertaking a consultation on proposals to reform the role of magistrates, now is the time to reaffirm a commitment to the central role that lay justice occupies within our legal system; but also to reconsider how magistrates' justice can be better adapted to facilitate a problem-solving approach, and how government can more fully discharge *its* responsibilities in providing the necessary conditions for this to take place.

In England and Wales, the relatively limited scrutiny that problem-solving and court specialisation has so far received is because problem-solving justice is an emerging phenomenon, that has largely been undertaken in a piecemeal, ad hoc fashion but in a way which, arguably, follows a similar arc to US court specialisation (Berman and Fox 2010). In fact it would be a fair reflection to say that the criteria for the adoption of genuine and substantive problem-solving justice has to date not been met: the characteristics required in order to satisfy a problem-solving approach are *not yet in existence* in England and Wales. From a conceptual perspective, scant attention has been paid to theorising problem-solving court praxis. There is currently no organised understanding or model of how problem-solving courts/justice do or do not influence defendants, and specific models of how the courts influence offenders are not well defined (Weiner *et al.* 2010). The lack of robust data collection on the impact and effectiveness of existing problem-solving courts (particularly on recidivism rates and rehabilitation) is also a significant limitation. Yet we have seen that serious efforts are now underway to redress this balance. Problem-solving advocates have recognised that if problem-solving justice is to be implemented, it must be an empirically validated framework for praxis rather than simply an aspirational idea.

As I have identified, a number of legal scholars have argued that the application of therapeutic or problem-solving principles is, in essence, designed to correct the flaws/failures of social service systems (Meekins 2006). Yet while I accept this dimension of the argument on problem-solving justice, it is not the whole story.

Problem-solving and court specialisation   141

Problem-solving courts set out to mitigate the penal consequences of arrest and prosecution, and undoubtedly they do offer access to scarce resources, including medical and social services. Eric Miller, in his foreword to this text, has thus described the 'courtification' of social service provision, whereby the criminal justice system becomes an important gateway for accessing services and treatment that are otherwise difficult to obtain. Moreover, the evolution of the criminal court system has occurred in response to public and professional dissatisfaction with the legal process, particularly with regard to the perceived failure of traditional magistrates' courts to deal effectively with offenders by responding to the underlying causes of criminal behaviour; and to impact upon recidivism levels and the 'revolving door' phenomenon of repeat offenders. However, rather than viewing developments in problem-solving justice as a response to the dwindling influence of traditional social institutions or the failure of court systems or welfare agencies, problem-solving courts ought to be seen as 'windows of opportunity' to attempt to transform the lives of those who enter the court system. Empirical research from the US and Australia is increasingly being able to evidence that, given the right conditions, problem-solving courts are able to impact upon recidivism levels as well as making efficiency savings. While the precise combination of which features deliver what type of 'success' requires further empirical study, the findings from existing studies are encouraging. One of the main objectives of this book was also to consider whether a problem-solving approach might transform the way we think about punishment, the role of the courts and criminal justice itself. My position is that problem-solving justice should, without question, be seen as transformative. In both the US and the UK, problem-solving justice represents a subversive counter-trend that stands in opposition to existing narratives on punitivism. Above all, however, problem-solving justice is transformative in the sense that it aims to recalibrate the substantive nature of punishment to make it more socially meaningful; to provide those historically marginalised defendants with greater voice in the justice process; and to reclaim justice as a fundamental element of *local neighbourhoods* rather than central government.

Notes

1 For example, in the Family Courts, the *Family Justice Review*, Interim Report (2011b) noted that:

> the lack of IT and management information is astonishing, with the result – among other things – that little is known about performance and what things cost. The system, in short, is not a system.... There is an almost unbelievable lack of management information at a system-wide level, with little data on performance, flows, costs or efficiency available to support the operation of the system ... These are the symptoms of a situation that simply cannot be allowed to continue.
>
> (p. 3: paras 13–14)

2 One magistrate for example, noted a potential problem-solving style being adopted in case management hearings where magistrates' Chairmen are beginning to 'mediate' between and challenge solicitors' requests regarding the number of witnesses, the need for police officers to attend and the need for a full record of taped interview for example.

References

Adler, M. (2003) 'A Socio-Legal Approach to Administrative Justice', *Law and Policy*, 25 (4): 323–52.

Aizer, A. (2008) 'Neighborhood Violence and Urban Youth: Working Paper' no. 13773 (Cambridge, MA: National Bureau of Economic Research). Available at: http://nber.org/papers/w13773.pdf

Aldrich, L. and H. Kluger (2010) 'New York's One Judge-One Family Response to Family Violence', *Juvenile and Family Court Journal*, 61 (4): 77–86.

Ali, S., W.E. Davis and J. Lee (2011) 'Multi-Stakeholder Dispute Resolution: Building Social Capital Through Access to Justice at the Community Level' *Pepperdine Dispute Resolution Law Journal*, 11.

Allen, A. (2002) 'Power, Subjectivity and Agency: Between Arendt and Foucault', *International Journal of Philosophical Studies*, 10: 131.

Allen, F. (1981) *The Decline of the Rehabilitative Ideal: Penal Policy and Social Purpose*, New Haven: Yale University Press.

Almquist, L. and E. Dodd (2009) *Mental Health Courts: A Guide to Research Informed Policy and Practice*, New York: Council of State Governments Justice Center New York.

American Bar Association Coalition for Justice (ABACJ) (2008) 'Road Map to Problem-solving Courts', American Bar Association Coalition for Justice.

Ames, A., R. Szyndler, K. Burston, R. Phillips, J. Keith, R. Gaunt, S. Davies and C. Mottman (2011) *The Strengths and Skills of the Judiciary in the Magistrates' Courts*, London: Ipsos Mori.

Anleu, S.R. and K. Mack (2005) 'Magistrates' Everyday Work and Emotional Labour', *Journal of Law and Society*, 32: 590.

Anleu, S.R. and K. Mack (2007) 'Magistrates, Magistrates Courts, and Social Change', *Law and Policy*, 29 (2): 183–209.

Ard, K.L. and H.J. Makadon (2011) 'Addressing Intimate Partner Violence in Lesbian, Gay, Bisexual, and Transgender Patients', *Journal of General Internal Medicine* August 2011, 26 (8): 930–3.

Arrigo, B.A. (2004) 'The Ethics of Therapeutic Jurisprudence: A Critical and Theoretical Enquiry of Law, Psychology and Crime', *Psychiatry, Psychology and Law*, 11: 23, 37.

Ashworth, A. (1994) 'Justifying the grounds of mitigation', *Criminal Justice Ethics*, 13 (1): 5–10.

Ashworth, A. (2004a) 'Criminal Justice Reform: Principles, Human Rights and Public Protection', *Criminal Law Review*, 516.

Ashworth, A. (2004b) 'General Principles of Criminal Law' in D. J. Feldman (ed.), *English Public Law*, Oxford: Oxford University Press.

References   143

Ashworth, A. (2010) *Sentencing and Criminal Justice*, Cambridge: Cambridge University Press.

Ashworth, A. (2013) Annual Roger Hood Lecture, 'Why Sentencing Matters'. University of Oxford, 23 May 2013.

Ashworth, A. and M. Redmayne (2005) *The Criminal Process*, Oxford: Oxford University Press.

Aspen, M.E. (1993) 'The Search for Renewed Civility in Litigation', *Valparaiso University Law Review*, 28: 513.

Auburn, T., G. Hanley Santos, J. Annison and D. Gilling (2013) 'Problem Solving and Its Role in a Community Justice Court', SLSA Annual Conference, University of York 26–28 March, 2013.

Australian Productivity Commission, Steering Committee for the Review of Government Service Provision (SCRGSP) (2012), *Report on Government Services 2012*.

Baldwin, J. (1997) *Small Claims in the County Courts in England and Wales: The Bargain Basement of Civil Justice*, Oxford: Clarendon Press.

Baldwin, J. and M. McConville *Negotiated Justice* (London: Martin Robertson, 1977)

Bambrough, S., M. Shaw and S. Kershaw (2013) 'The Family Drug and Alcohol Court service in London: a new way of doing Care Proceedings', *Journal of Social Work Practice: Psychotherapeutic Approaches in Health, Welfare and the Community*.

Barker, V. (2009) *The Politics of Imprisonment: How the Democratic Process Shapes the Way America Punishes Offenders*, Oxford: Oxford University Press.

Bazemore, G. and C.T. Griffiths (1997) 'Conferences, Circles, Boards, and Mediations: The "New Wave" of Community Justice Decision-making', Fed. Probation.

Bean, P. (1996) 'America's Drug Courts: A New Development in Criminal Justice', *Crime Law Review*, 718.

Bean, P. (1998) 'Drug courts and drug treatment', *Journal of Clinical Forensic Medicine*, 5 (4): 172–5.

Bean, P. (2002) *Drugs and Crime*, Cullompton: Willan.

Bean, P. (2004) *Drugs and Crime, Second Edition*, Cullompton: Willan.

Becker, D. and M.D. Corrigan 'Moving Problem-Solving Courts into the Mainstream', 18 Ct. Manager 6 (2003).

Beckerman, A. and L. Fontana (2002) 'Issues of race and gender in court-ordered substance abuse treatment', *Drug Courts in Operations: Current Research*, 33: 45.

Beckert, J. and F. Wehinger (2013) 'In the shadow: illegal markets and economic sociology', *Socio-Economic Review*, 11 (1): 5–30.

Belenko, S. (1998) 'Research on drug courts: A critical review', *National Drug Court Institute Review*, 1: 1–26.

Belenko, S. (2001) *Research on Drug Courts: A Critical Review 2001 Update*, National Center on Addiction and Substance Abuse, Columbia University.

Belenko, S., N. Fabrikant and N. Wolff (2011) 'The Long Road to Treatment: Models of Screening and Admission Into Drug Courts', *Criminal Justice and Behavior*, 38 (12): 1222–43.

Berlin, I. (1969) 'Two Concepts of Liberty' in *Four Essays on Liberty*, 118. Oxford: Oxford University.

Berlins, M. and C. Dyer (1989) *The Law Machine*, London: Penguin.

Berman, G. (2004a) *The Hardest Sell? Problem-Solving Justice and the Challenges of Statewide Implementation*, New York: Centre for Court Innovation.

Berman, G. (2004b) 'Redefining Criminal Courts: Problem-Solving and the Meaning of Justice', *American Criminal Law Review*, 41: 1313–19.

144   References

Berman, G. and J. Feinblatt (2001) 'Problem-Solving Courts: A Brief Primer', *Law and Policy*, 23: 125.

Berman, G. and J. Feinblatt (2002) 'Problem-solving justice: a quiet revolution', *Judicature*, 86: 182.

Berman, G. and J. Feinblatt (2005) *Good Courts: The Case for Problem Solving Justice*, New York: New Press.

Berman, G. and A. Fox (2009) *Lasting Change or Passing Fad? Problem Solving Justice in England and Wales*, London: Policy Exchange.

Berman, G. and A. Fox (2010) 'The Future of Problem-Solving Justice: An International Perspective', 10 *University of Maryland Law Journal* 1.

Blagg, H. (2008) 'Problem-Oriented Courts', Law Reform Commission of Western Australia, research paper.

Boldt, R.C. (2010) 'The Tomahawk and the Healing Balm: Drug Treatment Courts in Theory and Practice', *University of Maryland Law Journal of Race, Religion, Gender and Class*, 10: 45.

Booth, L., A. Altoft, R. Dubourg, M. Gonçalves and C. Mirrlees-Black (2012) *North Liverpool Community Justice Centre: Analysis of re-offending rates and efficiency of court processes*, London: Ministry of Justice.

Bottoms, A. (1995) 'The Philosophy and Politics of Punishment and Sentencing', in C. Clarkson and R. Morgan (eds) *The Politics of Sentencing Reform*, 17–49, Oxford: Clarendon Press.

Bowen, P. (2013) 'How Courts Can Use Prison More Intelligently', *Huffington Post*. Available at: www.huffingtonpost.co.uk/phil-bowen/courts-prison_b_3907229.html.

Bowen, P. and J. Donoghue (2013) 'Digging up the grassroots? The impact of marketisation and managerialism on local justice, 1997 to 2013', *British Journal of Community Justice*, 11 (2–3): 9–20.

Bowen, P. and S. Whitehead (2013) *Better Courts: Cutting Crime Through Court Innovation*, London: New Economics Foundation (NEF) and the Centre for Justice Innovation.

Bowers, J. (2008) Contraindicated Drug Courts, *UCLA Law Review*, 55: 783–835.

Bozza, J.A. (2007) 'Benevolent behavior modification: Understanding the nature and limitations of problem-solving courts', *Widener Law Journal*, 17: 97.

Bradley, K. (2009) 'The Bradley Report: Lord Bradley's review of people with mental health problems or learning disabilities in the criminal justice system', London: Department of Health.

Braithwaite, J. (1989) *Crime, Shame and Reintegration*, Cambridge: Cambridge University Press.

Braithwaite, J. (2002) *Restorative Justice and Therapeutic Jurisprudence Criminal Law Bulletin*, 38: 244.

British Broadcasting Company (BBC) News (2013) 'Save North Liverpool Community Justice Centre call'. Available at: www.bbc.co.uk/news/uk-england-merseyside-23870847.

Broome, S. (2012) Social Sentencing. Available at: www.thersa.org/fellowship/journal/archive/spring-2012/features/social-sentencing.

Brown, R. and S. Payne (2007) *Process Evaluation of the Salford Community Justice Initiative*, Ministry of Justice Research Series 14/7, London: Ministry of Justice.

Brunton-Smith, I. and P. Sturgis (2011) 'Do Neighborhoods Generate Fear of Crime? An empirical Test Using the British Crime Survey', *Criminology*, 49 (2): 331–69.

Burdon W.M, J.M. Roll, M.L. Prendergast and R.A. Rawson (2001) 'Drug courts and contingency management', *Journal of Drug Issues*, 31 (1): 73–90.

References 145

Bureau of Crime Statistics and Research (BOCSAR) (2008) 'The NSW Drug Court: A re-evaluation of its effectiveness', New South Wales Bureau of Crime Statistics and Research (BOCSAR).

Burns, R.P. (2009) *The Death of the American Trial*, Chicago: University of Chicago Press.

Burns, S.L. (2011) 'The Future of Problem-Solving Courts: Inside the Courts and Beyond', *University of Maryland Law Journal*, 10: 73.

Burns, S.L. and M. Peyrot (2003) 'Tough love: Nurturing and coercing responsibility and recovery in California drug courts', *Social Problems*, 50 (3): 416–38.

Burns, S.L. and M. Peyrot (2008) 'Reclaiming Discretion: Judicial Sanctioning Strategy in Court-Supervised Drug Treatment', *Journal of Contemporary Ethnography*, 37 (6): 720–44.

Bursik, R.J. (1988) 'Social Disorganisation and Theories of Crime and Delinquency: Problems and Prospects', *Criminology*, 26: 519.

Burton, M. (2006) 'Judicial Monitoring of Compliance: Introducing "Problem Solving" Approaches to Domestic Violence Courts in England and Wales', *International Journal of Law, Policy and the Family*, 20 (3): 366–78.

Cabinet Office (2009) *Engaging Communities in Criminal Justice*, Green Paper, April 2009, London: Cabinet Office.

Callahan, L., H. Steadman, J. Henry, S. Tillman and R. Vesselinov (2013) 'A multi-site study of the use of sanctions and incentives in mental health courts', *Law and Human Behavior*, 37 (1): 1–9.

Caplow, T. and J. Simon (1999) 'Understanding Prison Policy and Population Trends', in M. Tonry and J. Petersilia (eds) *Prisons*, 63–120. Chicago: University of Chicago Press.

Cappeletti, M. and B. Garth (1976) 'Civil Procedure: XVI', *Encyclopedia of Comparative Law*, 31–2.

Carr, H. and D. Cowan (2006) 'Labelling: Constructing Definitions of Antisocial Behaviour?', in J. Flint (ed.) *Housing, Governance and Antisocial Behaviour*, Bristol: Policy Press.

Carr, P.J. (2003) 'The New Parochialism: The Implications of the Beltway Case for Arguments Concerning Informal Social Control', *American Journal of Sociology*, 108: 1249.

Carr, P.J., L. Napolitano and J. Keating (2007) '"We Never Call the Cops and Here Is Why": A Qualitative Examination of Legal Cynicism in Three Philadelphia Neighbourhoods', 45 *Criminology* 445.

Casey, P.M. (2006) *Strategies to expand the problem-solving court approach*, 21 NASJE News Quarterly, 2.

Casey, P.M. and D.B. Rottman (2005) 'Problem-Solving Courts: Models and Trends', *The Justice System Journal*, 26: 35.

Casey, T. (2004) 'When Good Intentions are Not Enough: Problem-Solving Courts and the Impending Crisis of Legitimacy', *Southern Methodist University Law Review*, 57: 1516.

Center for Professional Responsibility (CPS) (2007) *Model Code of Judicial Conduct*, Chicago: American Bar Association.

Centre for Justice Innovation (2012) *Payback with a Purpose*, London: Centre for Justice Innovation. Available at: www.courtinnovation.org/sites/default/files/documents/Payback%20with%20a%20Purpose%20final.pdf.

Chase Deborah J. and P.F. Hora. (2000) 'The Implications of Therapeutic Jurisprudence for Judicial Satisfaction', *Court Review*, Spring 37 (1): 12.

146   *References*

Chase, D. and P.F. Hora (2009) 'The best seat in the house: The court assignment and judicial satisfaction', *Family Court Review*, 47 (2): 209–38.

Chase, O.G. (2002) 'American Exceptionalism and comparative procedure', *American Journal of Comparative Law*, 50: 277.

Cissner, A., M. Labriola and M. Rempel (2013) *Testing the Effects of New York's Domestic Violence Courts*, New York: Centre for Court Innovation.

Clamp, K. and C. Paterson (2011) 'Rebalancing Criminal Justice: Potentials and Pitfalls for Neighbourhood Justice Panels', *British Journal of Community Justice*, 9 (1/2): 21–35.

Clarke, C. and J. Neuhard (2004) 'From Day One: Who's in Control as Problem-Solving and Client-Centered Sentencing Take Center Stage?', *New York University Review of Law and Social Change*, 29: 11.

Clarke, C. and J. Neuhard (2005) 'Making the Case: Therapeutic Jurisprudence and Problem-Solving Practices Positively Impact Clients, Justice Systems and Communities They Serve', *St. Thomas Law Review*, 17: 781.

Clinks (2011) *'Big Judges' in England and Wales: Sentencer Involvement in Offender Management*, London: Clinks.

Crawford, A. (1997) *The Local Governance of Crime: Appeals to Community and Partnerships*, Oxford: Clarendon Press.

Crichton, J. and S. Fidler (2004) 'Court in Two Minds', *Druglink* January/February: 12–13.

Cohen, S. (1985) *Visions of Social Control: Crime, Punishment, and Classification*, Cambridge: Polity Press.

Cohen, S. and J. Young (1981) *The Manufacture of News: Social Problems, Deviance and the Mass Media*, London: Sage.

Conference of Chief Justices and Conference of State Court Administrators (2000) 'CCJ Resolution 22 COSCA Resolution for In Support of Problem-solving Courts', *Journal of the Center for Families*, 22–3.

Cook, P.W. (2009) *Abused Men: The Hidden Side of Domestic Violence*, US: Greenwood.

Cook, D., M. Burton, A. Robinson and C. Vallely (2004) *Evaluation of Specialist Domestic Violence Courts/Fast Track Systems*, London: Crown Prosecution Service and the Department for Constitutional Affairs.

Cook, D., M. Burton and A. Robinson (2005) 'Enhancing "Safety and Justice": The Role of Specialist Domestic Violence Courts in England and Wales', *British Journal of Criminology*, Vol. 7 Conference Edition.

Cooper, C., B. Franklin and T. Mease (2010), 'Establishing drug treatment courts: strategies, experiences and preliminary outcomes', *Organization of American States–CICAD*, 1: 6.

Cotterrell, R. (2002) 'Subverting Orthodoxy, Making Law Central: A View of Socio-legal Studies', *Journal of Law and Society*, 29 (4): 632–44.

Cowan, D., S. Blandy, E. Hitchings, C. Hunter and J. Nixon (2006) 'District Judges and Possession Proceedings', *Journal of Law and Society*, 33 (4): 547–71.

Crawford, A. and T. Newburn (2003) *Youth Offending and Restorative Justice*, Devon: Willan.

Crown Prosecution Service (CPS) (2008) *Specialist Domestic Violence Courts Review 2007/08*, London: CPS.

Crown Prosecution Service (CPS) (2012) *Violence against Women and Girls Crime Report 2011–12*, London: CPS.

Daicoff, S. (2000) 'Afterword: The Role of Therapeutic Jurisprudence Within the

References 147

Comprehensive Law Movement', *Practicing Therapeutic Jurisprudence* (ed.) D.P. Stolle, D.B. Wexler and B.J. Winick, Carolina: Carolina Academic Press.

Daicoff, S. (2002) 'The Comprehensive Law Movement', Touro Law Review, 19: 825.

Daicoff, S. (2005) 'Law as a Healing Profession: The Comprehensive Law Movement', *Pepperdine Dispute Resolution Law Journal*, 6–12.

Dalley, J. (2013) ' "One family, one judge": Towards a new model for access to justice for families facing violence in BC', *Appeal: Review of Current Law and Law Reform*, 18: 3.

Daly, K. (2011) *Conventional and innovative justice responses to sexual violence*, Melbourne: Australian Institute of Family Studies.

Davies, M. (2005) 'A new training initiative for the lay magistracy in England and Wales—a further step towards professionalisation?', *International Journal of the Legal Profession*, 12 (1): 93–119.

Davis, W. (2003) 'Special Problems for Speciality Courts', *American Bar Association Journal*, 89: 34.

de Souza Briggs, X. (2008) *Democracy as Problem Solving: Civic Capacity in Communities Across the Globe*, Boston: Massachusetts Institute of Technology.

Department for Communities and Local Government (DCLG) (2006) *Strong and Prosperous Communities*, London: DCLG.

DCLG (2008) *Creating Strong, Safe and Prosperous Communities: Statutory Guidance*, London: HMSO.

Department for Constitutional Affairs (DfCA) (2005a) *Supporting Magistrates to Provide Justice: Response Paper*, London: DfCA.

Department for Constitutional Affairs (DfCA) (2005b) *Supporting Magistrates' Courts to Provide Justice, Cm6681*, London: HMSO.

Derbyshire, P. (2011) *Sitting in Judgement: The Working Lives of Judges*, Oxford: Hart Publishing.

Devlin, P. (1979) *The Judge*, Oxford: Oxford University Press.

Dewhurst, D. (2010) Justice Foundations for the Comprehensive Law Movement, *International Journal of Law and Psychology*, 33: 463–74.

Diesfeld, K. and I. Freckelton (eds) (2003) *Involuntary detention and therapeutic jurisprudence: International perspectives on civil commitment*, Aldershot: Ashgate Publishing.

Diesfeld, K. and B. McKenna (2007) 'The Unintended Impact of the Therapeutic Intentions of the New Zealand Mental Health Review Tribunal? Therapeutic Jurisprudence Perspectives', *J. L. and Med*, 14: 566.

Donoghue, J. (2008) 'Antisocial Behaviour Orders (ASBOs) in Britain: Contextualizing Risk and Reflexive Modernization', *Sociology*, 42 (2): 337–55.

Donoghue, J. (2012) 'Anti-Social Behaviour, Community Engagement and the Judicial Role', *British Journal of Criminology*, 52: 591–610.

Dorf, M.C. (2003) 'Legal Indeterminacy and Institutional Design', *New York University Law Review*, 78: 875.

Douglas, R. and K. Laster (1992) *Reforming the People's Court: Victorian Magistrates' Reactions to Change*, Australian Criminology Research Council Grant 13/90.

Draca, M., S. Machin and R. Witt (2011) 'Panic on the Streets of London: Police, Crime, and the July 2005 Terror Attacks', *American Economic Review*, 101 (5): 2157–81.

Drug Policy Alliance (DPA) (2011) *Drug courts are not the answer: Toward a health-centered approach to drug use*, United States: Drug Policy Alliance.

Duffy, B., R. Wake, T. Burrows and P. Bremner (2008) *Closing the Gaps: Crime and Public Perception*, London: IPSOS MORI.

148   *References*

Ellen, I.G. (2012) 'Crime and Community Development', Open Forum: Voices and Opinions from Leaders in Policy, the Field and Academia. Available at: www.whatworksforamerica.org/ideas/crime-and-community-development/.

Ellsberg, M., H.A. Jansen, L. Heise, C.H. Watts and C. Garcia-Moreno (2008) 'Intimate partner violence and women's physical and mental health in the WHO multi-country study on women's health and domestic violence: an observational study', *Lancet*, 371 (9619): 1165–72.

Erickson, S.K., A. Campbell and S. Lamberti (2006) 'Variations in Mental Health Courts: Challenges, Opportunities, and a Call for Caution', *Community Mental Health Journal*, 42 (4): 335–44.

Eriksson, A. (2009) *Justice in Transition: Community Restorative Justice in Northern Ireland*, Collumpton: Willan Publishing.

Fagan, J. and V. Malkin (2003) 'Theorizing Community Justice Through Community Courts', *Fordham Urban Law Journal*, (30): 857–953.

Farrall, S., J. Jackson and E. Gray (2009) *Social Order and the Fear of Crime in Contemporary Times*, Oxford: Oxford University Press.

Farrell, G., A. Tseloni, J. Mailley and N. Tilley (2011) 'The Crime Drop and the Security Hypothesis', *Journal of Research in Crime and Delinquency*, 48 (2): 147–75.

Fahy, P. (2013) 'Responsible Citizens', Reform. Available at: http://10years.reform.co.uk/essays/Responsible-citizens.pdf.

Farole, Jr. D.J. and M. Rempel (2008) 'Problem-solving and the American Bench: A National Survey of Trial Court Judges', *The Justice System Journal*, 50–69.

Fazel, S. and K. Seewald (2012) 'Severe mental illness in 33 588 prisoners worldwide: systematic review and meta-regression analysis', *The British Journal of Psychiatry*, 200: 364–73.

Feinblatt, J. (2000) 'Judicial Innovation at the Crossroads: The Future of Problem-Solving Courts', *Court Manager*, 15: 28.

Field, S. (2006), 'State, Citizen, and Character in French Criminal Process', *Journal of Law and Society*, 33: 522–46.

Fisher, S.Z. (1993) 'Just the Facts, Ma'am: Lying and the Omission of Exculpatory Evidence in Police Reports', *New England Law Review*, 28: 1.

Finigan, M., W. Shannon, M. Carey and A. Cox (2007) *Impact of a Mature Drug Court Over 10 Years of Operation: Recidivism and Costs* (Final Report), Portland, OR: NPC Research.

Flint, J. (ed.) (2006) *Housing, Urban Governance and Antisocial Behaviour*, Bristol: Policy Press.

Fox, C. and K. Albertson (2012) 'Is payment by results the most efficient way to address the challenges faced by the criminal justice sector?', *Probation Journal*, 59 (4): 355–73.

Frank, J. (1973) *Courts on Trial: Myth and Reality in American Justice*, Princeton: Princeton University Press.

Frankel, M.E. (1974) 'Search for Truth: An Umpireal View', *University of Pennsylvania Law Review*, 123 (103): 1974–5.

Freckelton, I. (2007) 'Therapeutic Jurisprudence Misunderstood and Misrepresented: The Price and Risks of Influence', *Thomas Jefferson Law Review*, 30: 575.

Freedman, M.H. (1975) 'Judge Frankel's Search for Truth', *University of Pennsylvania Law Review*, 5: 1060.

Freeman, K. (2001) *New South Wales drug court evaluation: interim report on health and well-being of participants*, Contemporary Issues in Crime and Justice: 2001, 53, NSW Bureau of Crime Statistics and Research.

References 149

Freeman-Wilson, K., R. Tuttle and S.P. Weinstein (2001) *Ethical Considerations for Judges and Attorneys in Drug Court*, Alexandria, VA: National Drug Court Institute.

Freiberg, A. (2001) 'Problem-Oriented Courts: Practical Solutions to Intractable Problems?' *Journal of Judicial Administration*, 11: 1.

Freiberg, A. (2003) 'Therapeutic Jurisprudence in Australia: Paradigm Shift or Pragmatic Incrementalism', *Law in Context*, 20 (2): 6.

Froestad, J. and C. Shearing (2007) 'Conflict Resolution in South Africa: A Case Study. A South African Innovation: The Zwelethemba Model', in G. Johnstone and D. Van Ness (eds) *The Handbook of Restorative Justice*, Collumpton: Willan Publishing.

Fung, A. (2004) *Empowered Participation: Reinventing Urban Democracy*, Princeton, NJ: Princeton University Press.

Galaway, B. and J. Hudson (1996) *Restorative Justice: International Perspectives*, NY: Criminal Justice Press/Willow Tree Press.

Galligan, D.J. (1996a) *Due Process and Fair Procedures*, Oxford: Clarendon Press.

Galligan, D.J. (1996b) *A Reader on Administrative Law*, Oxford: Oxford University Press.

Garcia-Moreno, C., H.A. Jansen, M. Ellsberg, L. Heise and C.H. Watts (2006) 'Prevalence of intimate partner violence: findings from the WHO multi-country study on women's health and domestic violence', *Lancet*, 368 (9543): 1260–9.

Garland, D. (1990) *Punishment and Modern Society: A Study in Social Theory*, Chicago: Chicago University Press.

Garland, D. (2001) *The Culture of Control*, Oxford: Oxford University Press.

Gavrielides, T. (2008) 'Restorative justice—the perplexing concept: Conceptual faultlines and power battles within the restorative justice movement', *Criminology and Criminal Justice*, 8 (2): 165–83.

Gebelein, R.S. (2000) *The Rebirth of Rehabilitation: Promise and Perils of Drug Courts, Sentencing and Corrections: Issues for the 21st Century*, Washington, DC: NIJ.

Gelsthorpe, L. and A. Morris (2002) 'Restorative Youth Justice: The last vestiges of welfare?' in J. Muncie, G. Hughes and E. McLaughlin (eds) *Youth Justice: Critical Readings*, Buckinghamshire: Open University.

Genders, E. and E. Player (1995) *Grendon: A Study of a Therapeutic Prison*, Oxford: Oxford University Press.

Gerber, R.J. (1987) 'Victory vs. Truth: The Adversary System and Its Ethics', *Arizona State Law Journal*, 19: 3.

Gibbs, P. (2013) *Managing Magistrates' Courts – has central control reduced local accountability?*, London: Transform Justice.

Gilbert, P. (2010) *Compassion Focused Therapy*, Oxon: Routledge.

Gilling, D. and M. Jolley (2012) 'A Case Study of an English Community Court', *British Journal of Community Justice*, 10 (2): 55–69.

Goldberg, S. (2005) *Judging for the 21st Century: A Problem-solving Approach*, Ottawa: National Judicial Institute.

Goldkamp, J.S. (2000) 'The Drug Court Response: Issues and Implications for Justice Change', *Albany Law Review*, 63: 947.

Goldkamp, J. (2003) 'The impact of drug courts', *Criminology and Public Policy*, 2: 197–206.

Goldkamp, J.S. and C. Irons-Guynn (2000) *Emerging judicial strategies for the mentally ill in the criminal caseload: Mental health courts in Fort Lauderdale, Seattle, San Bernadino and Anchorage*, Washington: U.S. Department of Justice.

Gonzales, A.R., R. Schofield and G. Schmitt (2006) *Drug courts: The second decade*

150 *References*

[Special Report], U.S. Department of Justice, Office of Justice Programs: National Institute of Justice.

Goodpaster, G. (1987) 'On the Theory of American Adversary Criminal Trial', *Journal of Criminal Law and Criminology*, 78: 118.

Goriely, T.P., P. MCrone, A. Duff, C. Tata, A. Henry, M. Knapp, B. Lancaster and A. Sherr (2001) *The Public Defence Solicitors' Office: An Independent Evaluation*, Edinburgh: Scottish Executive.

Gover, A.R., E.M. Brank and J.M. MacDonald (2007) 'A specialised domestic violence court in South Carolina: An example of procedural justice for victims and defendants', *Violence Against Women*, 13: 603.

Gottfredson, D.C., B.W. Kearley, S.S. Najaka and C.M. Rocha (2007) 'How Drug Treatment Courts Work' *Journal of Research in Crime and Delinquency*, 44 (1): 3–35.

Greater London Authority (GLA) (2012) *Minutes of the London Violence Against Women and Girls Panel*, London: GLA.

Griller, G.M. (2011) *The Quiet Battle for Problem-Solving Courts*, Williamsburg, VA: National Center for State Courts.

Griffin, P.A, H.J. Steadman and J. Petrila (2002) 'The Use of Criminal Charges and Sanctions in Mental Health Courts', *Psychiatric Services*, 53 (10).

Griffith, J.D., G.A. Rowan-Szal, R.R. Roark and D.D. Simpson (2000) 'Contingency management in outpatient methadone treatment: a meta-analysis', *Drug and Alcohol Dependence*, 58: 55–66.

Guzman, D.E. (2012) *Drug Courts: Scope and Challenges of an Alternative to Incarceration, IDPC Briefing Paper*, International Drug Policy Consortium.

Halliday, S. (2004) *Judicial Review and Compliance with Administrative Law*, Oxford: Hart Publishing.

Hanley-Santos, G., T. Auburn, J. Annison and D. Gilling (2013), 'Problem-solving in an English Community Justice Court: Therapeutic Jurisprudence in Practice?', poster presented at Howard League 'What Is Justice?' conference, Oxford University, 1 October 2013.

Hardcastle, G.W. (2003) 'Adversarialism and the Family Court: A Family Court Judge's Perspective', *University of California Davis Law Review*, 9: 57.

Harlow, C. and R. Rawlings (1997) *Law and Administration* (2nd edition), London: Butterworths.

Harman, K. and I. Paylor (2002) 'A shift in strategy', *Criminal Justice Matters*, 47 (Spring): 8–9.

Harwin, J., M. Ryan and J. Tunnard, with S. Pokhrel, B. Alrouh, C. Matias and S. Momenian-Schneider (May 2011) *The Family Drug and Alcohol Court (FDAC) Evaluation Project Final Report*, Brunel University.

Hawken, A. and M. Kleiman (2009) *Managing Drug Involved Probationers with Swift and Certain Sanctions: Evaluating Hawaii's HOPE*, Washington, DC: National Institute of Justice.

Hennessy, A.M. (2008) 'Specialist Domestic and Family Violence Courts: The Rockhampton Experiment'. Available at: http://archive.sclqld.org.au/judgepub/2008/Hennessy160608.pdf

Henry, K. and D. Kralstein (2011) *Community Court: The Research Literature*, New York: Center for Court Innovation.

Her Majesty's Courts Service, *Her Majesty's Courts Service Annual Report and Accounts 2008/09*, London: The Stationery Office.

Her Majesty's Courts Service, *Her Majesty's Courts Service Business Plan 2010–11*, London: HMCS, March 2010.

References   151

Her Majesty's Treasury (2013) *Spending Round 2013: next stage in government's plan to move from rescue to recovery*, London: HM Treasury.

Hester, M. (2011) 'The Three Planet Model: Towards an Understanding of Contradictions in Approaches to Women and Children's Safety in Contexts of Domestic Violence', *British Journal of Social Work*, (41): 837–53.

Hester, M., J. Pearce and N. Westmarland (2008) 'Early Evaluation of the Integrated Domestic Violence Court, Croydon', *Ministry of Justice Research Series 18/08*, London: Ministry of Justice.

Hickert, A.O., S.W. Boyle and D.R. Tollefson (2009) 'Factors That Predict Drug Court Completion and Drop Out: Findings From an Evaluation of Salt Lake County's Adult Felony Drug Court', *Journal of Social Service Research*, 35: 2.

Higgins, S.T. and K.E. Silverman (1999) *Motivating behavior change among illicit-drug abusers*, Washington, DC American Psychological Association.

Hillian, D., M. Reitsma-Street and J. Hackler (2004) 'Conferencing in the Youth Criminal Justice Act of Canada: Policy Developments in British Columbia', *Canadian Journal of Criminology and Criminal Justice*, 46: 343.

Hoffman, M.B. (2000) 'The Drug Court Scandal', *North Carolina Law Review*, 78: 1437.

Hoffman, M.B. (2001) 'The Rehabilitative Ideal and the Drug Court Reality', *Federal Sentencing Reporter*, 14: 172.

Hollingworth, M. (2008) 'An examination of the potential impact of the Drug Rehabilitation Requirement on homeless illicit drug-using offenders', *Probation Journal*, 55 (2): 127–38.

Hood, R. (1962) *Sentencing in Magistrates' Courts*, London: Tavistock.

Hood, R. (1972) *Sentencing the Motoring Offender*, London: Heinemann.

Hood, R. (1992) *Race and Sentencing*, Oxford: Oxford University Press.

Hora, P.F. (2009) 'Through a Glass Gavel: Predicting the Future of Drug Treatment Courts', *Court Review*, 12.

Hora, P.F. (2011) *Courting New Solutions Using Problem-Solving Justice: Key Components, Guiding Principles, Strategies, Responses, Models, Approaches, Blueprints and Tool Kits*, Blueprints and Tool Kits: 1–46.

Hora, P.F. and T. Stalcup (2007) 'Drug Treatment Courts in the Twenty-First Century: The Evolution of The Revolution in Problem-Solving Courts', 42 *Georgia Law Review* 717.

Hora, P.F., W.G. Schma and J.T. Rosenthal (1998) 'Therapeutic jurisprudence and the drug treatment court movement: Revolutionizing the criminal justice system's response to drug abuse and crime in America', *Notre Dame Law Rev*, 74: 439.

Hough, M., A. Clancy and T. McSweeney (2003) *The Impact of Drug Treatment and Testing Orders on Offending: Two-Year Reconviction Results*, HORSD Findings 184. London: Home Office.

Hough, M. and J. Roberts (1999) 'Sentencing Trends in Britain. Public Knowledge and Public Opinion', *Punishment and Society*, 1 (1): 11–26.

Hough, M. and J. Roberts (2012) 'Public Knowledge and Opinion, Crime and Justice', in M. Maguire, R. Morgan and R. Reiner (eds), *The Oxford Handbook of Criminology*, Oxford: Oxford University Press.

Howard League for Penal Reform (2012) *Community Sentences*, London: HLPR.

Hunter, C., J. Nixon and S. Shayer (2000) *Neighbour Nuisance, Social Landlords and the Law*, London: Chartered Institute of Housing.

Hunter, S., J. Douard, S. Green and Larry Bembry (2012) 'New Jersey Developments: New Jersey's Drug Courts: A fundamental shift from the war on drugs to a public health approach for drug addiction and drug-related crime', *Rutgers Law Review*, 64: 795.

152   References

Husak, D. (2011) 'Lifting the Cloak: Preventive Detention as Punishment', *San Diego Law Review*, (48): 1173.

Huxley-Binns, R. and J. Martin (2013) *Unlocking the English Legal System* (3rd edition), Oxon: Routledge.

Holland, P. (2011) 'Lawyering and Learning in Problem-Solving Courts', *Washington University Journal of Law and Policy*, 34: 185.

Holloway, K., T.H. Bennett and D.P. Farrington (2008) *Effectiveness of Treatment in Reducing Drug-Related Crime*, Stockholm: Swedish National Council for Crime Prevention.

Home Office (2002) *Justice For All, Cm 5563*, London: The Stationery Office.

Home Office (2003) *Safety and Justice: The Government's Proposals on Domestic Violence Cm 5874*, London: HMSO.

Home Office (2004) *The Benefits of Community Engagement*, London: Home Office.

Home Office (2005) *Supporting Magistrates' Courts to Provide Justice, Cm 6681*, London: Home Office.

Home Office (2008) *Justice with Safety. Specialist Domestic Violence Courts Review 2007–2008*, London: Home Office.

Home Office (2010a) *Breaking the Cycle*, London: Home Office.

Home Office (2010b) *Call to End Violence to Women and Girls*, London: Home Office.

Home Office (2010c) *2009/10 British Crime Survey*, London: Home Office.

Home Office (2011) *Call to End Violence to Women and Girls: An Action Plan*, London: Home Office.

Home Office (2012a) *Problem-Oriented Partnerships: Tilley Awards 2012 Guidance for Entrants*, London: Home Office.

Home Office (2012b) *Putting Victims First: More Effective Responses to Anti-Social Behaviour*, London: Home Office.

Home Office (2013) *Police Recorded Crime (PRC) Open Data Tables*, London: Home Office.

Hough, M. and J. Roberts (1999) 'Sentencing Trends in Britain', *Punishment and Society*, 1: 11.

Hough, M., B. Bradford, J. Jackson and J.R. Roberts (2013) *Attitudes to sentencing and trust in justice: exploring trends from the crime survey for England and Wales*, Ministry of Justice analytical series, London: Ministry of Justice.

House of Commons (2013) *Child sexual exploitation and the response to localised grooming – Home Affairs Committee*, London: House of Commons.

Hudson, B. (2003) *Justice in the Risk Society: Challenging and Re-affirming Justice in Late Modernity*, London: Sage.

Husak, D. (2011) 'Retributivism, Proportionality, and the Challenge of the Drug Court Movement', in *Retributivism Has a Past: Has It a Future?* Michael Tonry (ed.), USA: Oxford University Press, 214.

Indemaur, D. and L. Roberts (2003) 'Drug Courts in Australia: The First Generation', *Current Issues in Criminal Justice*, 15 (2): 136–54.

Institute for Economics and Peace (IEP) (2013) *2013 Global Peace Index*, New York: IEP.

James, D.V. (2010) 'Diversion of mentally disordered people from the criminal justice system in England and Wales: An overview', *International Journal of Law and Psychiatry*, 33: 241–8.

Jarvis, D., N. Berkeley and K. Broughton (2011) 'Evidencing the Impact of Community Engagement in Neighbourhood Regeneration: The Case of Canley, Coventry', *Journal of Community Development*, 2: 46.

References 153

Jennings, W., S. Farrell and S. Bevan (2012) 'The economy, crime and time: An analysis of recorded property crime in England and Wales 1961–2006', *International Journal of Law, Crime and Justice*, 40: 192.

Jewkes, Y. (2010) *Media and Crime*, London: Sage.

Johnston, L. (2011) 'Theorizing Mental Health Courts', University of Florida Levin College of Law (unpublished).

Johnson, S.L. (1987–8) 'Unconscious Racism and the Criminal Law', *Cornell Law Review*, 73: 1016.

Jolliffe, D. and D. Farrington (2009) *Initial evaluation of reconviction rates in Community Justice Initiatives*, London: Ministry of Justice.

Judge, Lord Chief Justice Lord (2011) Summary Justice In and Out of Court: The Police Foundations' John Harris Memorial Lecture. Available at: www.judiciary.gov.uk/media/speeches/2011/lcj-speech-john-harris-memorial-lecture-07072011.

Judge, Lord Chief Justice Lord (2013) *Letter to The Right Honourable Keith Vaz MP – Home Affairs Committee Inquiry into Child Sexual Exploitation and the response to localised grooming*, London: Judiciary of England and Wales. Available at: www.judiciary.gov.uk/Resources/JCO/Documents/letter-lcj-to-keith-vaz-mp.pdf.

Judiciary of England and Wales (2013a) *Training for magistrates and legal advisers*. Available at: www.judiciary.gov.uk/training-support/judicial-college/how-the-judicial-college-is-governed/magisterial-committee.

Judiciary of England and Wales (2013b) *Guidance for Magistrates involved in scrutiny of out of court disposals*, London: Judiciary of England and Wales.

Justice Policy Institute (JPA) (2011) *Addicted to courts: How a growing dependence on drug courts impacts people and communities*, Washington: Justice Policy Institute.

Kagan, R.A. (2003) *Adversarial Legalism: The American Way of Law*, Harvard: Harvard University Press.

Kalich, D. and R.D. Evans (2006) 'Drug court: An effective alternative to incarceration', *Deviant Behavior*, 27: 569–90.

Kane, P.S. (1993) 'Why Have You Singled Me Out? The Use of Prosecutorial Discretion for Selective Prosecution', *Tulsa Law Review*, 67: 2293.

Karp, D. (2001) 'Harm and Repair: Observing Restorative Justice in Vermont', *Justice Quarterly*, 18: 727.

Karp, D., G. Bazemore and J. D. Chesire (2004) 'The Role and Attitudes of Restorative Board Members: A Case Study of Volunteers in Community Justice', *Crime and Delinq.*, 50: 487.

Karp, D. and T.R. Clear (2000) 'Community Justice: A Conceptual Framework', *Boundaries changes in criminal justice organizations*, 2: 323–68.

Kelitz, S., R. Guerrero, A.M. Jones and D.M. Rubio (2001) *Specialization of Domestic Violence Case Management in the Courts: A National Survey*, NCJ Publication 186192, Washington, DC: National Center for State Courts, National Institute of Justice.

Kempinen, B. (2011) 'Problem-Solving Courts and the Defense Function: The Wisconsin Experience', *Hastings Law Journal*, 62: 1149.

Kennedy, R. (1997) *Race, Crime and the Law*, New York: Pantheon.

Kerr, J., C. Tompkins, W. Tomaszewski, S. Dickens, R. Grimshaw, N. Wright and M. Barnard (2011) *The Dedicated Drug Courts Pilot Evaluation Process Study*, London: Ministry of Justice.

King, M., A. Freiberg, B. Batagol and R. Hyams (2009) *Non-Adversarial Justice*, Sydney: Federation Press.

154 References

King, M. and B. Batagol (2010) 'Enforcer, Manager or Leader? The Judicial Role in Family Violence Courts', *International Journal of Law and Psychology*, 33: 409.

King, R. and J. Pasquarella (2009) *Drug courts – A review of the evidence*, Washington: The Sentencing Project.

King, M. (2009) *Solution-Focused Courts Bench Book*, Melbourne: The Australasian Institute of Judicial Administration.

Kirby, A., T. McSweeney, P. Turnbull and B. Bhardwa (2010) *Engaging Substance Misusing Offenders: A Rapid Review of the Substance Misuse Treatment Literature*, Institute for Criminal Policy Research, London.

Kleinhesselink, R. and C. Mosher (2003) 'A Process Evaulation of the Clark County Domestic Violence Court', *Violence Against Women Online Resources*.

Kralstein, D. (2005) 'Community court research: a literature review', Center for Court Innovation, New York.

Kury, H. (ed.) (2008) *Fear of Crime—Punitivity. New Developments in Theory and Research*, Crime and Crime Policy Vol. 3, Bochum: Universitätsverlag Brockmeyer.

Labriola, M., M. Rempel and R.C. Davis (2005) *Testing the Effectiveness of Batterer Programs and Judicial Monitoring, Final Report*, Washington DC: National Institute of Justice.

Lacey, N. (1992) 'The Jurisprudence of Discretion: Escaping the Legal Paradigm' in K. Hawkins (ed.), *The Uses of Discretion*, Oxford: Clarendon Press.

Lacey, N. (2008) *The Prisoners' Dilemma*, Cambridge: Cambridge University Press.

Lacey, N. and H. Pickard (2012) 'From the Consulting Room to the Court Room: Taking the Clinical Model of Responsibility of Without Blame into the Legal Realm', *Oxford Journal of Legal Studies*.

Langbein, J.H. (2003) *The Origins of Adversary Criminal Trial*, Oxford: Oxford University Press.

Langer, M. (2005) *The rise of managerial judging in international criminal law*, AM. J. Comp. L. 835.

Lanni, A. (2005) 'The Future of Community Justice', 40 *Harvard Civil Rights–Civil Liberties Law Review*.

Lempert, R. (1989) 'The dynamics of informal procedure: The case of a public housing eviction board', *Law and Society Review*, 23: 347–98.

Livingstone, I. (2013) 'Community Justice in Action in Plymouth'. Available at: www. clinks.org/community/blog-posts/community-justice-action-plymouth

Lösel F. A., J. A. Koehler, L. Hamilton, D. K. Humphreys and T. D. Akoensi (2011) *Strengthening Transnational Approaches to Reducing Reoffending: Final Report*, Cambridge: University of Cambridge Institute of Criminology.

Luban, D. (1983) 'The Adversary System Excuse', *The Good Lawyer: Lawyers' Roles and Lawyers' Ethics 83*, Totowa: Rowman & Littlefield.

Luskin, M.L. (2013) 'More of the same? Treatment in mental health courts', *Law and Human Behavior*, 37 (4): 255–66.

Lynch, M. (2011) 'Mass incarceration, legal change, and locale', *Criminology and Public Policy*, 10 (3): 673–98.

Lynch, J.P. and A. Pridemore (2011) 'Crime in International Perspective', in J.Q. Wilson and J. Petersilia (eds) *Crime and Public Policy*, Oxford: Oxford University Press.

Mazur, R. and L. Aldrich (2003) 'What Makes a Domestic Violence Court Work? Lessons from New York', *Judges' Journal* 42 (2).

McBarnet, D. (1981) *Conviction*, Basingstoke: Palgrave Macmillan.

McConville, M., J. Hodgson, L. Bridges and A. Pavlovic (1994) *Standing Accused,* Oxford: Clarendon Press.

References   155

McCoy, C. (2003) 'The Politics of Problem-Solving: An Overview of an Origins and Development of Therapeutic Courts', *American Criminal Law Review*, 40: 1513.

McCubbins, M.D., R.G. Noll and B.R. Weingast (1989) 'Structure and Process, Politics and Policy: Administrative Arrangements and the Political Control of Agencies', *Virginia Law Review*, 75: 431–82.

McDermott, D. (2001) 'The Permissibility of Punishment', *Law and Philosophy*, (20): 403.

McEwan, J. (2011) 'From Adversarialism to Managerialism: Criminal Justice in Transition', *Legal Studies*, 4: 51.

McGuire, J. (2001) 'What Works in Correctional Intervention? Evidence and Practical Implication', *Offender rehabilitation in practice: Implementing and evaluating effective programs*, 25–43.

McIvor, G. (2009) 'Therapeutic jurisprudence and procedural justice in Scottish Drug Courts', *Criminology and Criminal Justice*, 9 (1): 21–9.

McIvor, G. (2010) 'Reconviction Among Drug Court Participants', *Review of the Glasgow and Fife Drug Courts: Report*, Edinburgh: Scottish Government Community Justice Services.

McIvor, G., L. Barnsdale, S. Eley, M. Malloch, R. Yates and A. Brown (2006) *The Operation and Effectiveness of the Scottish Drug Court Pilots*, Crime and Criminal Justice Research Findings 81, Edinburgh: Scottish Executive.

McIvor, G., S. Eley, M. Malloch and R. Yates (2003) *Establishing Drug Courts in Scotland: Early Experiences of the Pilot Drug Courts in Glasgow and Fife*, Crime and Criminal Justice Research Findings 71, Edinburgh: Scottish Executive.

McKeana, J. and K. Warren-Gordona (2011) 'Racial Differences in Graduation Rates From Adult Drug Treatment Courts', 9 *Journal of Ethnicity in Criminal Justice* 41.

McKenna, K. (2007) *Evaluation of the North Liverpool Community Justice Centre*, London: Ministry of Justice.

McNeill, F. (2011) 'Probation, Credibility and Justice', *Probation Journal*, 58: 9.

McNeill, F. and B. Whyte (2007) *Reducing Reoffending: Social Work and Community Justice in Scotland*, Cullompton: Willan.

McNichol, E., P. Oliff and N. Johnson (2011) *States Continue to Feel Recession's Impact*, Washington, DC: Center on Budget and Policy Priorities.

McSweeney, T., A. Stevens, N. Hunt and P.J. Turnbull (2008) 'Drug testing and court review hearings: Uses and limitations', *Probation Journal*, 55: 39.

McSweeney, T., P. Meadows, H. Metcalf, P. Turnbull and C. Stanley (2009) *The feasibility of conducting an impact evaluation of the Dedicated Drug Court pilot*, National Institute of Economic and Social Research and the Institute for Criminal Policy Research, London: Kings College.

McVie, S. (2011) 'Alternative models of youth justice: lessons from Scotland and Northern Ireland', *Journal of Children's Services*, 6 (2): 106–114.

Macdonald, S. (2006) 'The Principle of Composite Sentencing: Its Centrality to, and Implications for, the ASBO', *Criminal Law Review*, 791–808.

Machin, S., O. Marie and S. Vujić (2011) 'The Crime Reducing Effect of Education', *The Economic Journal*, 121: 463–84.

Machin, S. and C. Meghir (2004) 'Crime and economic incentives', *Journal of Human Resources*, 39 (4): 958–79.

Magistrates' Association (MA) (2011) *Magistrates in the Community Annual Report 2010/11*, London: MA.

Magistrates' Association (MA) (2012) *Active, Accessible, Engaged: The Magistracy in the 21st Century*, London: MA.

156   *References*

Magistrates Association (MA) (2013) *What about training?* Available at: www. magistrates-association.org.uk/about-magistrates/training/.

Maguire, M. (2012) 'Criminal Statistics and the Construction of Crime', M. Maguire, R. Morgan and R. Reiner (eds), *The Oxford Handbook of Criminology* (5th edition), 206–44, Oxford: Oxford University Press.

Mair, G. and M. Millings (2011) *Doing Justice Locally: The North Liverpool Community Justice Centre*, London: Centre for Crime and Justice.

Mair, G. and H. Mills (2009) *The Community Order and the Suspended Sentence Order Three Years On*, London: Centre for Crime and Justice Studies.

Malkin, V. (2005) 'The End of Welfare as We Know It: What Happens When the Judge is In Charge*, 25 Critique of Anthropology*, 380.

Mansky, A. (2004) 'Straight out of Red Hook: A Community Justice Centre Grows in Liverpool', *Judicature*, 87 (5): 255.

Marchetti, E. and K. Daly (2004) 'Indigenous Courts and Justice Practices in Australia', *Trends and Issues in Crime and Criminal Justice*, 277: 1–6.

Marlowe, D.B., D.S. Festinger, K.L. Dugosh and P.A. Lee (2005) 'Are Judicial Status Hearings a "Key Component" of Drug Court? Six and Twelve Months Outcomes', *Drug and Alcohol Dependence*, 79 (2): 145–55.

Marlowe, D. (2010) *Research Update on Adult Drug Courts*, Alexandria, VA: National Association of Drug Court Professionals.

Marshall, T. (1991) 'Victim-Offender Mediation', *Research Bulletin*, 30: 9–15.

Martinson, R. (1974) 'What Works? Questions and Answers about Prison Reform', *The Public Interest*, 22–54.

Martinson, R. (2003) 'What works?', *Crime: Critical Concepts in Sociology*, 1: 200.

Maruna, S. (2001) *Making Good: How Ex-Convicts Reform and Rebuild Their Lives*, Washington, DC: American Psychological Association Books.

Maruna, S. and T.P. LeBel (2002) 'Welcome Home? Examining the Re-entry Court Concept from a Strengths-based Perspective', *Western Criminology Review*, 4: 91.

Maruna, S. (2011) 'Judicial Rehabilitation and the "Clean Bill of Health" in Criminal Justice', *European Journal of Probation,* 3 (1): 97–117.

Meekins, T.M. (2006) 'Specialized Justice: The Over-Emergence of Specialty Courts and the Threat of a New Criminal Defense Paradigm', *Suffolk University Law Review*, 40: 1.

Mills, A., R. Meek and D. Gojkovic (2011) 'Exploring the relationship between the voluntary sector and the state in criminal justice', *Voluntary Sector Review*, 2 (2): 193–211.

Mooney, G. and S. Neal (2010) 'Welfare worries: mapping the directions of welfare futures in the contemporary UK', *Research, Policy and Planning*, 27 (3): 141–150.

Morgan, R. and N. Russell (2000) 'The Judiciary in the Magistrates' Courts', London: Home Office.

Mayor's Office for Policing and Crime (MOPAC) (2013) *Consultation for the Second Mayoral Strategy on Violence Against Women and Girls (2013–17)*, London: MOPAC.

Matczak, A., E. Hatzidimitriadou and J. Lindsay (2011) *Review of Domestic Violence policies in England and Wales*, London: Kingston University and St George's, University of London.

Matrix Knowledge Group (2008) *Dedicated Drug Court Pilots: A Process Report*, Ministry of Justice Research Series 7/08, London: Ministry of Justice.

Matthews, R. (2005) 'The myth of punitiveness', *Theoretical Criminology*, 9 (2): 175–201.

References 157

Meadows, L., K. Clamp, A. Culshaw, N. Cadet, K. Wilkinson and J. Davidson (2010) *Evaluation of Sheffield City Council's Community Justice Panels Project.* Project Report. Sheffield, Sheffield Hallam University.

Meekins, T.M. (2006) 'Specialized Justice: The Over-Emergence of Speciality Courts and the Threat of a New Criminal Defense Paradigm', *Suffolk University Law Review*, 40: 1.

Meekins, T.M. (2007) 'Risky Business: Criminal Speciaity Courts and the Ethical Obligations of the Zealous Criminal Defender', *Berkeley Journal of Criminal Law*, 12: 75.

Menkel-Meadow, C. (1984) *Toward Another View of Legal Negotiation: The Structure of Problem-Solving*, 31 *U.C.L.A Law Review* 754.

Menkel-Meadow, C. (1996) 'The Trouble with the Adversary System in a Postmodern, Multi Cultural World', 38 *William and Mary Law Review*, 5, 30 (1996–7).

Merrall, E.L.C. and S.M. Bird (2009) 'A Statistical Perspective on the Design of Drug-Court Studies', *Evaluation Review*, 33 (3): 257–80.

Miller, A.R. (1984) 'The Adversary System: Dinosaur or Phoenix', 69 *Minnesota Law Review* 1 (1984–85).

Miller, E.J. (2004) 'Embracing Addiction: Drug Courts and the False Promise of Judicial Interventionism', *Ohio State Law Journal*, 65: 1479.

Miller, E.J. (2007) 'The Therapeutic Effects of Manageria. Re-entry Courts', *Federal Sentencing Reporter*, 20 (2): 127–35.

Miller, E.J. (2009) 'Drug Courts and the New Penology', 20 *Stanford Law and Policy Review* 417.

Miller, E.J. (2012) *A Criminal Revolution? Problem Solving Courts in Theory and Practice*, paper presented to the Oxford University Criminal Law Discussion Group, March 2012.

Miller, L. (2008) *The Perils of Federalism: Race, Poverty, and the Politics of Crime Control*, Oxford: Oxford University Press.

Millie, A., J. Jacobson, E. McDonald and M. Hough (2005) *Anti-social behaviour strategies: finding a balance*, London: Joseph Rowntree Foundation.

Millie, A., J. Tombs and M. Hough (2007) 'Borderline sentencing: A comparison of sentencers' decision making in England and Wales and Scotland', *Criminology and Criminal Justice*, (7): 243–67.

Ministry of Justice (2008) *Dedicated Drug Courts: A Process Report*, London: Ministry of Justice.

Ministry of Justice (2009) 'Table 6.9, Offender Management Caseload Statistics 2009', Ministry of Justice.

Ministry of Justice (2010a) *Green Paper Evidence Report: Breaking the Cycle: Effective Punishment, Rehabilitation and Sentencing of Offenders*, London: Ministry of Justice.

Ministry of Justice (2010b) *Breaking the cycle: effective punishment, rehabilitation and sentencing of offenders Cm7972*, London: Ministry of Justice.

Ministry of Justice (2010c) *Criminal Statistics, England and Wales 2008*, London: Ministry of Justice.

Ministry of Justice (2011a) *Proven Re-Offending Statistics Quarterly Bulletin, July 2010 to June 2011, England and Wales*, London: Ministry of Justice.

Ministry of Justice (2011b) *Family Justice Review: Interim Report*, London: Ministry of Justice.

Ministry of Justice (2012a) *Swift and Sure: The Government's Plans for Reform of the Criminal Justice System*, London: Ministry of Justice.

158   References

Ministry of Justice (2012b) *Punishment and Reform: Effective Community Sentences*, Cm 8334, London: Ministry of Justice.

Ministry of Justice (2012c) 'Table 1, Cost per place and cost per prisoner by individual prison, National Offender Management Service Annual Report and Accounts 2011–2012: Management Information Addendum', London: Ministry of Justice.

Ministry of Justice (2013a) *Proven Re-offending Statistics Quarterly Bulletin, October 2010 to September 2011, England and Wales*, London: Ministry of Justice.

Ministry of Justice (2013b) *Press Release – Damian Green: Reforming the Role of Magistrates*, London: Ministry of Justice.

Ministry of Justice (2013c) *Serving as a Magistrate: A detailed guide to the role of JP*. Available at: www.direct.gov.uk/prod_consum_dg/groups/dg_digitalassets/@dg/@en/documents/digitalasset/dg_072742.pdf.

Ministry of Justice (2013d) Written ministerial statement, Wednesday 17 July 2013, Ministry of Justice: *North Liverpool Community Justice Centre*, London: Ministry of Justice.

Ministry of Justice (2013e) Home Office and the Office for National Statistics (ONS) *An Overview of Sexual Offending in England and Wales: Statistics Bulletin (January 2013)*, London: Ministry of Justice.

Ministry of Justice (2013f) *Press Release: Reoffending is up while fewer people enter the criminal justice system*. Available at: www.gov.uk/government/news/reoffending-is-up-while-fewer-people-enter-the-criminal-justice-system.

Mirsky, L. (2006) 'The Chard and Ilminster Community Justice Panel: Restorative Community Justice', *Restorative Practices E-Forum* 1–2.

Mitchell O., D.B. Wilson, A. Eggers *et al.* 'Assessing the effectiveness of drug courts on recidivism: a meta-analytic review of traditional and non-traditional drug courts', *Journal of Criminal Justice: 2012*, 60–71.

Moore, D. (2007) 'Translating Justice and Therapy. The Drug Treatment Court Networks', *British Journal of Criminology*, 47 (1): 42–60.

Murphy, J. (2012) 'The Continuing Expansion of Drug Courts: Is That All There is? *Deviant Behavior*, 33 (7): 582–8.

National Audit Office (NAO) (2009) *HM Courts Service – Administration of the Crown Court Report by the Controller and Auditor General HC 290 Session 2008–09*, London: NAO.

National Crime Council (2007) *Problem Solving Justice: The Case for Community Courts in Ireland*, Dublin: Stationery Office.

National Housing Federation (NHF) (1999) *Housing and Crime: Safe as Houses*, London: NHF.

National Institute for Health and Clinical Excellence (2007) *Drug Misuse: Psychosocial Management of Drug Misuse*, NICE guideline. Draft for consultation, London: NICE.

National Legal Aid and Defender Association (NLADA) (2003) Ten Tenets of Fair and Effective Problem Solving Courts' (Washington, D.C. National Legal Aid and Defender Association.

National Association of Criminal Defense Lawyers (NACDL) (2009) America's Problem-solving Courts: The Criminal Costs of Treatment and the Case for Reform Washington, D.C.: NACDL.

National Offender Management Strategy (NOMS) *Working with Personality Disordered Offenders: A Practitioner's Guide*, London: NOMS.

Nieto, M. (1998) *Probation for Adult and Juvenile Offenders: Options for Improved Accountability*, California State Library, California Research Bureau.

Newburn, T. (2002) 'Atlantic crossings "Policy transfer" and crime control in the USA and Britain', *Punishment and Society*, 4 (2): 165–94.

References   159

Newburn, T. (2012) 'Disaster averted but questions remain over courts' response to riots', *The Guardian* 3 July 2012. Available at: www.theguardian.com/uk/2012/jul/03/questions-remain-court-response-riots.

Newbury, A. (2011) '"I Would Have Been Able to Hear What They Think": Tensions in Achieving Restorative Outcomes in the English Youth Justice System', *Youth Justice*, 11 (3): 250–65.

Nolan, J.L. (1998) *The Therapeutic State: Justifying Government at Century's End*, NY: NYU Press.

Nolan, J.L. (2001) *Reinventing Justice: The American Drug Court Movement*, Princeton NJ: Princeton University Press.

Nolan, J.L. (2002) *Drug Courts in Theory and in Practice*, New York: Walter de Gruyter.

Nolan, J.L. (2003) 'Redefining Criminal Courts: Problem-Solving and the Meaning of Justice', 40 *American Criminal Law Review* 1541.

Nolan, J.L. (2009a) *Legal Accents, Legal Borrowing: The International Problem-Solving Court Movement*, Princeton NJ: Princeton University Press.

Nolan, J.L. (2009b) *Reinventing Justice: The American Drug Court Movement*, Princeton NJ: Princeton University Press.

Nonet, P. and P. Selznick (1978) *Law and Society in Transition: Toward Responsive Law*. New Jersey: Transaction Publishers.

Neff, K. (2011) *Self-Compassion*, London: Hodder and Stoughton.

Newmark, L., M. Rempel, K. Diffily and Kane, K. (2001) *Specialized Felony Domestic Violence Courts: Lessons on Implementation and Impacts from the Kings County Experience*, Urban Institute of Justice Policy Center.

O'Hear, M.M. (2009) 'Rethinking Drug Courts: Restorative Justice as a Response to Racial Injustice', *Stanford Law and Policy Review*, 20: 101.

O'Malley, P. (2008) 'Experiments in risk and criminal justice', *Theoretical Criminology*, 12 (4): 451–69.

Office of the Deputy Prime Minister (ODPM) (2003) *Sustainable Communities: Building for the Future*, London: HMSO.

Office for National Statistics (ONS) (2013) *Crime Survey for England and Wales, Year Ending March 2013*.

Padfield, N. (2011) 'Wither the rehabilitation revolution?' *Criminal Justice Matters*, 86: 17.

Packer, H.L. (1964) 'Two Models of the Criminal Process', *University of Pennsylvania Law Review*, 113: 1–2.

Parenti, C. (1999) *Lockdown America: Police and Prisons in an Age of Crisis*, New York: Verso.

Pawson, R. (2006) *Evidence-based Policy: A Realist Perspective*, London: Sage.

Peeples, R. and H. Nyheim (2008) 'Beyond the Border: An International Perspective on Business Courts', *Business Law Today*, 17: 35.

Petrucci, C.J. (2002) 'Respect as a Component in the Judge-Defendant Interaction in a Specialised Domestic Violence Court that Utilises Therapeutic Jurisprudence', 38 *Criminal Law Bulletin* 263.

Petrila, P. (1993) 'Paternalism and the Unrealized Promise of Essays in Therapeutic Jurisprudence', *New York Law School Journal of Human Rights*, 10: 877.

Petrila, J. (2003) 'An introduction to special jurisdiction courts', *International Journal of Law and Psychiatry*.

Pepinsky, H. (1978) 'Discretion and Crime Legislation', in M. Evans (ed.) *Discretion and Control*, London: Sage.

160 References

Perreault, S. (2013) *Police reported crime statistics in Canada, 2012*, Ontario: Statistics Canada.

Pew Center on the States (2011) *State of Recidivism: The Revolving Door of America's Prisons*, Washington, DC: The Pew Charitable Trusts.

Phelan, A. (2003) 'Solving Human Problems or Deciding Cases? Judicial Innovation in New York and its Relevance to Australia: Part 1', 13 *Journal of Judicial Administration* 98.

Pinard, M. (2004) 'Broadening the Holistic Mind Set: Incorporating Collateral Consequences and Re-Entry Into Criminal Defense Lawyering', *Fordham Urban Law Journal*, 31: 1067.

Pinard, M. (2006) 'An Integrated Perspective on the Collateral Consequences of Criminal Convictions and Reentry Issues Faced by Formerly Incarcerated Individuals', *Boston University Law Review*, 86: 623.

Popovic, J. (2002) 'Judicial Officers: Complementing Conventional Law and Changing the Culture of the Judiciary', *Law in Context* 20: 128 (special edition on *Therapeutic Jurisprudence*, edited by M. McMahon and D. Wexler).

Poulin, A.B. (2001) 'Prosecutorial Inconsistency, Estoppel, and Due Process: Making the Prosecution Get Its Story Straight', *California Law Review*, 89: 1423.

Portillo, S., D.S. Rudes, J. Viglione and M. Nelson (2013) 'Front-Stage Stars and Backstage Producers: The Role of Judges in Problem-Solving Courts', *Victims and Offenders*, 8 (1): 1–22.

Pratt, J. (2002) *Punishment and Civilization*, London: Sage.

Pratt, J. (2005) *The New Punitiveness: Trends, Theories and Perspectives*, Oxon: Willan Publishing.

Priestley, P. and M. Vanstone (2010) *Offenders or Citizens? Readings in Rehabilitation*, Cullompton: Willan.

Prison Reform Trust (2013) 'Crime and Courts Bill – Schedule 15'. Available at: http://www.prisonreformtrust.org.uk/Portals/0/Documents/PRT%20Briefing%20-%20Crime%20and%20Courts%20Bill%20HoC%20Second%20Reading%2014%20January%202013.pdf

Pycroft, A. (2012) 'Relationship and rehabilitation in a post-what works era', in A. Pycroft and S. Clift (eds) *Risk and Rehabilitation: Management and Treatment of Substance Misuse and Mental Health Problems in the Criminal Justice System*, London: Policy Press.

Quinn, M.C. (2000) 'Whose Team Am I on Anyway? Musings of a Public Defender About Drug Treatment Court Practice', *New York University Review of Law and Social Change*, 26: 37.

Quinn, M. (2006) 'Revisiting Anna Moscowitz Kross's Critique of New York City's Women's Court: The Continued Problem of Solving the "Problem" of Prostitution with Specialized Criminal Courts', *Fordham Urban Law Journal* 33: 665.

Quinn, M.C. (2008) 'Anna Moscowitz and the Home Term Part: A Second Look at the Nation's First Criminal Domestic Violence Court', *Akron Law Review*, 41: 733.

Quinn, M.C. (2009) 'The Modern Problem-Solving Court Movement: Domination of Discourse and Untold Stories of Criminal Justice Reform', *Washington University Journal of Law and Policy*, 31: 57.

Rabinovich-Einy, O. and R. Tsur (2010) 'The Case for Greater Formality in ADR: Drawing on the Lessons of Benoam's Private Arbitration System', *Vermont Law Review*, 34: 529.

Raine, J.W. and P. Keasey (2012) 'From Police Authorities to Police and Crime Commissioners: Might Policing Become More Publicly Accountable?', *Internationational Journal of Emergency Services*, 1 (2): 122–34.

References 161

Redlich, A. (2013) 'The Past, Present, and Future of Mental Health Courts' in R.L. Wiener and E.M. Brank (eds) *Problem Solving Courts: Social Science and Legal Perspectives*, New York: Springer.

Redlich, A.D., S. Hoover, A. Summers and H.J. Steadman (2010) 'Enrollment in Mental Health Courts: Voluntariness, Knowingness, and Adjudicative Competence', *Law and Human Behavior*, 34 (2): 91–104.

Redlich, A.D., H.J. Steadman, J. Monahan, J. Petrila and P.A. Griffin (2005) 'The Second Generation of Mental Health Courts', *Psychology, Public Policy, and Law*, 11 (4): 527–38.

Reed, J. (1992) *Review of mental health and social services for mentally disordered offenders and others requiring similar services: Vol. 1: Final summary report*, Cm. 2088. London: HMSO.

Rempel, M., M. Green and D. Kralstein (2012) 'The impact of adult drug courts on crime and incarceration: findings from a multi-site quasi-experimental design, *Journal of Experimental Criminology*, 8 (2): 165–92.

Restorative Justice Council (RJC) (2013) 'Legislation for Restorative Justice'. Available at: www.restorativejustice.org.uk/news/importan_milestone_for_rj/

Roberts, J. (2008) 'Sentencing Policy and Practice: The Evolving Role of Public Opinion', *Penal populism, sentencing councils and sentencing policy,* 15.

Roberts, J. and M. Hough (2005) *Understanding Public Attitudes to Criminal Justice*, New York: McGraw-Hill International.

Roberts, J. and M. Hough (2011) 'Custody or Community? Exploring the Boundaries of Public Punitiveness in England and Wales', *Criminology and Crime Justice*, 11 (2): 181–97.

Rodriguez, N. (2005) 'Restorative Justice, Communities, and Delinquency: Whom do we Reintegrate?', *Criminology and Public Policy*, 4: 103.

Rose, D.R. and T. Clear, 'Incarceration, Reentry, and Social Capital: Social Networks in the Balance', prepared for the conference From Prison to Home: The Effect of Incarceration and Reentry on Children, Families and Communities (Washington, DC: U.S. Department of Health and Human Services, 2001). Available at: http://aspe.hhs.gov/hsp/prison2home02/Rose.htm.

Rothman, E.F., D. Exner and A.L. Baughman (2011) 'The Prevalence of Sexual Assault Against People Who Identify as Gay, Lesbian, or Bisexual in the United States: A Systematic Review', Trauma Violence Abuse April 2011 12 (2): 55–66.

Royal Commission on the Justices of the Peace (1948) London: HMSO.

Safer Future Communities (2012) *How the Voluntary, Community and Social Enterprise Sector Can Help Reduce Crime and Keep Communities Safe in Your Area: Our Offer to Police and Crime Commissioners*, London: Clinks. Available at: www.clinks.org/assets/files/PDFs/SFC/VCSE%20Sector%20offer%20final_eng.pdf].

Sahl, J. (2011) 'Behind Closed Doors: Shedding Light on Lawyer Self-Regulation – What Lawyers Do When Nobody's Watching?', *San Diego Law Review*, 48: 447.

Sampson, R.J. and C. Loeffler (2010) 'Punishment's place: the local concentration of mass incarceration', *Daedalus* 139 (3): 20–31.

Sanders, A. and I. Jones (2007) 'The Victim in Court' in S. Walklate (ed.) *Handbook of Victims and Victimology*, Oxon: Routledge.

Sampson, R., S. Raudenbush and F. Earls (1997) 'Neighborhoods and Violent Crime: A Multilevel Study of Collective Efficacy 1997', *Science*, 277 (5328): 918–24.

Sanders, A. and R. Young (2007) *Criminal Justice*, Oxford: Oxford University Press.

Sarteschi, C., M., Michael, G. Vaughn and K. Kim (2011) 'Assessing the effectiveness of

162   References

mental health courts: A quantitative review', *Journal of Criminal Justice*, 29 (1): 12–20.

Schiff, M., G. Bazemore and M. Brown (2011) 'Neighborhood Accountability Boards: The Strength of Weak Practices and Prospects for a "Community Building" Restorative Model', *Washington University Journal of Law and Policy*, 36: 17.

Schneider, R.D. (2009) Mental Health Courts, *Wiley Encyclopedia of Forensic Science*, New York: John Wiley and Sons.

Schneider, R.D. (2010) 'Mental health courts and diversion programs: A global survey', *International Journal of Law and Psychiatry*, 33 (4): 201–6.

Scraton, P. and K. Chadwick (1987) *Law, Order and the Authoritarian State: Readings in Critical Criminology*, Buckinghamshire: Open University Press.

Scraton, P. and K. Chadwick (2001) 'Authoritarian Populism' and 'Critical Criminology' in J. Muncie and E. McLaughlin (eds) *The Sage Dictionary of Criminology*, London: Sage.

Sevigny, E.L., K. Brian, F. Fuleihan and V. Ferdik (2013) 'Do drug courts reduce the use of incarceration?: A meta-analysis' *Journal of Criminal Justice*, 41 (6): 416–25.

Shapland, J. and M. Hall (2007) 'What Do We Know About the Effects of Crime on Victims?', *International Review of Victimology*, 14 (2): 175–217.

Shapland, J., A. Atkinson, H. Atkinson, E. Colledge, J. Dignan, M. Howes, J. Johnstone, G. Robinson and A. Sorsby (2006) 'Situating restorative justice within criminal justice', *Theoretical Criminology*, 10 (4): 505–32.

Shute, S., R. Hood and F. Seemungal (2005) *A Fair Hearing? Ethnic Minorities in the Criminal Court*, Cullompton: Willan.

Simon, L.M.J. (1995) 'A Therapeutic Jurisprudence Approach to the Legal Processing of Domestic Violence Cases', *Psychology, Public Policy and Law*, 1: 57.

Simon, J. (1999) 'They Died With Their Boots On: The Boot Camp and the Limits of Modern Penality', *Social Justice*, 22: 25–48.

Simon, J. (2001) 'Entitlement to Cruelty: Neo-Liberalism and the Punitive Mentality in the United States', in K. Stenson and R. Sullivan (eds) *Crime Risk and Justice* 125–43, Cullompton: Willan.

Simon, J. (2002) 'Crime, Community, and Criminal Justice, *California Law Review*, 90: 1415.

Skyrme S.T. (1991) *History of the Justices of the Peace*, Chichester: Barry Rose, 2: 232–6.

Skeem, J.L., S. Manchak and J.K. Peterson (2011) 'Correctional Policy for Offenders with Mental Illness: Creating a New Paradigm for Recidivism Reduction', *Law and Human Behavior*, 35: 2.

Skogan, W.G. (1974) 'The Validity of Official Crime Statistics: An Empirical Investigation', *Social Science Quarterly*, 55 (1): 25–38.

Slinger, E. and R. Roesch (2010) 'Problem-solving courts in Canada: A review and a call for empirically-based evaluation methods', *International Journal of Law and Psychiatry*, 33 (4): 258–64.

Slobogin, C. (1995) 'Therapeutic Jurisprudence: Five Dilemmas to Ponder', *Psychology, Public Policy and Law*, 1: 219.

Smith, A. (2003) 'The Difference in Criminal Defense and the Difference It Makes', *Washington University Journal of Law and Policy*, 11: 83.

Snacken, S. and E. Dumortier (eds) (2011) *Resisting Punitiveness in Europe?: Welfare, Human Rights and Democracy*, Oxon: Routledge.

Snacken, S. (2010) 'Resisting punitiveness in Europe?', *Theoretical Criminology*, 14 (3): 272–92.

References   163

Sommerlad, H. (2004) 'Some Reflections on the Relationship between Citizenship, Access to Justice, and the Reform of Legal Aid', *Journal of Law and Society*, 31 (3): 345–68.

Sparrow, P. and G. McIvor (2013) 'Sentencing drug offenders under the 2003 Criminal Justice Act: Challenges for the probation service', *Criminology and Criminal Justice*, 13: 298.

Spinak, J.M. (2003) 'Why Defenders Feel Defensive: The Defender' Role in Problem-Solving Courts', *American Criminal Law Review*, 40: 1617.

Stahlkopf, C. (2008) 'Political, Structural, and Cultural Influences on England 's Youth Offending Team Practices', *International Criminal Justice Review*, 18: 455.

Statistics Canada (2012) *Uniform Crime Reporting Survey (UCR) 2012*, Canada: Government of Canada.

Steadman, H.J. (2005) *A Guide to Collecting Mental Health Court Outcome Data*, New York: Council of State Governments.

Steadman, H.J., A.D. Redlich, P. Griffin, J. Petrila and J. Monahan (2005) 'From referral to disposition: Case processing in seven mental health courts', *Behavioral Sciences and the Law*, 23 (2): 215–26.

Steadman, H.J., F. Osher, P.C. Robbins, B. Case and S. Samuels (2009) 'Prevalence of Serious Mental Illness Among Jail Inmates', *Psychiatric Services*, 60: 761–5.

Steadman, H.J., A. Redlich, L. Callahan, P.C. Robbins and R. Vesselinov (2011) 'Effect of mental health courts on arrests and jail days: a multisite study', *Archives of General Psychiatry*, 68 (2): 167–72.

Stempel, J.W. (2010) 'Feeding the Right Wolf: A Niebuhrian Perspective on the Opportunities and Limits of Mindful Core Concerns Dispute Resolution', *Nevada Law Journal*, 10: 472.

Stenson, K. and A. Edwards (2004) 'Policy Transfer in Local Crime Control: beyond naïve emulation', in T. Newburn and R. Sparks (eds) *Criminal Justice Political Cultures*, Oxon: Willan.

Stewart, J. (2005) *Specialist Domestic/Family Violence Courts Within the Australian Context*, Issues Paper 10. Sydney, Australia: Australian Domestic and Family Violence Clearinghouse, University of New South Wales.

Stewart, J. (2011) *Specialist Domestic Violence Courts: What we Know Now – How Far Have Australian Jurisdictions Progressed?* Sydney, Australia: Australian Domestic and Family Violence Clearinghouse, University of New South Wales.

Stevens, A., M. Trace and D. Bewley-Taylor (2005) *Reducing Drug Related Crime: An Overview of the Global Evidence (Report 5)*. London: The Beckley Foundation Drug Policy Foundation.

Sharkey, P. (2010) 'The Acute Effect of Local Homicides on Children's Cognitive Performance', *Proceedings of the National Academy of Sciences of the USA*, 107 (26): 11733–8.

Stafford, M., T. Chandola and M. Marmot (2007) 'Association between Fear of Crime and Mental Health and Physical Functioning', *American Journal of Public Health*, 97 (11): 2076–81.

Stolle, D.P., D.B. Wexler and B.J. Winick (eds) (2000) *Practicing Therapeutic Jurisprudence: Law as a Helping Profession*, Carolina: Carolina Academic Press.

Sward, E.E. (1988) 'Values, ideology and the evolution of the adversary system', *Indiana L. J.*, 64: 301 (1988–9) at 32.

Tata, C. (2008) *Transformation, Resistance and Legitimacy: the role of Pre-Sentence Reports in the Production (and Disruption) of Guilt and Guilty Pleas*, Paper Presented to the European Society of Criminology, Annual Conference 2008.

164 *References*

Tata, C. (2013) 'Beyond the Revolving Court Door: Is it time for Problem-Solving Courts in Scotland?', *Scottish Justice Matters*, (1): 17.

Tata, C., T. Goriely, P. Duff, A. Henry, P. McCrone and M. Knapp (2004) 'Does Mode of Delivery Make a Difference to Criminal Case Outcomes and Client Satisfaction? The Public Defence Solicitor Experiment', *Criminal Law Review*, 2: 5.

The Right Honourable Lord Justice Auld (2001) *Review of the Criminal Courts of England and Wales*, London: HMSO.

Tomasic, R. and M. Feeley (1982) *Neighborhood justice: assessment of an emerging idea*, New York: Longman.

Tonry, M. (1994) 'Racial Disproportion in US Prisons', *British Journal of Criminology*, 34: 97–115.

Tonry, M. (1995) *Malign Neglect*, New York: Oxford University Press.

Tonry, M. (2007) 'Determinants of Penal Policies', *Crime and Justice*, 36 (1): 1–48.

Tonry, M. and R. Hood (1996) *Crime, Race and Ethnicity*, Chicago: University of Chicago Press.

Took, G. (2005) 'Therapeutic Jurisprudence and the Drug Courts: Hybrid Justice and its Implications for Modern Penality', *Internet Journal of Criminology* 1.

Tseloni, A., J. Mailley, G. Farrell and N. Tilley (2010) 'Exploring the international decline in crime rates', *European Journal of Criminology*, 7 (5): 375–94.

Turnbull, P.J., T. McSweeney, R. Webster, *et al.* (2000) *Drug Treatment and Testing Orders: The Final Evaluation Report*, Research Study 212, London: Home Office.

Tutty, L., J. Ursel and F. Douglas (2008) 'Specialized domestic violence courts: a comparison of models', in J. Ursel, L.M. Tutty and J. Lemaistre (eds), *What's Law Got to Do with It? The Law*, Specialised Courts and Domestic Violence in Canada, Cormorant Press: Toronto, 69–94.

Tyler, T.R. (1992) 'The Psychological Consequences of Judicial Procedures: Implications for Civil Commitment Hearings', *Southern Methodist University Law Review*, 46: 433.

Umbreit, M.S. and A.W. Roberts (1996) Mediation of Criminal Conflict in England: An Assessment of Services in Coventry and Leeds – Executive Summary.

United Nations Office on Drugs and Crime (UNODC) (2008) *Handbook for Prison Managers and Policymakers on Women and Imprisonment*, New York: United Nations

van Caenegem, W. (2003) 'Adversarial Systems and Adversarial Mindsets: Do We Need Either?', *Bond Law Review*, 15.

van Dijk, J., A. Tseloni and G. Farrell (eds) (2012) *The International Crime Drop: New Directions in Research (Crime Prevention and Security Management)*, Basingstoke: Palgrave Macmillan.

von Hirsch, A. (1993) *Censure and Sanctions*, Oxford: Oxford University Press.

von Hirsch, A. and A. Ashworth (1998) (eds) *Principled Sentencing*, London: Hart Publishing.

von Hirsch, A. and J. Roberts (1997) 'Racial Disparity in Sentencing: Reflections on the Hood Study', *The Howard Journal of Criminal Justice*, 36 (3): 227–36.

Wacquant, L. (2000) 'The New "Peculiar Institution": On the Prison as Surrogate Ghetto', *Theoretical Criminology*, 4 (3): 377–89.

Wacquant, L. (2001a) 'The Penalisation of Poverty and the Rise of Neo-liberalism', *European Journal on Criminal Policy and Research*, 9 (4): 401–12.

Wacquant, L. (2001b) 'Deadly Symbiosis when Ghetto and Prison Meet and Mesh', *Punishment and Society*, 3 (1): 95–133.

Wacquant, L. (2004) *Punir les pauvres: Le nouveau gouvernement de l'insécurité sociale*, Paris: Editions Dupuytren.

References   165

Wacquant, L. (2006) 'Penalization, Depolitization and Racialization: On the Overincarceration of Immigrants in the European Union', pp. 83–100, in S. Amstrong and L. McAra (eds) *Perspectives on Punishment: The Contours of Control*, Oxford: Oxford University Press.

Walker, S. and D. Louw (2003) 'The South African court for sexual offences', *International Journal of Law and Psychiatry*, 26 (1): 73–85.

Walker, S. and D. Louw (2005a) 'The South African court for sexual offences: Perception of the victims of sexual offences', *International Journal of Law and Psychiatry*, 28 (3): 231–45.

Walker, S. and D. Louw (2005b) 'The South African court for sexual offences: Perception of the families of victims', *International Journal of Law and Psychiatry*, 28 (4): 418–29.

Watson, A., P. Hanrahan, D. Luchins, M.J. Heyrman and A. Lurigio (2001) 'Mental health courts and complex issues of mentally ill offenders', *Psychiatric Services*, 52 (4): 477–81.

Wendell Holmes Jnr, O. (1897) 'The Path of the Law', *Harvard Law Review*, 10: 457.

Wenzel, M., T.G. Okimoto, N.T. Feather and M.J. Platow (2007) 'Retributive and Restorative Justice', *Law and Human Behavior*, 32: 375.

Werb, D., R. Elliot, B. Fischer, E. Wood, J. Montaner and T. Kerr (2007) 'Drug treatment courts in Canada: an evidence-based review', *HIV/AIDS Policy and Law Review*, 12 (2/3).

Western, B. (2004) 'Politics and Social Structure in The Culture of Control', *Critical Review of International Social and Political Philosophy*, 7 (2): 22–41.

Wexler, D.B. (1990) *Therapeutic Jurisprudence: The Law as a Therapeutic Agent*, Carolina: Carolina Academic Press.

Wexler, D.B. (1992) 'Putting Mental Health into Mental Health Law: Therapeutic Jurisprudence', *Law and Human Behavior*, 16 (27): 32.

Wexler, D.B. (1993) 'Therapeutic Jurisprudence and the Criminal Courts', *William and Mary Law Review*, 35: 279.

Wexler, D.B. (1995) 'Reflections on the Scope of Therapeutic Jurisprudence', *Psychology, Public Policy and Law*, 1: 236.

Wexler, D.B. 'Therapeutic Jurisprudence and the Criminal Courts', *William and Mary Law Review*, 35: 279.

Wexler, D.B. (2010) 'Therapeutic Jurisprudence and its Application to Criminal Justice Research and Development', *Irish Probation Journal*, 7: 94.

Wexler, D. (2012) 'New Wine in New Bottles: The Need to Sketch a Therapeutic Jurisprudence "Code" of Proposed Criminal Processes and Practices', *Arizona Legal Studies Discussion Paper*, 12–16.

Wexler, D.B. and B.J. Winick (eds) (1996) *Law in a Therapeutic Key: Developments in Therapeutic Jurisprudence*, Carolina: Carolina Academic Press.

Winick, B.J. and D.B. Wexler (2001) 'Drug treatment court: Therapeutic jurisprudence applied', *Touro Law Review*, 18: 479.

Winick, B.J. and D.B. Wexler (2003) *Judging in a Therapeutic Key: Therapeutic Jurisprudence and the Courts*, Durham, NC: Carolina Academic Press.

Weiner, R L., B.J. Winick, L.S. Georges and A. Castro (2010) 'A testable theory of problem solving courts: Avoiding past empirical and legal failures', *International Journal of Law and Psychology*, 33: 417.

Winick, B.J. (1997) 'The Jurisprudence of Therapeutic Jurisprudence', *Psychology, Public Policy and Law*, 3: 184–5.

166　*References*

Winstone, J. and F. Pakes (2010) *Process evaluation of the Mental Health Court pilot, Ministry of Justice Research Series 18/10*, London: Ministry of Justice.

Winstone, J. and F. Pakes (2012) 'Community Orders and the Mental Health Court Pilot: A service user perspective of what constitutes a quality, effective intervention' in A. Pycroft and S. Clift (eds) *Risk and Rehabilitation: Management and Treatment of Substance Misuse and Mental Health Problems in the Criminal Justice System*, London: Policy Press.

Wood, D. (2013) 'Swift and sure: McJustice for a consumer society' *Criminal Justice Matters*, 91 (1): 10–11.

Wolf, R.V. (2007) *Principles of Problem-Solving Justice*, New York: Bureau of Justice Assistance. Available at: www.courtinnovation.org/sites/default/files/Principles.pdf.

Wolf, R.V. (2009a) 'A New Way of Doing Business: A Conversation about the Statewide Coordination of Problem-solving Courts', *Journal of Court Innovation*, 2: 191.

Wolf, R.V. (2009b) 'Race, Bias, and Problem-Solving Courts', 21 *National Black Law Journal* 27.

Wolff, N. and Pogorzelski, W. (2005) 'Measuring the effectiveness of mental health courts: Challenges and recommendations', *Psychology, Public Policy and Law*, 11 (4): 539–69.

Worrall, A. (1987) *Gender, Crime and Justice*, in A. Worrall and P. Carlen (eds), Milton Keynes: Open University Press.

Wright, M. (1996) *Justice for Victims and Offenders: A Restorative Response to Crime*, Winchester: Waterside Press.

Wu, J. and C. Spohn (2008) 'Interdistrict Disparity in Sentencing in Three U.S. District Courts', *Crime and Delinquency*, 56: 290.

Young, J. (2002) 'Identity, Community and Social Exclusion', *Crime, Disorder and Community Safety*, 26.

Young, J. (2007) *The Vertigo of Late Modernity*, London: Sage.

Zacharias, F.C. (2009a) 'Integrity Ethics', *Georgetown Journal of Legal Ethics*, 22: 541.

Zacharias, F.C. (2009b) 'True Confessions About the Role of Lawyers in a Democracy', *Fordham Law Review*, 77: 1591.

Legislation

Children and Young Persons Act 2008
Courts Act 2003
Crime and Courts Act 2013
Justice of the Peace Act 1949
Localism Act 2011
Offender Rehabilitation Bill

Statutory instruments

The Criminal Procedure Rules 2013 No. 1554 (L. 16)

Index

adversarial model 41–3

Bradley Report, The (2009) 112–13, 115–16, 117
Breaking the Cycle: Effective Punishment, Rehabilitation and Sentencing of Offenders 23

Centre for Court Innovation in New York 14–15
community: court review of community orders 54–7; courts 52, 94; effects of crime on 13–14; empowerment of 96; engagement results 105, 106, 107; inconsistent sentencing 52–3; justice panels 21; magistrates' role 50–1, 52–4; Payment by Results (PbR) model 26; Plymouth Community Justice Court 102–4; Red Hook Community Justice Centre (RHCJC) 104–5
Community Harm Statement (CHS) 107
Community Impact Statements (CISs) 106
community justice initiatives 94–5, 97; CJSSS (Criminal Justice – Simple, Speedy, Summary) 101; evaluation 99; North Liverpool Community Justice Centre (NLCJC) 96–101; Plymouth Community Justice Court 101
community orders 54–7
court closures 52, 125
court listing practices 57–8
court reforms: development of 44–6; magistrates' courts 46–7, 52–4; past decade 31; reasons for 44
court specialisations: adversarial model 41–3; development of 45–6; variables and overlaps 41
Crime and Courts Act (2013) 24–5; *Part 2,* 27

crime rates : factors involved 2; recidivism 2–3; sources and figures 1

defence counsel 38–40, 67
disadvantaged groups 67; *see also* 'hard to reach' groups
domestic violence (DV/IPV): research findings 81; *Violence against Women and Girls Crime Report 2011–12,* 86
domestic violence courts: differing models 81–2; Family Drug and Alcohol Courts (FDACs) 88–9; Integrated Domestic Violence Courts (IDVCs) 82, 87; Specialist Domestic Violence Courts (SDVCs) 81
drug courts xi, 63; disadvantaged groups 67; Drug Rehabilitation Requirements (DRRs) 71–2; Drug Treatment and Testing Orders (DTTOs) 70; effectiveness 68–70; funding 77; intermediate sanctions 134–5; mental health issues 'dual diagnosis' 116; pilot schemes evaluation 72–5; punitive approach 65–6; therapeutic approach 66–7
drug crime recidivism 62–3, 65
Drug Rehabilitation Requirements (DRRs) 71–2
Drug Treatment and Testing Orders (DTTOs) 70

Engaging Communities in Criminal Justice (2009) 101

Family Drug and Alcohol Courts (FDACs) pilot study evaluation 88–9
funding 29, 77, 137–8; *see also* public sector reform

'hard to reach' groups 107; *see also* disadvantaged groups

168 *Index*

Integrated Domestic Violence Courts (IDVCs) 82; pilot study and evaluation 87

judicial review: drug courts 64; Integrated Domestic Violence Courts (IDVCs) 82; judge's role and significance 37–8, 44

lay magistrates *see* magistrate
local justice *see* community

magistrates 47–51; changing role 53–4; effects of court closures 52; Neighbourhood Justice Panels (NJPs) 125–9; out of court disposals 120–1; sentencing 52–3; *Swift and Sure Justice* 53; training xvi , 48–9, 101, 105–6, 131
magistrates' courts: listing practices 57–9; out of court disposals 120–1; reform of 46–7, 52–4
mental health: *Bradley Report (2009)* 112–13, 115–16, 117; statistics for offenders 108
Mental Health Courts (MHC): drug misuse 'dual diagnosis' 116; need for 111–13; pilot schemes 113–16; scalability 116; voluntary participation 115
Mental Health Courts (MHCs) in USA: effectiveness assessments 110–11; establishment of 108–9; voluntary participation 109–10

Neighbourhood Justice Panels (NJPs) : cases 123–4; contentious issues 126–8, 131; description 121–2; introduction of 118–19; magistrates' involvement 125–9; pilot schemes 122–3; research 119, 122; response to court closures 125; 'Swift and Sure Justice' 123, 125
North Liverpool Community Justice Centre 96–8; closure 101; evaluation 99–100

out of court disposals 120–1

Payment by Results (PbR) model 26–7
Plymouth Community Justice Court 101, 102; independent study 102–3; therapeutic jurisprudence 103–4
probation 139
problem-solving courts 13–14, 16–17, 35, 141; community orders legislation 54–7; concerns regarding 67; effectiveness 34, 68–70; judicial behaviour 37–8;

punitivism 22, 65–6; restorative justice 26, 37; specialist courts 31–2; teamwork 75; therapeutic approach 35–6, 66–7; USA 14–15, 33–4; *see also* drug courts; Integrated Domestic Violence Courts (IDVCs); Family Drug and Alcohol Courts (FDACs); specialist Sexual Violence Courts (SVCs)
problem-solving justice 13–14, 17–18; judicial independence 133–4; in USA 14–15
public sector reform : effects of court closures 52; target driven centralisation 51, 58, 68
punitivism : drug court 65–6; forms and variations 18–20; non-punitivism 20–1; problem-solving court 22

recidivism: *Breaking the Cycle* 23; crime rates 2–3; drug crime 62–3, 65
Red Hook Community Justice Centre (RHCJC) 104–5
rehabilitation 22–4
restorative justice 3 principles of 36; Neighbourhood Justice Panels (NJPs) 118
restorative justice legislation: amendments to the *Powers of Criminal Courts (Sentencing) Act 2000*; *Ministry of Justice 2012a* 35
review hearings 17

sentencing: continuity 64, 76, 91, 92; effectiveness 78–81; guidelines 52; inconsistency 52–3; selectivity in 67
specialist courts 31–3
Specialist Domestic Violence Courts (SDVCs) 81–2; evaluation 83–4, 86; National Resource Manual 84–5; sentencing continuity 91, 92; *see also* domestic violence courts
specialist Sexual Violence Courts (SVCs): child sex abuse 90–1; jurisdiction issues 90, 91; model 89, 90; MOPAC survey 89
Swift and Sure Justice 53; Neighbourhood Justice Panels (NJPs) 123, 125

therapeutic jurisprudence in: community courts 95; Plymouth Community Justice Court 103–4; problem-solving courts 35–6
training: magistrates 48–9, 101, 105–6; problem-solving justice xvi

Violence against Women and Girls Crime Report (2011–12) 86